THE BUDDHIST SECTS
OF JAPAN

Daibutsu or "Great Buddha," Kamakura

THE BUDDHIST SECTS
OF JAPAN

THEIR HISTORY, PHILOSOPHICAL
DOCTRINES AND SANCTUARIES

BY

E. STEINILBER-OBERLIN

WITH THE COLLABORATION OF
KUNI MATSUO

TRANSLATED FROM THE FRENCH BY
MARC LOGÉ

GREENWOOD PRESS, PUBLISHERS
WESTPORT, CONNECTICUT

The Library of Congress cataloged this book as follows:

Steinilber-Oberlin, Émile, 1878–
    The Buddhist sects of Japan, their history, philosophical doctrines and sanctuaries, by E. Steinilber-Oberlin with the collaboration of Kuni Matsuo. Translated from the French by Marc Logé. Westport, Conn., Greenwood Press ₁1970₁

      303 p. illus. 23 cm.

      Reprint of the 1938 ed.
      Translation of Les sects bouddhiques japonaises.
      Includes bibliographical references.

      1. Buddhist sects—Japan.   I. Matsuo, Kuninosuke, 1899–joint author. II. Title.

BL1440.S72 1970   294.3′9′0952   78–109854
ISBN 0–8371–4349–7   MARC

Library of Congress   71 ₁7₁

Originally published in 1938 by George Allen & Unwin Ltd., London

Reprinted from an original copy in the collections of the Brooklyn Public Library

Reprinted by Greenwood Press, Inc.

First Greenwood reprinting 1970
Second Greenwood reprinting 1976

Library of Congress Catalog Card Number 78-109854

ISBN 0-8371-4349-7

Printed in the United States of America

LETTERS ADDRESSED TO THE AUTHOR BY
EMINENT JAPANESE BONZES AND PROFESSORS

". . . I congratulate you in having undertaken the study and expounding of Japanese Buddhism. Everyone will understand that Japanese Buddhism must be envisaged in its relation to the ideas and spiritual needs born on Nippon soil.

All the spiritual life of Japan—its art, literature and morals —is impregnated with Buddhist Philosophy, without which it cannot be understood. Does the stranger realise all the importance this philosophy has acquired in all the domains of our national life? If one extirpated Buddhism from the Japanese soul, our civilisation and life would lose half their value. We can but rejoice to see a foreigner take an interest in the Buddhist doctrine (and not stop at the manifestations of vulgar piety which too often proceed from denatured conceptions) and study the different characteristics and nuances of philosophical Buddhism, of universal tendencies.

H. UI,

Professor at the Imperial University of Tohoku."

". . . I approve your study of Buddhism and your effort to make your compatriots understand it.

Although Japanese Buddhism is, in a general way, the heir of Chinese Buddhism, itself issued from Hindu Buddhism, our Buddhist doctrines, born during the epoch of Kamakura (1186-1332), have developed in a particularly interesting way.

Japanese Buddhism is inspired by the spiritual needs of Japan, and constitutes a Japanese creation, whilst preserving a high universal value. The sects each present their own particular physiognomy, and differ a great deal the one from the other, whilst accusing, nevertheless, a common tendency: the preoccupation of avoiding useless philosophical complications, of going directly to the most simple conceptions and practices, and of affirming before all a human philosophy. All Buddhist

5

philosophy is made for man *by* man. It constitutes a natural religion. Buddha does not exist in a transcendent way outside of our own thought—and that is what distinguishes Buddhism from other religions. *Buddhism is the crystallisation of the spiritual effort of Humanity.*

H. ONO,

Professor at the Faculty of Letters of Taishô."

CONTENTS

ILLUSTRATIONS

INTRODUCTION

THIS book is merely a philosophical inquiry.

My task has been limited to obtaining explanations, to group them methodically and reproduce them in the most faithful way possible. When a certain point seemed obscure to me I sought the necessary explanations. When the exposed system included a Mystery, I respected it. Different or opposed points of view were presented to me. I listened to imaged, poetical or charming propositions and to others which were austere, complex and technical. I have noted both the ones and the others. I always took care to persuade my interlocutor to sketch the essential part of his doctrine *in relievo*, whilst allowing him, if he judged proper, to reserve certain perspectives and shadowed zones. I myself have taken great care to respect, in the case of each doctrine, its special charm, and if I may express myself thus, its perfume, its colour and its light.

To the reader who *sincerely* wishes to understand the philosophical doctrines of modern Buddhism I deliver the result of this inquiry, which I might have entitled "Living Buddhism : Its smiling and deep philosophy."

The idea of making an inquiry on this subject came to me after having read the criticisms which Western writers have so often formulated against "philosophical Buddhism," or "Superior Buddhism." The amused traveller has never failed to note the picturesque aspects of popular Buddhism as well as its naïve practices. But if peradventure one began to speak of some highly philosophical aspect of Buddhism—such as the Tendai or the Zen sects—one was immediately confronted by the barrier erected by certain renowned authors.

Appropriating the terms of yet another critic, Basil Hall Chamberlain declared that "these doctrines were almost unintelligible and impossible to express in clear terms."

"It is a religion of metaphysicians," said Lafcadio Hearn, "a religion of scholars so difficult to understand even by persons of a certain philosophical culture, that it may easily be confounded with a system of universal negation."

Other critics are more displeasing.

"It is a tissue of solemn nonsense," declares A. Roussel, Professor of Sanskrit, author of several works on Buddhism, who concludes as follows: "If it be true that all Japanese sects are a defiance to common sense, the Zen sect is by far the most audacious of them all."

In presence of all these various judgments, it therefore seemed to me that it would be equitable if not to put matters right, which I do not pretend to do, at least to modestly propose a sufficiently precise basis of explanation to all those who have preserved the taste of philosophical and spiritual things, and whose thought is free of foregone conclusions.

I went to Japan provided with flattering references, on a mission for the *Society for Franco-Japanese Intellectual Rapprochement*. The French Minister of Foreign Affairs was kind enough to recommend me to his diplomatic agents and to inform them that I "wished to pursue philosophical studies and researches." He also asked them to lend me their kind aid if I thought wise to have recourse to them. But although I greatly appreciated the moral value of these recommendations, I must add that they were practically of little use to me. I soon understood that there was only one effective way of going about my work, and that was to frequent in all confidence, and if I may express myself thus, in all simplicity of heart, Buddhist bonzes, monks and pilgrims.

Therefore in order to undertake this inquiry, I lived in Japan as a Buddhist—studying and meditating with the bonzes and monks, amongst whom I am honoured to possess some true friends. For it must be understood that it was less a question of explaining the texts, than of expressing in clear terms actual and living Buddhist philosophical conceptions, such as they exist in the thought of enlightened Buddhists of our times, and such as they explained them to me. On the other hand, it was only in Japan that I could usefully pursue my investigations. Indian Buddhism is, in fact, almost extinct. The southern communities, such as those of Ceylon, practise what is more or less exactly called Primitive Buddhism (Hinayana)—or in any case a form of ancient and undeveloped Buddhism. Chinese Buddhism, which flourished before the Tang and Sung dynasties, has since entered into an era of decadence. Of the thirteen sects it counted formerly, there only remain formations resulting from the fusion of older elements, or which are impregnated with Thibetan mysticism. And even if Chinese Buddhism sought, as we are told it does, to reaffirm itself at this present moment, it would nevertheless be necessary to leave the renovators the time to accomplish their work before speaking of it.

This investigation which I undertook in the land of pink cherry trees and red maples, amongst "pure-hearted people," was the occasion of innumerable delights. I have lived in monasteries the life of Buddhist monks, and I have practised with those dear and gentle comrades, whom I shall never forget, the spiritual exercises and meditations prescribed by a common discipline. On the road leading to the sanctuaries I intended to visit, I have shared my bowl of rice with other pilgrims, humble folk ; like them I donned the *Kasa*—the large reed hat —and on wet days I slipped on the picturesque straw raincoat. Together we purified ourselves in the basin of lustral water placed at the entrance of the temples, and tasted the ineffable joy, of which I will speak at length later, of feeling one's soul renewed. I have loved the Buddhist evening peace in the calm temple-grounds, near lotus-covered ponds, and I have culled from the smiling lips of bonzes whose faces were penetrated with spirituality the secret of their peaceful hearts.

On moonlight nights I have known the emotion of discovering on mountain slopes the distant, twinkling lights of hospitable little temples—mere wooden shelters covered with thatch. I have seen an old bonze who watered his flags with love, whilst remarking to me with a smile and conformably to the faith, "*Flowers also can become Buddhas.*" And I have seen other priests obeying the Buddhist respect of life, avoid walking on mole-hills or disturbing the bees pilfering the heart of a peony.

In the depths of celebrated temples, replete with works of art, amidst gilded lacquer work and flowers, in an atmosphere heavy with incense and dreams, in which the thought of centuries seems to be condensed, I bowed piously before the golden or bronze Buddhas—images of *Him who was great because He loved Peace.*

In the sixth century of our era, Buddhism, born in India, then acclimatised in China, penetrated Japan, coming from Korea. The Japanese became acquainted with it through Chinese texts and commentaries.

The new religion found in the person of the Prince Regent Shōtoku (572-621), the Constantine of Japan, a zealous partisan. He adhered to it both by conviction and by policy, being persuaded that the conceptions of wisdom, and the ideas of charity, unity and spiritual harmony it professed, might be profitably opposed to the clan spirit which then divided the country. Fundamentally tolerant, Buddhism agreed well with Shintō, the ancient ancestor worship (which is still traditionally practised today), and gradually penetrated the society, the customs, the arts—in fact the whole soul of Japan. Japanese civilisation became essentially, profoundly Buddhist, and well could one speak of a "Buddhist Humanism."

But this result was only attained because the Japanese *milieu* reacted in its turn upon Buddhism—and this is precisely what interests us here. Elementarily, the fundamental and primitive themes of Buddhism can be resumed in the affirmation that "*Life is pain.*" Everything in Life is fleeting, passing, unstable, and this very impermanence of things results in still more pain. The origin of suffering is the desire to exist. Because of this desire we reincarnate ourselves eternally, and mill around in the unending Ocean of Transmigrations, which perpetuates suffering. Our Karma passes like a fluid which assumes different forms. Our destiny, for better or for worse, is the consequence of our preceding lives, in which we accomplished either good or evil. Each cause produces its own effect, and we obtain the retribution of our acts. In order to put an end to this succession of painful lives, one must kill in oneself the desire to exist. Then one reaches Illumination or Nirvâna, which is in reality the state of supreme wisdom, non-suffering and non-desire.

According to different spheres, this theory could become either a sterile and mortal pessimism, or a human philosophy full of charm, rich in delicate nuances, in dreams, and a very elevated method of attaining serenity of soul. Japan understood it in this second manner. But how was this transformation of adjustment accomplished? What exactly becomes of Buddhism, of the ancient pessimistic doctrine of India, in the human, smiling, living and vivifying Japanese atmosphere?

To this question my investigation brings an answer.

In order to understand clearly the pages one is about to read, it should not be forgotten that Buddhism, by posing as a *fact* that life is suffering, constitutes before all a method of salvation for human beings—a way, a "vehicle" as the Buddhists say, destined to lead us to the refuge, to the calm haven where suffering, and the desire which are its causes, no longer exist. To advance towards the supreme goal in the way of perfection, ends at what a mathematician would call the *limit point*, and what Buddhists call Nirvâna. One will readily admit that several ways may lead to this goal—just as several paths lead to the eternally pure summit of Fuji-Yama—and that these ways may be more or less easy or direct of access, and exact of the faithful more or less personal effort. The whole basis of Buddhism, which is but an attitude assumed before life, can be elementarily resumed thus : to escape from suffering and reach a calm, pure haven.

The ways and methods are numerous. There exists a whole gamut of them. Each Japanese sect has its own philosophy, its classical themes of meditation, its own particular spiritual manner. Branches or sub-sects still further diversify its interpretations. A Buddhist is not at all embarrassed, however, by this diversity in which contradictions sometimes appear. On the contrary, he is proud of it. He compares the multiplicity of doctrines and sects to flowers of different colours and perfume growing side by side, in the field of Buddha. Did not Buddha himself vary his teachings so as to adapt them to the intellectual capacity of his hearers ? One would offend a Christian, the adept of a revealed religion, by pretending that his religion was not definitive and that it is ceaselessly transforming itself. But on the contrary a Buddhist like Mr T. Suzuki, bonze and professor at the Buddhist College of Otani, states as a principle "that a religion must either adapt itself to the genius of the people who adopts it or else disappear."

It was precisely the gamut of these diverse aspects, of these philosophical doctrines and ways of spiritual salvation, which the Japanese bonzes and monks kindly consented to explain to me during our conversations and walks together. One knows that Buddhists have classically divided their conceptions into two schools : Hinayana or Little Vehicle (Japanese: *Shōjō*) and Mahayana, Great Vehicle (Japanese: *Daijō*).

The Hinayana is often called Primitive Buddhism or Buddhism of the South. It is characterised by the practice of austere disciplines which recall their monastic origin, by the acquisition of personal merits, and by long meditations on nihility—all things which he who aspires to Buddhahood, that is to say to Nirvâna, pursues throughout successive lives during innumerable *Kalpas*, or cosmic periods, whilst manifesting an almost positivist indifference to all high philosophical speculations, both general and co-ordinated, and to all true metaphysics.

The Mahayana on the contrary, broadening into idealistic or pantheistic metaphysical conceptions, by affirming generously a community of origin and essence between the creatures and Buddha, brings theoretically and practically to men in their march towards light, encouraging facilities and hopes which are sometimes radiant. One discovers in it a sort of democratic evolution. *All men can become Buddha!*

With the Mahayanist doctrines opens an era of more or less facilitated universal liberation. Certain of these doctrines assume the aspect of a gospel. At their origin these conceptions provoked in Japan controversies which were as impassioned as those which raged in France around the famous question of predestination and grace. They triumphed. Japan is Mahayanist, the characteristic Hinayana sects—Kusha and Jō-Jitsu—which had implanted themselves on its territory, disappeared, and with them those which drew their inspiration solely from the negative Indian philosophy (Sanron sect).

To be astonished by this would be to disregard the virtue of the Japanese atmosphere, of the physical and moral aspect of this adorable country, both subtle and positive, special but human. One must have travelled in this land of Japan, the landscapes of which are sometimes as vaporous as the snow on the cherry trees in springtime, or as the pink morning haze on the islands of the Inland Sea, and sometimes as clear-cut as those shrunken pines and those picturesque rocks which detach their black silhouettes, outlined in Indian ink, on a mother-of-pearl background. One must have walked in the company of Japanese friends—bonzes, merchants, officials or men of the people—who always, at their hour, reveal themselves poets, friends of ephemeral things—falling flowers, fleeting clouds, running water, the flight of a butterfly through the morning dew—and one must have discovered in other circumstances in this same friend a soul disciplined unto death, the iron will of a Samurai. One must have visited those wooden temples, so often consumed by fire, destroyed by earthquakes, but always rebuilt again, in order to understand that the Japanese soul and the physical *milieu*, which reflect in each other, are composed of impermanency and eternity, of dream and of solidity, of all that which, transposed to the plane of philosophy, is called *nihility and absolute*. In such a sphere Buddhism is modelled, transformed and polished. It reacts upon the morals, civilisation and art. It impregnates itself with them so as to express itself in infinitely varied and human formulas, bathing in its light the illusion and vacuity of this world, whilst safeguarding an essential reality and a luminous hope—just as an artist reserves a golden value on a black lacquered surface.

Let us now present to our readers the Buddhist doctrines which will be spoken of in the course of the following interviews, grouped summarily according to their philosophical characteristics. This is naturally a simple, unpretentious order of classification, the writer taking great care not to encroach upon the explanations which will follow, and which must preserve their direct value, their unexpected and fresh charm.

These doctrines of the Kusha, Jō-Jitsu and Sanron sects prescribe essentially the ancient method of long meditations on nihility or vacuity, during innumerable *kalpas* or cosmic periods. Supreme wisdom and Nirvâna are only reached when the illumined one has understood the nihility of all things, and has assimilated himself to vacuity. It is perfect intelligence, difficult to acquire, which saves the ego from the ocean of painful transmigrations. These philosophies are purely Hindu, but uttered by Japanese lips they become smiling and poetic. Their deceiving and pessimistic basis remains nevertheless what it was in the time of their founders, the celebrated sages of India. Imported into Nippon, the sects which professed exclusively these doctrines have become extinct. Their sacred books remain, however, inseparable from the Buddhist fund, even be it Japanese, and their thought still subsists. I recall the observation made to me by a bonze : *"Japan never rejects anything. It assimilates."*

I therefore beg my reader to do as much, and not to reject the doctrines of these sects by declaring summarily that the absent are always in the wrong, but to remember that wisdom has consisted in all times in becoming conscious of the nihility of all things, and that he himself doubtless belongs to the religion, one of whose sacred texts declares : *"Vanity of vanities, all is vanity and vexation of spirit."*

But as I have said above, the exclusive thought of absolute void, of black nihility, is not Japanese. How many times, having scaled a mountain which sheltered on its slopes some monastery or other, have I not turned back to look at the distance I have travelled ? The haze bathed the valley, yet always some object or other emerged here or there—a tree, a rock, a roof, or, as in the engravings of Hiroshige, a bridge—a lilliputian bridge— something to which life was clinging. Thus with the Hosso sect we will assist at the restoration of an *Absolute* : Thought. The Kusha and Jō-Jitsu doctrines were, as we will see, *phenomenalist*. The Sanron doctrine was *nihilist*. The Hosso doctrine will be *idealist* and *subjectivist*, long before the Idealist Schools of the West. Still more venturesome, the other sects —Kegon, Tendai, Shingon and Zen—will be *pantheist*, and will proclaim the consequence of our community of origin and essence with Buddha. All creatures are by their very nature potential Buddhas. From this moment Buddhism changes of aspect. The Japanese smile reappears like light following a fog. The sky was dark and empty, now it lightens again, becoming blue and radiant. Yet one must not forget that it is the same sky. The community of essence and origin of all beings, including Buddha—salvation for all, whence optimism—accessible methods—the way to Nirvâna rendered practicable to all—synthetic doctrines which not only do not exclude any of the preceding aspects of Buddhist thought, but which each even pretend to incorporate them—a religion with universal tendencies—such are the ideas which we find most frequently from henceforth and which give the general tone.

But if, abandoning this general point of view, we examine each doctrine separately, what varieties of conceptions present themselves to our mind! The Kegon doctrine with its astounding visions of thousands of Buddhas who eternally preach throughout the universe the Good Law to mankind! The Tendai doctrine whose pantheism can be paralleled to that of Spinoza, and which also sometimes rejoins the thought of Hegel! The mystical Shingon doctrine to which I have added, to amuse myself, marginal notes culled from Saint Teresa of Avila and Maeterlinck! The Zen philosophy, so original, individualistic and intuitive, which one quite naturally compares with the philosophies of Nietzsche and Bergson— that Zen which appeals to poets, artists and dilettanti, and which was nevertheless the religion of the intrepid Samurais of yore, and which now numbers millions of adepts!

Lastly, there are the sects of the Pure Land (the Jôdo and Shinshu sects), the doctrines of the grace and of the mercy of Amida-Buddha, which are situated at the extreme point of the evolution tending towards optimism, and the simplification of the methods of worship. Their essential thought may be resumed as follows: access to the Pure Land (Paradise in which one reaches Nirvâna and therefore where one becomes a Buddha) is promised after death to all men without exception, whether they be worthy or sinners, on the sole condition of their having implored Amida-Buddha *with a sincere heart*, by pronouncing his name. Faith replaces philosophy. The faithful no longer reaches the supreme refuge by the painful "holy way"—but without effort, allowing himself to be carried on "Amida's barque of Love." The practices of the cult are reduced to the utmost—to a simple recitation of three words—"*Namu Amida Butsu,*" which is assuredly within the reach of all, even of simple or busy folk.

Thus the most difficult religion of the world has become for the adepts of the Pure Land, the most simple and practical which it is possible to imagine—a sort of pietism devoid of formalities or impediments. And that also is a revolution gently accomplished in the heart of Buddhism. Here one cannot help establishing a comparison with Christianity. I did not fail to draw the attention of the bonzes of the sect to this point. They partially recognised it, and in particular Messrs Kawasaki and Fujioka of the Shinshu sect, both bonzes of the celebrated Hongwanji sanctuary at Kyôto, and Mr Kanei Okomoto, bonze of the Jôdo sect, belonging to the no less famous monastery of Chion-in. One will read their answers. Let us add that, by reason of their practical simplification, these sects seem able to adapt themselves particularly well to the exactions of active and absorbing modern life. That is doubtless one of the reasons of their success, and why they actually number more than ten million perpetual members.

It would be difficult to determine in what measure the sects of the Pure Land—purely Japanese creations, but whose canonical texts are ancient sutras bearing expressly those simplifications of doctrine and practice which they advocate— have themselves, and by the effect of a natural evolution, become adapted to the exigencies of contemporary life, and in what measure their religious leaders, alarmed by Christian rivalry, have very legitimately been able to voluntarily accentuate their modernistic tendencies. Those who will study this question must not forget what has just been said about the evolution of Buddhism in the sense of accessibility and facility —evolution which dates since long. Nor should they ignore that the Nichiren sect—a creation of the Japanese saint whose name it bears, and the resolute adversary of the Pure Land doctrines—has nevertheless, like the latter, opened the way of easy salvation to all, and simplified religious practices to such an extent as to consist merely in the utterance of a few words.

The tendencies we have just spoken of are general, and characterise the religious evolution of Japan.

In order to understand these different doctrines and their spiritual and practical value, the reader must make a personal effort of comprehensive sympathy and sincerity of soul. He will not be content with noting their structure, with criticising them or erecting systems of logical arguments for or against them. He will place himself in the light which each sheds and will in his conscience extract with sympathy the living impression of that doctrine, just as one intensifies the perfume of a flower by holding its corolla in one's hand. One of these doctrines, for instance, may be only a theme for meditation; one should therefore meditate upon this theme. Another expresses the mystery of the world by appropriate ritualistic mysteries; one should feel this mystery. Another appeals to intuition: one should therefore reawaken primordial qualities in oneself. Under the varied appearance of things the Oriental—and the Japanese in particular—perceives a fundamental unity, a continuity, a Karma, where the Westerner only sees most often opposed and even contradictory values. One must therefore take this fact into account. The shades revealed by Far-Eastern psychology are extraordinarily rich. One must not forget it. *And if it should sometimes seem that the Western and Far-Eastern thought are not always situated on the same plane, the reader should, by an effort of sympathy, strive to accede to the next plane. He will certainly gain by so doing, for intelligence likes new horizons, and the heart enriches itself by its contact with other hearts.*

I do not wish to end these pages of introduction without expressing my deep admiration for the members of the Buddhist clergy, and my sincere gratitude towards those Japanese bonzes and monks who welcomed me with so much kindness and delicacy. And on certain evenings when I was exhausted after my pilgrimages, some of them gave me the same proofs of care and solicitude that old friends one has just met again might give one.

A great number of bonzes are true scholars versed in the study of texts. Besides Chinese, Sanskrit and Thibetan they have also a knowledge of one or more European languages. They are, moreover, professors in the Imperial Universities or in Free Faculties. Their high intellectual value is enhanced by an extreme modesty which we are not always accustomed to meet in Europe. Thus one of my friends, a Japanese bonze, whose name I will not mention out of discretion, corrects the works of a famous French Sanskrit scholar.

The knowledge of Western things possessed by these Japanese priests is an unfailing source of astonishment. Thus Mr Nukariya, bonze and professor at the Faculty of Kyôto, quotes and discusses Bergson. Mr Yamabe, professor and bonze in the same town, who is very learned in all Christian doctrines, speaks of the Gospel of Saint Mark as if it was quite a familiar text. My friend Mr Yoshida, a Buddhist monk, offered me one day the treatises of a Japanese priest, remarking quite naturally : "It will remind you in many points of the philosophy of Plotinus."

Another day I saw my friend Mr Fujioka, who is also a bonze and who specialises in social questions, plunged in the study of voluminous files which I recognised as documents belonging to the *Assistance Publique* of Paris. And—shall I say it ?—one evening I surprised Mr Yamaguchi, bonze, professor and scholar of a universal reputation, absorbed in a French book he was reading with an indulgent smile. I was indiscreet enough to glance at the title : it was *Le Livre de Mon Ami*, by Anatole France !

It should be known in France and in the West that nothing is so false as the occidental prejudice that a bonze is a being intellectually separated from the rest of humanity, whose brain is immobilised by dead ideas. Japanese bonzes constitute an *élite*. They are the perfect representatives of one of the greatest spiritual values of the world. Assuredly all bonzes cannot be great scholars. But the humble bonze of a small temple, who lives in solitude, will, to say the least, set one an example of wisdom, of simplicity of life and candour of soul, which I cannot recall without deep emotion.

Buddhism is *the highest moral value* man has discovered exclusively *in* man. It has a right to our respect and to our sympathy, as have also all the systems of ideas and beliefs which bring to humanity a principle of wisdom, a hope or a consolation. No one knows what tomorrow may be made of, and the road is uncertain. It therefore does not behoove us to deprive the human mind of any of its spiritual values. On the contrary, we should strive to preserve for it *all* its avenues of Light.

And to consider only one of these—Buddhism—I would resume my thought thus. Buddhism possesses a pacifying virtue which cannot be contested. Its true goal is peace of soul. Peace! How many of us in the confusion of their hearts could say like the Shonin Shinran before he founded the sect of the Pure Land :

"*I am he who has lost his way in the mountain and who is drowning in the water of the tempest.*"

Who could deny that wisdom dwells in these Buddhist sanctuaries ?

Have we therefore the right to ignore this wisdom, we men of Europe, who have drowned the world in blood ?

E. STEINILBER-OBERLIN.

Paris, 1930.

During my stay in Japan, I never failed to receive the warmest and most sympathetic welcome from all the Buddhist monks, bonzes and professors I consulted.

I therefore address my deepest gratitude to them as well as to my friend Mr Kuni Matsuo, who was my faithful companion during my visit to Japan.

THE BUDDHIST SECTS OF JAPAN

CHAPTER I

THE KUSHA SECT

(1) The Kusha Sect. (2) One evening in the sacred park of Nara Mr K. Koyama, bonze and scholar, explains to me the principle of the Kusha philosophy: the inexistence of the 'ego,' and the reality of those elements the assemblage of which forms the world. The theory of the *dharmas* according to the *Book of Metaphysical Treasure*. (3) On red maples reflected in the Tatsuta river. How one becomes a Buddha.

1. *The Kusha Sect*

The Kusha doctrine was brought to Japan in the year 658 of our era, by two Japanese priests, Chitsu and Chitatsu, who, during a sojourn in China, had become the disciples of Chinese teachers.

The canonical text of this sect, translated into Japanese, is the *Book of Metaphysical Treasure* (Sanskrit: *Abhidarma Kosa Shastra*) composed by Vạsubandhu, one of the most celebrated sages of India, who lived in the fourth and fifth centuries of our era. The Kusha sect derived its name, which is a Japanese transcription of the Sanskrit term, from the title of this book. Kosa signifies "treasure."

Although the Kusha sect is extinct, the above-mentioned text is still considered one of the most important works of the sacred literature of Buddhism, and is still studied in Japanese universities.

2. *In the Sacred Park of Nara*

Today I visit the temple of Nara with my Buddhist master and teacher, the bonze Koyama, a most learned philosopher and poet.

The shades of evening are falling in the sacred park. A few stone lanterns are lit. The wind has subsided. The great peace of Buddha descends upon the motionless trees and penetrates one's very soul. Tame deer come and eat out of our hands the rice cakes we have bought for them at a little booth. Shadows seem to hover under the secular cryptomerias. Shintō temples adjoin Buddhist shrines, for in Nara all is peaceful, tolerant, sympathetic and heart soothing. Oh the indefinable charm of Buddhist serenity!

Indicating this dream scenery with a discreet gesture of his hand, the bonze remarks smilingly:

"Buddhist peace."

I am particularly affected by the silence of the old park. It is not an absolute or mortal silence. It is rather the silence of life appeased. By listening intently I can catch the murmur of things, and sometimes the echo of a wooden gong which priests are striking in a near-by temple.

We gradually yield to that Buddhist charm composed of spirituality and art, which lulls our spirit. I seem to see again the venerable temples of black and red lacquer, against a leafy background already mellowed by autumn, through which we sauntered all that day—and the Dai-Butsu, the colossal Buddha with his beatific smile, seated on an immense lotus. I recall the interior of Buddhist sanctuaries—sudden revelations of a strange weirdness filled with golds, flowers, precious ornaments, and naïve offerings dulled with blue incense. Nara, ancient centre of Japanese Buddhism! In truth there exists here a deep and human conception which one must learn if one does not wish to pass through Japan either as a blind man or as a bounder.

Let he who wishes to do so travel hurriedly, tourist fashion. I for my part have come religiously to the sanctuary of Nara, drawn hither by my love of souls, and because I wish to strive through sympathy to understand the souls of others.

Having witnessed extraordinary upheavals, I come as a man

of my time to ask those who are worthy of it to reveal to me the secret of their inner peace.

And this evening in particular, in company of this sensitive and intelligent Japanese priest, I would deem any other attitude either a betrayal or an insolence.

As we walk the bonze remarked:

"I brought you to Nara this evening because I believed that in this sacred park I could explain to you better than elsewhere the philosophical doctrines of the sects of Kusha, Jō-Jitsu and Sanron, the object of my lesson. These sects were founded at Nara, and it was here that they developed themselves. Nara was, as you know, the brilliant capital of Japan between the years 710 and 794 of our era, and Buddhism was its very soul. At that epoch it counted no less than 500,000 inhabitants. Its magnificent court encouraged and protected religion, literature and art. The splendour of Nara has passed, as all things pass, impermanence being the law of the world. That which represents spirit alone subsists, in spite of having experienced different material vicissitudes : these old temples, such as the Todaiji and Kofukuji founded at that epoch—the Hōryūji, which is still more ancient, the monumental statue of Buddha in gold and bronze, and a few other treasures.

"The three Buddhist sects of Kusha, Jō-Jitsu and Sanron, of which I am about to speak to you, no longer exist. They are dead sects."

I gaze surprised at the bonze who, impressive as ever, clad in black, wrapped in a silken stole, treads softly on the fallen leaves. His shaven head gleams like pale ivory, and his face shines as with a spiritual light.

"Do I astonish you?" he asks. "Yet, believe me, it is not useless to speak of these dead sects. It is necessary to know their doctrine if one wishes to understand present-day Buddhism. The canonical texts of these sects imported from India have remained substantial works of Japanese Buddhism, which has rejected nothing, but has been content to assimilate, modify, diversify and synthesise. These philosophical acquisitions, amalgamated to others, have created the doctrines of the living sects. In short, the essential thought of the dead sects subsists. Does not the past always subsist ? This old park is bathed in mysterious shadows because it is full of memories, because vanished causes and effects interpenetrate each other unfathomably. When the moon veils her face the shadows disappear. Yet have they left no trace whatever ? Who can say what may be the action of an instant of shadow upon a blade of grass ? Around you in this shadowed park, where the moonlight filters through the branches, a subtle play of shades and shadows superimpose themselves and intermingle with each other. Thus it is also with human thought.

"It is necessary to know what has been, in order to fathom what *is*."

The bell of Todaiji vibrated gravely.

"It has rung thus for twelve centuries," said the bonze.

And this remark still further deepened my emotion.

"I will now," he continued, "give you an account of the philosophy of the Kusha sect. It was founded in Japan in 625, and its text-book, composed by the Indian scholar Vasubandhu, is entitled the *Book of Metaphysical Treasure*. What is this *Treasure* ? A conception of nihility, the meditation of which, by freeing us from the vanities of this world, allows us to acquire, thanks to the tribulations of life and adversity, a soul as indifferent, as detached and as subtle as the pollen of flowers in springtime.

"The principle of this philosophy may be resumed thus: the 'ego' does not exist. It is merely an illusion. Man is only the aggregate of diverse elements such as sensation, memory, intelligence, which each constitute a reality, and all together, Reality. Man is, so to speak, made up of different parts. Yet all these parts united do not create a distinct personality—an 'ego.' The term 'ego' is void of sense—or rather it expresses merely a dream, a lie."

"So, I do not exist?" I asked.

"That which interests you most in yourself, your 'ego' does not exist. But I repeat that each of the different elements of which you are formed—such as sight, hearing, smell, touch, desire, intelligence, memory—really exist. These elements are classically designed by the Sanskrit word *dharmas* (Japanese: *Hō*). The most concentrated formula of the Kusha philosophy is finally the following: The non-existence of the 'ego' and the reality of *dharmas*."

"I have some difficulty in admitting that I am deprived of an 'ego,'" I observed. "Won't you please develop your thought?"

"One might compare the ego to a cloud of fireflies in the night. What is it in reality? A gathering of fireflies. As a distinct being it does not exist. Yet one might mistake it for a distinct creature, fantastic and luminous, which lives, extends or contracts itself, and floats against the black sky. Yet it is only a word. In the same way a swarm of bees hanging to a pine branch is but an aggregate of bees, and the green mass of the pine itself is but a compound of fine seeds, just as our body and spirit are compounds of multiple elements which are perceived under a material or spiritual aspect. An aggregate does not make a person. The ego is merely an illusion."

Whilst the bonze was speaking, a procession of fairies, lit by a lantern, passed in the distance. These were the sacred dancers of the near-by Shintō temple, clothed in white and red, their hair decked with camellias. Suddenly their lantern went out and the fairy vision disappeared. My teacher looked at me with a smile. We both had the same thought: "Thus does illusion fly away."

"In the *Milindapanha*," continued the bonze, "a celebrated book of Hindu Buddhism, the wise Nagasena explains to King Milinda the non-existence of the 'ego' by means of a comparison which has since become classical.

29

'Venerable man,' said the King, 'I came in a chariot.'

'What is a chariot?' asked the sage. 'How can one conceive it?
Is the pole the chariot?'

'By no means, venerable one.'

'Are the wheels the chariot?'

'By no means, venerable one.'

'Is the body the chariot?'

'By no means, venerable one.'

'Is the yoke the chariot?'

'By no means, in truth, venerable one.'

'I beg thee, O King, to tell me whether the pole, the axle, the
wheels, the body, the yoke united form the chariot?'

'Truly not, venerable one.'

'Therefore, O King, is there anything other than the pole, the
axle, the wheels, the body and the yoke which is the chariot?'

'By no means, in truth, venerable one.'

'King, although I have questioned thee very closely, I am unable
to discover this chariot. In truth the word "chariot" is but an
empty word.'

"Just as the Hindu sage takes his chariot to pieces," continued the bonze, "so the author of the *Book of Metaphysical
Treasure*, the canonical text of the Kusha sect, takes the Universe
to pieces by means of a more abstract and less familiar process.
He does so, however, with the same object, which is to
demonstrate that outside of the pieces which compose the
Universe there is nothing. You will find in the text the
enumeration of the seventy-five *dharmas* and five aggregates
(Sanskrit: *Skandhas*) which constitute man and the world. I
quote at random some of the former: sensation, form, desire,
intelligence, memory, ignorance, selfishness, faith, lack of evil,
energy, life, birth, destruction, space, etc. These are grouped
into five aggregates: form, sensation, ideas, concepts and
understanding, the first of which is material, whilst the others
are spiritual. As it often happens in Buddhist books, the
categories, divisions and subdivisions are given here in a very
detailed way. Thus there exists pure *dharmas* and impure
dharmas;—conditioned *dharmas* (*samskrita*) and unconditioned
dharmas (*asamskrita*);—the *dharmas* belonging to the realm of

passion, of good or evil, of incertitude, etc. These precisions may seem to you idle scholasticism. Do not let us forget that every race and every epoch has possessed its own methods of reasoning. The author of the *Book of Metaphysical Treasure* wished to place at our disposal a complete set of elements and conditions allowing us to reconstitute a being, in order to show up strikingly the absence of 'ego.' In reality these elements cross and intercross each other, and it is their point of junction which we call a being and which produces the illusion of an 'ego.'"

"But," I objected, "by thus insisting on the nothingness of man, does not one risk introducing the darkest pessimism and sadness into one's mind?"

"Let us beware of the mirage of words," said the bonze. In order to understand Buddhism, one must cease to be a maniac of so-called reality, a builder on emptiness. One must know how to contemplate nothingness. Does the illusion of an 'ego' make you happy? By no means. The 'ego' is merely a source of suffering. Yet it is for this phantom that so many men struggle, lament and fret themselves painfully in vain. Meditate one hour only on the inexistence of the 'ego,' and you will already feel like another man—like an appeased and serene intelligence; your misfortunes will strike against emptiness. What would it be if you had meditated for long—or, according to the classical term, during incalculable *kalpas* (cosmic periods)? Meditation upon the *dharmas* and non-existence of the 'ego' is rewarded by peace of soul, and not by sadness."

"A negative joy," I objected.

"That of the wise man. For what intelligent man could wish to torment himself about his ghost?"

3. *How one becomes a Buddha*

A few days after this conversation, chance led our steps to the banks of the Tatsuta river, sung by the poets. In it were reflected raspberry-coloured autumn maples. The water, the foliage, were both red, as if incandescent. One could not distinguish the point where the river was reddened by the reflection of the maples, or where the fallen leaves made a purple carpet.

Pointing to the river, the bonze remarked softly :

"A mantle of brocade."

The celebrated poem by the bonze Noin came to my mind : "*Carried by the wind, the maple leaves of Mimora weave brocades on the waters of the Tatsuta.*"

No doubt my teacher shared this thought.

"One could almost believe it *is* brocade," he remarked. "Yet it is only an illusion. This brocade exists no more than our 'ego.' We see there in truth but different elements—maple leaves—reflections upon the water."

Then the stars began to shine and their light fell on the water. I noticed that the surfaces of water bearing maple leaves remained opaque, and did not reflect the starry heavens. Yet, farther on, one could distinguish quite clearly the flowing water reflecting the stars and red maples, from water covered with a sheet of red leaves.

The bonze remarked with a laugh :

"The end of Illusion is . . . Illumination."

We pursued our philosophical walk in silence for a while.

Meditation on the subject proposed to me—the non-existence of the 'ego'—absorbed me for a long time. I was undertaking the experience wholeheartedly. I said to myself : "This evening I want to follow the advice of this bonze, and to liberate my thought. If I am merely 'vacuity,' I wish to taste fully the charm, the intoxication of vacuity. How often does it happen to us in the course of our life to live one of those rare moments of absolute sincerity towards ourselves, and to escape from our prejudices and foregone conclusions ? What I first understood was that, contrarily to all reason, Western education renders us unfit for meditation. Today no Westerner, except priests, knows how to meditate. We are paralysed by the mean demon of a positive and misunderstood utilitarianism—by a still more vulgar irony and by ready jest. Then certain philosophical objections came to my mind. My teacher forestalled them by saying :

"It is at first difficult to admit that sensation, intelligence, memory, existing really as such, should not be *my* sensation, *my* intelligence and *my* memory. To admit the reality of the elements, causes of my illusion, and not admit the ' ego ' which one believes to be their centre and support, and thus reverse the vulgar belief, requires a power of meditation which is not acquired in a day.

"It is only by successive and prolonged meditative exercises that you will succeed in freeing your thought from the mist producing the mirage. Gradually your consciousness will become enlightened. Then one day the absurd illusion will fall away like the red maple leaves in autumn and you will be flooded by the peaceful light of heaven. But before reaching this point, the 'holy way' you must follow is both long and difficult.

"Here is, according to the teaching of the Kusha sect, how one becomes a Buddha.

"The *Shō-mon* (mere hearers of the word) will escape the confusion in which so many men are floundering, only after three successive births, if they constantly practise meditation. But if they are careless or narrow-minded, they will have to pass through sixty *kalpas* (cosmic periods) before reaching enlightenment. The *En-Gaku* (individual Buddhas) and the *Bosatsu* (Bodhisattvas or Future Buddhas) reach Illumination after a probation, the duration of which is proportionate to their faculty. In any case, it is only after innumerable *kalpas*, consecrated to meditation, that the Bosatsu, by practising the *Rokudo*, or Six Perfections (meditation, morality, charity, energy, patience and wisdom), will at last reach Buddhahood."

CHAPTER II

THE JŌ-JITSU SECT

(1) The Jō-Jitsu Sect. (2) A Buddhist priest explains to me the principle of this sect: the 'ego' does not exist, neither do the elements which compose beings and the world. The theme of the two nothingnesses. "This world of dew."

1. *The Jō-Jitsu Sect*

The doctrine of this sect was imported to Japan by the Korean bonzes, Kwanroku and Ekwan, about the year 625 of our era. Its canonical text is *The Book of the Perfection of Truth*, in Japanese *Jō-Jitsu-Ron*, from which it takes its name (Sanskrit: *Sayta-siddhi-Shastra*). It is a collection of interpretations of the conceptions of primitive Buddhism, composed in the fourth century by the Hindu sage Harivarman. It was later translated into Chinese. This sect, like the preceding one, no longer exists, but the interest of the above-mentioned work is still great, as the philosophical thought of this sect marks an intermediate position between the Kusha doctrine and the Sanron doctrine which we will examine later.

2. *The Doctrine*

Dawn sprinkled the alleys of Nara with pink splashes of colour. A fragrant smell emanated from the pines. The ground was littered with small crinkled objects resembling dried leaves. These were *uzumi*, or the empty shells of cicadae. Everyone knows that in autumn Japanese cicadae throw off their light shells just as they would discard a faded garment. Poets see in these fragile empty envelopes an image of life.

I thought of the tiercet by the poet Jōsō : "*Oh the autumn cicadae, dead beside its empty shell!*" Sadness. Smiling nihility.

"You believed," objected my teacher, "that having meditated upon the Kusha philosophy you had reached an understanding of nothingness. But for an adept of the Jō-Jitsu sect you have only reached half-way. The Kusha doctrine teaches that the 'ego' alone is illusory, but that the *dharmas* are real. *The Jō-Jitsu doctrine teaches that both the 'ego' and the dharmas are equally illusions.*"

"It is therefore complete nihility ?"

"Yes, but with nevertheless a subtle ideal and theoretical difference which I will explain in a moment. Practically the Jō-Jitsu sect convenes you to a double meditation on the following classical theme : 'True *dharmas*, in which no 'ego' exists, are like an empty vase. And as the substance of the vase does not exist in itself, just so the *dharmas* are inexistent in themselves.'

"This theme of meditation, which brings to the spirit a sense of liberating detachment, is called the Meditation on the Two Nothingnesses. The empty cicadae shells in autumn reminded me a moment ago of the nothingness of all things. The *dharmas* are like this empty shell."

"What about that subtle difference you were going to explain to me ?"

"Well, here it is. It resides in the demonstration of the second nothingness—that is in the inexistence of everything in itself. On this point the sect's doctrine is as follows : the past no longer exists—the future does not exist as yet—the present moment alone is real. But what *is* the present moment ? Does not the present vanish as soon as it is born ? Everything *is* and *is not* at the very moment we think of it. Everything is born and destroys itself immediately. What we call reality would therefore seem to be but a moment's flash.

"Now the moment of reason (Japanese : *setsuna*) escapes us. It possesses merely a theoretical value. Yet we speak of reality. How can we even have the illusion of it ? Because millions of successive instants give us the illusion of continuity. And this is illusory because there is only a succession—a series—of distinct phenomena, but never an identity or a real continuity. The burning end of a rope which I twirl like a sling gives the illusion of a rope of fire. So it is with the aspect of the world."

"Therefore everything is illusion," I remarked, "except, perhaps, that flash of reason that is and is not at the same instant, and which, in consequence, I would not know what to do with. This seems to be an *instantaneous* philosophy which reaches the limits of nihilism ?"

"Yes. I'll add that by thus disjoining the dream of the world, the doctrine divides the illusions into three classes. I have just spoken of it from the point of view of duration. That is the illusion of continuous phenomena (*Sozoku-ne*). Two or more lines of apparent continuity meet each other, thus forming illusory combinations, since they themselves are but illusions. This is called the illusion of contingent phenomena (*Injoke*). Then men arrogantly establish relations between these illusions (*Sodaïke*)."

Drops of dew clung to the ends of twigs and blades of grass, then they fell, evaporating in the warm, pink mist of dawn. A whole scintillating vision of multicoloured fires vanished suddenly.

Japanese Buddhists have a proverbial and poetical expression to translate the impermanence, the flight of things towards nihility. And the bonze reminded me of it very aptly as he observed with a smile :

"This world of dew."

CHAPTER III

THE SANRON SECT

(1) The Sanron Sect. (2) A Buddhist priest explains to me the nihilistic principle of the Sanron philosophy. Nothing exists. All is vacuity. Nagarjuna, the negator. The Parable of the Man with Diseased Eyes. (3) The Hōryūji sanctuary, the ancient centre of the sect. The Sanron philosophy versus the Japanese soul. (4) Mr Yamaguchi, a bonze and professor at Otani-Daigaku, the Buddhist Faculty of Kyōto, lecturer on the canonical book of the Sanron Sect, explains to me his personal point of view. The texts of Nagarjuna, the inexistence of the soul and the vacuity of things. (5) Moonlight before the pond of Sarusawa: a résumé of the philosophy of the dead sects.

1. *The Sanron Sect*

The Sanron sect (literally The Three Books) possesses, as its name tells us, three canonical texts. It was founded in Japan in A.D. 625 by the Korean bonze Ekwan, the same who had imported the fundamental texts of the Jō-Jitsu sect. Like these, the Sanron texts had previously been translated from Sanskrit into Chinese.

The three canonical works of this sect are, beginning with the most important, *The Book on the Meditation of the Middle Way* (Japanese: *Thû-Kwanron*; Sanskrit: *Madhyamika-Shastra*), composed by the celebrated Hindu philosopher Nagarjuna, who lived at the end of the second century A.D. *The Hundred Books* (Japanese: *Hyakuron*; Sanskrit: *Sata-Shastra*), by the same author. Lastly, *The Book of the Twelve Doors* (Japanese: *Junimonron*; Sanskrit: *Dvadasa-Nikâya-Shastra*), by the Hindu philosopher Deva.

The Sanron sect no longer exists, but the work of Nagarjuna, which is essential in the history and formation of Buddhist doctrines, still subsists. *The Book on the Meditation of the Middle Way*, which is particularly studied, recently formed the subject of a series of lectures given by Mr Yamaguchi, who, besides being a bonze, is also a great scholar and an eminent Sanskritist.

2. *A Buddhist priest explains to me the nihilistic principle of the Sanron philosophy. Nothing exists. All is vacuity*

Before penetrating into the temple of Hōryūji, the oldest sanctuary of Japan and ancient centre of the Sanron sect, now affected to the Hosso sect, the bonze spoke to me as follows:

"The Kusha doctrine denied the existence of the 'ego,' but admitted the existence of the *dharmas*. The momentaneistic doctrine of the Jō-Jitsu, which only considers the Present, merely conceded to these elements the real life of a moment of reason, the Present dying as soon as it is born.

"Thus the world had been pulverised into subtle dust atoms, and, so to speak, no longer existed. Yet this slight reality was still too much in the sight of Nagarjuna, the Hindu sage of the second century A.D., the most implacable negator, the greatest nihilist the world has ever seen.

"In truth, Nagarjuna vaunts himself of having no doctrine, no system. He is content to destroy the system of others. This is what one should understand by *The Middle Way*, the characteristic title of his most important work. Having criticised and rejected all the philosophical doctrines of his time, both realist and negative—both the belief in the existence as well as in the non-existence of things, and the affirmations of both right and left, if I may express myself thus—Nagarjuna takes his stand on another plane: *The Middle Way*, leading to the point of 'non-acquisition' (*Mutoku*), where the spirit identifies itself with absolute vacuity. The method of *The Middle Way*, which consists essentially in disavowing both those who believe in reality and those who affirm the non-existence of things, has played, and still plays an important part in Buddhistic speculation. But the term '*Middle Way*' covers, according to different authors and sects, different conceptions of a more or less extensive range. What is especially striking in Nagarjuna is, above all, his destructive dialectic which leaves the mind before a void, or, more exactly, makes a void of the mind.

"If you will question me now, I will endeavour to answer you by reading passages from the *Thû-Kwan-Ron*, the sacred book of the sect."

The autumn wind chased before us the dead leaves and the golden dust of the path.

"This morning," observed the bonze dreamily, "I noticed near the old temple a small bed of white and yellow chrysanthemums. A light breeze stripped the flowers, and thousands of petals strewed the earth, coloured fragments which reminded me of the appearance of the world when one has cleared away its illusions. Then the wind blew stronger, scattering the petals, dispersing the faded flowers. And suddenly before my eyes, all was emptiness."

I understood the poetical allusion. Thus the distinctive genius of Nagarjuna swept away all systems before it.

I questioned methodically:

"What about the 'ego'—the soul?"

"There is neither 'ego,' nor soul: only vacuity." (*He then proceeded to read Nagarjuna's text which he was carrying.*) "Where would the soul be if it existed? In each cell of the body supporting it, or enveloping it exteriorly? But whether it sustains the body or protects it like an armour, since the soul is immortal, the body under these conditions should also be immortal."

"What about matter?"

"There is no matter—only vacuity." (*Reading.*) "If matter exists, it would escape our understanding. The quality of extension conferred to it is an absurdity. The atom is indivisible? That is another absurdity: since it faces its neighbour on six sides, it possesses six parts. Extension cannot be explained. Forms and matter do not exist."

"What about the real elements of the world—the *dharmas* and the *aggregates*?"

"There are no elements—only vacuity." (*Reading.*) "The theory of real aggregates is indefensible. There can be neither conjunction nor separation of elements. To lend beings a nature is but a vain word. The physical and spiritual elements of this world of phantasmagorical illusions is equally unreal."

"Sensation, perception?"

"There is no sensation nor perception—only vacuity." (*Reading.*) "The concurrence of the object, the senses and understanding is impossible. Sensation, perception, are but vain words—illusions."

"Causes?"

"There are no causes—only vacuity." (*Reading.*) "The pretended relations of causes to effects is nihility, vanity, illusion. Either the thing is born of itself and would not cease from being born again, or it is born of others, and, in that case, one says an absurdity, as others cannot exist in reference to that which does not exist."

"Movement, change?"

"There is neither the one nor the other—only vacuity." (*Reading.*) "Who says change says unreality. If things were real they would be unmovable. Milk would already be butter —butter would still be milk."

"Yet . . . reason?"

"Is but an error. Everything passes. There is neither essence, nor phenomena, nor principles. Only vacuity— vacuity—vacuity."

"Still," I objected, "if everything is emptiness, then Buddha himself does not exist?"

"Nagarjuna foresaw that objection," replied the bonze. "The state of vacuity is precisely what is called Nirvâna. And as Nirvâna is the possession of Buddhahood, we are Buddhas by the very reason of our vacuity. I repeat that you are not yet in presence of a system, but in that of a method of reducing all affirmation *ab absurdo*. Nagarjuna once declared : 'If I presented any kind of thesis I would be at fault. But I have no thesis.' Vacuity is neither reality nor non-existence—neither affirmation nor negation. It is the point of non-acquisition (*Mutoku*)—the summit from which one no longer hears even that 'mental murmur' which Buddhist texts speak of."

There was silence, then the bonze remarked :

"I will tell you, to end, the Parable of the Man with Diseased Eyes, which is a classic text of Hindu Buddhism.

"A poor monk who suffered from a disease of the eyes thought he saw flies in his empty bowl, and was ceaselessly making the gesture of brushing away the annoying little insects. Seeing this, a passer-by asked him : 'Why dost thou make that gesture ?' The monk with diseased eyes answered : 'I am chasing the flies which are in my bowl.' The passer-by then declared : 'But there are no flies in thy bowl. It is absolutely empty.' But the sick man did not understand and continued to repeat his vain gesture."

"The passer-by is no doubt the Initiated who sees clearly ?" I asked.

"He is Buddha. The man with the diseased eyes is the ordinary man who lives in the world of illusions. All is empty. Enlightened understanding also is empty. The passer-by has not even the idea that there are flies or the appearance of flies in the bowl. From that point of view his thought is also empty. It is thus that Buddha sees the world.

"Do you understand now why the wise man can say neither 'yes' nor 'no,' and must finally make silence within himself ?"

Dusk was falling. The old temple of Hōryūji, of which we had just crossed the threshold, slept amidst the shadows. Oh, that Buddhist calm !

Almost imperceptibly the bonze murmured :

"The silence. . . ."

3. *In the Sanctuary of Hōryūji*

It is not without reason that we visit Hōryūji, the oldest
temple in Japan, the ancient centre of the Sanron sect, which is
occupied today by the priests of the Hosso sect.   A visit to this
temple poses the problem of how the Japanese spirit reacts in
presence of foreign importations.   At the sight of the artistic
treasures accumulated in its halls, in the pagoda, in the *kura*,[1]
many of which are of Hindu, Chinese and Korean inspiration,
one might fear the effect of this invasion of foreign influence
on Japanese taste, if one did not remember that Japan has
always known how to assimilate exterior ideas without ever
compromising its essential originality.

In a parallel manner I experienced the same fear, soon
allayed, however, concerning spiritual things.   In presence of
the doctrines of Hindu Buddhism, the Japanese mind has
reacted, as we shall see, with incomparable masterliness and
facility.   The Kusha, Jō-Jitsu and Sanron doctrines were too
charged with negative Hindu philosophy and with a depressing
nihilism to be accepted as such by the *nuancé* and practical mind
of the Japanese.   The canonical books of these sects subsist, but
the sects themselves are dead, and Japanese Buddhist thought,
pursuing its smiling and constructive evolution, has built its
spiritual home according to its own particular genius, and to
its own racial qualities.

A young priest does us the honour of the sanctuary with
perfect graciousness.   His engaging smile dispenses me with
presenting the credentials in which eminent Buddhists had
kindly recalled my sympathy to their faith.   We visit the
Ni-o-mon, the old two-storied gate, the *Kondo* temple and the
five-storied pagoda.   Then we enter the *Dai-Kodo*, or the
"Hall of Lectures," in which I find a striking proof of what I
have just been saying.   Am I in India ?   The very ancient
mural paintings are clearly of Hindu inspiration.   The expression of that Buddha on his throne, and of those divinities

[1] Store-room, treasure-house.

decked with tiaras, is full of lassitude and resignation. These are truly gods intoxicated with the perfume of some strange exotic flower, obsessed by some distant thought which has no relation with humanity. One might believe them to have been brought here direct from the temples of Ajunta. What a contrast with the products of Japanese art of which I see such graceful examples in other halls—statuettes in gilded wood or polychrome earthenware, both spiritual and realistic—as well as that adorable, smiling Kwannon, the Goddess of Mercy and Kindness.

The bonze draws a lesson from these surroundings.

"In these temples where, under an artistic aspect, Hindu philosophy appears in conflict with Japanese thought, I think it opportune to define the rôle of Nagarjuna in the internal evolution of Buddhism. It should be remembered that the destructive dialectics of the great negator had as unforeseen consequence, that of preparing the way for Mahayana Buddhism. I specify: the doctrines of the Hinayana (Kusha and Jō-Jitsu), by limiting the human horizon to strict phenomena, encircled the spirit which was thus unable to soar higher and remained earthbound. These doctrines constituted a sort of materialism or positivism, and barred the road to more ideal and merciful conceptions, and, in any case, lacked flight of imagination.

"Nagarjuna overthrew all obstacles. From henceforth it was necessary either to make shift with absolute void or take a different direction. It is here that the Japanese spirit gave its full measure. It rejected nothing, it adopted. But its genius repudiated Buddhist thought just as it renewed Chinese, Hindu or Korean art, of which you see so many marvellous examples in this temple, to the extent of forming an entirely distinct creation—personal—Japanese.

"Until now I have expounded to you essentially Hindu philosophies transplanted into Japanese soil, and already coloured by the tints seen through our atmosphere. By studying other sects—*the living sects of Japan*—you will see how

43

Japan, although seeking its sacred texts in India, progressively released Buddhistic conceptions out of its own heart and according to its practical needs. The Hindu and Chinese doctrines were passed like sand through a sieve in order to retain only the gold—and Japan melted this gold anew in the image of its multiform idealistic and realistic genius, which is both poetical, practical and constructive."

4. *Mr Yamaguchi, professor at the Buddhist College of Otani-Daigaku, lectures on the canonical book of the Sanron sect, and explains to me his personal point of view*

"Nagarjuna's philosophy, such as it is expounded in the *Thûron*" (*Book on the Meditation of the Middle Way*), said this eminent Sanskritist, "has not always been well understood. There has been a deplorable tendency to present it in an incomplete manner—to retain only half of it, if I may express myself thus—and to understand it simply in the sense (which in my opinion is inexact) that the celebrated Hindu philosopher contented himself, by means of remarkable dialectics, with denying the essence of things, be it matter or thought, as well as their appearance.

"Now this is not the way the thought of Nagarjuna should be understood. The negative thought of Nagarjuna is more complete, and by this very fact has a far greater range.

"The doctrine of the *Thûron* belongs essentially to that Buddhist school called the Middle Way—precisely because it accepts neither the realism of the ones, nor the negative affirmations of the others. It is outside of, and on another plane than that to which belong those who affirm that 'all exists,' or even that 'nothing exists.' It is the value of the affirmation as such which is here in cause, and that is what matters. If I trace upon a piece of paper (*and Mr Yamaguchi suits the action to the words*) the words 'negation of essence,' I have only expressed half the thought contained in the *Thûron*. In order to complete my exposition I must trace with regard to this formula, and giving them the same value, the words 'negation of negation.' Thus only can the theme of the canonical book of the Sanron sect be precisely, though elementarily stated."

"It is total void?"

"No, it is not total void, and I believe one has been wrong to abuse of this term. The plane on which the dominating preoccupation of Nagarjuna is situated is not that of metaphysics. It is a moral plane. What he wishes to say is that attachment to self, attachment to the act, creates illusion, the phenomenal world, and evil. One should detach oneself from it. The Hindu philosopher wishes to bring us to complete detachment. Now this spiritual position is fundamentally that of Buddhism."

"Since one should detach oneself from everything, does that mean that you believe life to be evil?"

"No. Life is not evil."

"You believe Life to be good?"

"No. Life is not good."

"Then . . . ?"

"We are speaking of a method and of nothing else. We are on the plane of a moral method and not on that of a system or of a metaphysical construction. In order to understand the true sense of the *Thû-Kwan-ron* a long and deep practice of it is necessary. Progressively, in proportion as Western scholars produce translations and studies on this subject (and certain excellent works have already appeared such as those of M. de la Vallée-Poussin, in French, and of Mr Walleser, in German), it will be possible for European readers to appreciate the exact depth and range of this aspect of Buddhist thought. When things concerning Buddhism are at stake, one must beware of too hasty judgments, and return to the sources, to the texts. It is fundamentally necessary to study the texts and always return to them."

I follow this advice and plunge into *The Book on the Meditation of the Middle Way*, of which the following passages are particularly characteristic:

On the Inexistence of the Soul.

Some say that sight, hearing, touch, exist because there is something that existed anteriorily to these manifestations. But how could sight, etc., proceed from that which does not exist? That is to say that one must admit that this being, the Soul, existed before these manifestations.

But this hypothesis of an anterior or independent existence of the soul is erroneous, because how could this being be known if it existed before sight, touch, etc.? If that being could exist without sight, etc., could this latter thing, which could only be known by a certain sign, exist before it was known? How could *this* exist without *that*, and how could *that* exist without *this*?

If this being called soul could not exist anteriorily to all such manifestations as sight, etc., how could it exist before each one of these taken individually?

If it is the same soul which sees, listens, touches, etc., one must admit that the soul existed anteriorily to each of these manifestations. Now this is not guaranteed by the facts.

If, on the other hand, the hearer is one person and the seer is another, he who feels must be yet another. Yet sight, hearing and feeling will be instantaneous, and that leads one to predicate a plurality of souls.

Besides, the soul does not exist in the element on which sight, hearing and feeling depend.

If sight, hearing and feeling have no soul which existed anteriorily to them, neither do they possess any existence in that quality. For how could *this* exist without *that*, as *that*? Both subject and object are mutually conditioned. The soul, such as it is, possesses no individual, independent, reality whatever. That is why the hypothesis which supports the existence of a personal soul anterior to sight, etc., or simultaneous with, or even posterior to, these manifestations, must be rejected as sterile. *A personal soul does not exist.*

On the Vacuity of Things.

Some people object to the Buddhist doctrine concerning the vacuity of things.

If everything is inexistent, and if there is neither creation nor destruction, one must conclude that the Four Holy Truths do not exist. The perception of Pain, the Cessation of Accumulation, the Realisation of this Cessation and the Progress of Discipline, must all be held as unrealisable. If all these together are unrealisable, neither of the Four States of Holiness can exist, and without these states there can be no person to aspire to them. If there be no wise men, the community of the faithful is henceforth impossible. Besides, since the Four Holy Truths do not exist there is no Good Law or Community. The existence of Buddha himself must be an impossibility. Consequently, those who speak of vacuity must be held as negators of the Triple Treasure. Vacuity destroys not only the law of causes and the general principle of retribution, but annihilates the possibility of a world of phenomena.

To these objections it should be answered: He alone is troubled by these arguments who does not understand the true sense and true range of vacuity.

The teaching of the Buddha rests upon the distinction between two sorts of truth: absolute and relative. Those who do not possess an adequate understanding of these are incapable of grasping the deep and subtle signification of Buddhism.

But no more than relative truth can absolute truth be attained—and when absolute truth is not reached, Nirvâna cannot be obtained.

The obtuse mind, not perceiving the truth, goes directly to its own destruction, for it is like a clumsy magician who gets caught by his own tricks—or an inexpert snake hunter who wounds himself. The honoured Master of the World knew well what was abstruse in the doctrine which is beyond the mental capacity of crowds, and he was in favour of not revealing it to them.

The objection that Buddhism adheres to vacuity, and that by so doing it exposes itself to grave errors, fails absolutely to reach its goal, for there are no errors in vacuity. Why? Because it is by reason of vacuity that all things are possible in fact, and without vacuity all things would be reduced to zero. Those who deny vacuity and see in it an error, resemble the horseman who forgets that he is on horseback.

If one believes that things exist by reason of their own essence, and not by reason of their vacuity, one would wish that things should be produced without cause. One destroys thus the relations which exist between the author, the act and the acted, and one also destroys the conditions which constitute the law of Birth and of Death.

All must be considered as a state of vacuity. [1]

---

[1] (*Translated from the Chinese by the Bonze T. Suzuki, professor at the Buddhist College of Otani, Kyōto.*)

5. *A résumé of the doctrines of the "dead sects" by moonlight before the Pond of Sarusawa*

One evening, some time later, we were dreaming on the banks of the Pond of Sarusawa. The moon threw a luminous pathway over the water.

The bonze resumed his thought in the following words:

"Look. One would think there was a luminous pathway under the moon. Yet that path does not exist. It is a mere reflection. But the water which supports it exists. So the Kusha doctrine tells us: 'Self is but illusion—the *dharmas* alone are real.' But the water ruffled by the wind is but a succession of wavelets and each little wave lives but an instant, and dies as soon as it is born. That is what the Jō-Jitsu observes. But the ponds themselves, like drops of dew, evaporate some day. What is the bottom of all things? Vacuity. . . . Such is the conclusion of the Sanron sect."

We remained silent.
The peace of vacuity descended upon us.

CHAPTER IV

THE HOSSO SECT

(1) The Hosso Sect. (2) Mr T. Nagano, bonze of the sect, explains to me the fundamental principle of the Hosso Sect: Thought alone is real, the rest is but a dream. A new visit to the Hōryūji temple, centre of the sect. The theory of the *Kings of the Intellect* is expounded before thousands of small Buddhas. "The Three Periods." (3) Visit to the sanctuaries of Yakushiji, of Kofukuji and to the Kyomidsu-dera.

1. *The Hosso Sect*

This sect was founded in Japan A.D. 653 by the monk Dōshō, on his return from China, where he had been taught by the celebrated pilgrim Hiouen-Thsang, who himself had brought the doctrine back from India. Another Japanese priest called Genbō preached the same teaching about the year 712. This doctrine was thus transmitted through two different lines.

The texts of the sect are numerous, but about nine centuries after Buddha, a "Sum" of them was compiled which was known in Japanese under the name of *Jo-Yui-Shiki-Ron* (Sanskrit: *Vijnaptimatrata-Siddhi-Shastra*).

The Hosso sect counts 44 temples and monasteries, 700 priests, more than 1000 perpetual subscribers, and more than 10,000 occasional subscribers who also practise Shintoism.

2. *Mr T. Nagano, bonze of the sect, explains to me the fundamental principle of the Hosso Philosophy. Thought alone is real. The rest is but a dream*

Mr T. Nagano, bonze of the Hosso sect, who accompanied Mr Koyama and myself during our last walks together, is about to instruct me in his turn. We all three pace slowly to and fro in front of the porch of the Hōryūji temple, which is the centre of the Hosso sect and the oldest Buddhist temple in Japan. This porch is supported by red columns resting on large, flat stones. Gazing at them, I am conscious of that same impression of strength which one experiences before Doric temples. Singular contrasts! I had just been introduced to a world of dew which volatilises itself, and yet here I was, looking at a solid, well-balanced architecture, more apt to suggest the idea of a firm and precise reality than that of a vaporous dream!

"The Japanese soul," remarked my Buddhist teacher, "presents diverse aspects. Like the Fuji-Yama, our sacred mountain, it is according to different hours hard as a rock, or vaporous as a dream. The Japanese likes what is poetical, such as the evanescent evening tints darkened by the shadow of a flying plover, the fleeting reflections of willows in water, under a light mist, the fluid snow of the cherry blossoms. But he also likes that which is positive, precise, reckoned, solid, such as, for example, the red columns of the Hōryūji porch resting upon their massive bases. He likes discipline, will-power, the steely soul of the Samurais. The vague and the precise both suit him equally well according to the case. Fuji-Yama, which is sometimes squat and massive, sometimes the play of clouds amongst clouds, is thus the symbol of our souls.

"It is possible that men and beasts express in a living form the physical *milieu* which witnessed their birth. A same rush of sap, a same sentiment seems to have produced Fuji-Yama with its various aspects (squat, austere, but also, when it drapes itself in the pink of dawn, pure as the eternal snows, melancholy as a dream in the mauve evenings, irradiating a universal glory in the setting sun or indescribably moving in the golden dusks), and the men of this land, who though sometimes proud, hard, tenacious and iron-hearted, occasionally reveal the delicate soul of a poet, tinted like a flight of gulls in a mother-of-pearl sky. Their temples are also made in their image. How could the thought of such men, accessible to dreams but in love with the concrete, ever lose itself in the nihility of abstraction or in the play of vain dialectics? Of these latter, the Japanese have kept the pulp and thrown away the skin as in the case of a fruit.

"Of the different Buddhist sects issued from India and China which established themselves in our territory, those alone subsist which, without losing anything of their universal value, modelled their philosophic teaching upon our racial and psychological exactions, and assumed, if I may express myself thus, the light and colour of our country. After this study of the Kusha, Jō-Jitsu and Sanron sects, too redolent with Hindu mentality, we might have foreseen that Japanese thought would reaffirm its contours, like Fuji after a fog. Effectively we are going to see the Hosso doctrine emerge from the clouds and reinstate an Absolute: *Thought*. It is said that nothing exists? Indeed something *does* exist: *Thought*. But as Thought creates the world, the latter being a projection of Thought, is nevertheless only a dream."

Then with perfect fitness, the bonze, who was striving to bring my mind to conceive that everything organises itself around a centre—as a preface to his philosophical explanations—led me before a sort of daïs in the *Dai-Kodo*, where statues and celebrated works of art are grouped around a marvellous Buddha.

The great bronze Buddha is seated, making the gesture of pacification. He was once placed at the entrance of a temple which has long since been destroyed by fire. But he is immortal. Since looking at him, I have distinctly the impression that he is the living centre of this place, and that the other statues are merely his emanations. Thus in a moment my teacher the bonze will, by means of rather dry technical precisions, demonstrate to me that Thought is the central element from which all is derived, and from which all irradiates. I find this same idea expressed here by other works of art, and by a great pagoda-shaped shrine, one of the artistic glories of the Hōryūji, sheltering around a central figure, thousands of tiny gold Buddhas seated on lotus flowers.

"The Hosso doctrine," continued the bonze, "teaches that the whole universe, all that we perceive by the senses and by the spirit, or the Three Worlds, the world of desire (*Yoru*), the world of form (*Shiki*), and the world that has no form (*Mu-Shiki*), exist only in thought, and that nothing exists outside of thought. Life is but a dream. All is illusion. The ego is certainly mere illusion, but the universal illusion has a spiritual support. The Hosso doctrine is a spiritual axis which affirms itself in the vanishing of things—the subject creating its own object and its own concepts. You will learn that there are seven kinds of thoughts or faculties, which all proceed in last analysis from an eighth thought—pure and primitive—which is precisely that subject, that ideal support called the *Araya-Shiki* (in Sanskrit *Alaya-Vijnâna*). This projects like a shadow upon a transparent blind, the illusion of reality: forms, colours, sounds, ideas, sentiments, in short the world. The Hosso doctrine is an idealism. Its mechanism has given rise to many discussions. The gamuts of tints, of subtle interpretations, is infinite and subjective.

"Since I am obliged to leave generalities I will give you a few technical details.

"According to the *Jo-Yui-Shiki-Ron*, or 'Sum' of the sect, the mechanism of the world can be taken to pieces and explained as follows:

"In the centre is the matrix-thought, the *Araya-Shiki*, from which all emanates. Truth to tell, in the text the latter is only cited at the end of the enumeration of the different elements forming the world. This method is in conformity with the oriental mind, whose natural tendency is to go from mystery towards light rather than first declare the truth, then project its light upon the different phenomena.

"The *Araya-Shiki* presents three aspects. Sometimes it is

active and emanates from things; sometimes it is passive, subjected in its turn to the effect of things. Let us compare it to the ocean whose flow and ebb do not change its nature, or to the rhythm of the heart dilating and contracting without ever ceasing to be the same heart. Sometimes the *Araya-Shiki* is will-power—it acts and marks its imprint. It is called the King of the Intellect, which title it shares, though unique in its essence, with seven other *Shikis*, or spiritual elements of understanding. Logically it should have been called the King of Kings, but that is not in the text.

"The seven other Kings of the Intellect which, despite their titles, are only the aids of *Araya-Shiki*, are the *Gen-Shiki* (perception of sight), the *Ni-Shiki* (perception of hearing), the *Bi-Shiki* (perception of smell), the *Zetsu-Shiki* (perception of taste), the *Shin-Shiki* (perception of touch), the *I-Shiki* (perception of sentiment or ideas), and the *Mana-Shiki* (perception perverted by ignorance, imagination, heredity, etc.).

"Nothing exists, or seems to exist, in the world but through the effect of these Kings. It is they who, like magicians, create the unreal enchantment of forms, colour, sounds, ideas, and of all that escapes the imagination—of all the things included in the following categories: intellectual forms (*Shiki-Hō*), intellectual qualities (*Shin-Jō-Hō*), that which escapes understanding (*Shin-Fu-So-Ō-Hō*), and Immateriality (*Mu-I-Hō*).

"If one pursues the analysis of the world, it is in these four classes that one will range the ninety-two *dharmas* which contribute to its formation. These, added to the eight Kings of the Intellect we have just spoken of, bring to one hundred the total of the elements said to belong to Matter (*Ji*) or to Reason (*i*), which constitute the whole of the Cosmos of Things and of Life. This analysis of the world throws into still greater relief the existence of what are called in Sanskrit the *Bijas*, virtualities which immediately engender their consequences. All these elements, such as they are explained by subtle controversies, 'impregnate' each other, or, in order to use a term employed in the Sanskrit texts, 'perfume' one

53

another. The theory of this reciprocal 'perfuming' (*Vasana*) of these elements is extremely subtle. The central idea is that the world is only an idealistic, and therefore a human conception."

We pursue our visit of the Hōryūji temple.

Amongst the artistic marvels of the *Dai-Kodo*, my Buddhist teacher draws my attention to a sort of shrine where a tiny golden Buddha, flanked by two of his disciples, stands on a lotus suported by a spiral stem. This is one of the treasures of which the Hōryūji is the most justly proud. As I examine it more closely, I become aware of its great charm. The gentle, smiling countenance of the little Buddha on his high-stemmed lotus transports us into the higher regions of metaphysics. On the contrary, his two disciples are of a rather heavy realism. Is this contrast voluntary? Perhaps. In any case my teacher seizes this pretext to continue his doctrinal exposition, the deep idea of which harmonises with the impression produced by the little golden Buddha, symbol of supreme intelligence, and of his two less refined disciples, who appear to have some difficulty in following their master to the heights from which he radiates.

"The Buddha," continued my teacher, "did not immediately teach his highest doctrine. His disciples could not have understood it. He proportioned the revelation of the truth to the unequal understanding of his auditors, and with this object in view he divided his teaching into Three Periods. Each of these teachings *is* Truth from a certain point of view, but the two first have only a very incomplete and preparatory value. The third alone is complete. It is Perfect Truth.

"The first period is called *U* (existence), because men then believe in the reality of the elements composing the world. The second period is called *Ku* (nihility), because during this stage men believe that all is absolute void or illusion. The third period is that during which the Buddha taught the *Thû-Dô* (Middle Way), that is to say when he uncovered to human understanding a deep spiritual synthesis in which appears the real and eternal essence (Thought), as well as the illusory character of the world, such as the Hosso doctrine explains it.

"When some ignorant person will affirm to you that things really exist—*laugh*. When some ignorant person tells you that they do *not* exist—*smile*. For you know that there is a third Truth—Perfect Truth—and you know of what it consists."

"Which of these three teachings do you teach first?" I asked the bonze.

He glanced at me, lifted a finger, and answered, smiling slyly:

"*Nin mité, hotoké.*" (Look at the hearer, then choose the doctrine.)

As we left the temple and skirted a small bed of chrysanthemums whose petals had been scattered by the wind, leaving only the stalks wet with the evening dew, the bonze again compared this evanescent world to dewdrops volatilising themselves.

"We Buddhists will not cease repeating that all is illusion and instability," he declared. "We do not condemn the Hindu meditations on nihility. We understand them differently, that is all. More than any other people the Japanese have been impressed by the impermanence of things—turn by turn terrible or poetical—such as an earthquake or the fall of ephemeral flowers. Our Buddhistic conceptions are indeed all penetrated by the sentiment of instability, by the vision of a world evaporating like dew. Yet we believe that under the fleeting mist of morn and night we discern an *eternal essence*. I like to believe that this is what the poet wished to express in the following tiercet:

This dewy world
Is in truth but a world of dew,
And yet . . ."

55

3. *A visit to the sanctuaries: the Yakushiji and the Kofukuji*

That day a fine rain was falling, drenching the trees and the temples of Nara in a dream-like atmosphere. Yet the tree-trunks remained very black and the lacquer sanctuaries were of a flaming red. A visit to the temples of Yakushiji and Kofukuji, of the Hosso sect, heightened in my eyes the contrast between the ephemeral and the permanent, the dream of an hour and the essential.

Alas, relentless Time has accomplished its work of destruction in the case of the first of these temples. It is not miraculous that these wooden buildings should last so long? But when I see those great bronze statues dating from the seventh century, the oldest in Nipponese art—Yakushi, Nikko and Gwakko Bosatsu, the adorable Kwannon who, 'tis said, was melted in gold extracted from Mount Meru, I then understand the thought of those faithful believers who entrusted the permanent values of Japan to this sanctuary.

I am glad to experience the same impression on entering the Kofukuji. Built in the eighth century, this temple was burnt in 1717. Fire and earthquake, and perhaps also those blossoming trees which form a snowy aureole to so many temples, remind the smiling souls of the Japanese of that evanescent character of things which Buddhism has transposed into wisdom. Oh, the sadness of fleeting things. Illusory life.

Behind the temple there is a little bridge called Sarusawa-no-Ike, from which, according to legend, a beautiful maiden, lovely as the moon, drowned herself for love. The enchantment of forms and of colours slips away towards nothingness. Yet in the park of the temple, Kōbō Daishi, the great Japanese saint, planted a pine tree which he dedicated to the gods, in a thought of eternity. And the statues of Kwannon and the Bosatsus seem eternal. Time, fire, cataclysms have destroyed many things, for it is in the nature of things to perish. *Thought subsists.*

The visit to the two temples was for me a mute lesson of Hosso philosophy : *Thought alone is essential.*

At the Kyomidsu-dera.

Leaning against the wooden balustrades, pilgrims gaze long at the blue distances. It is impossible to describe the charm of this unique temple, so original in structure, with its great roof and its galleries amidst its verdant settings. One would like to pass one's life there as a Buddhist artist, poet or dreamer. Yet enchanting as this vision is under whatever angle one examines it, and however delightful may be the corners one discovers, its lines are always pure and the foregrounds of any of its different aspects detach themselves like a clear thought. Thus in Japanese engravings charm never excludes precision. In this luminous land reverie never leads to the abdication of mind. A latent energy, a human and solid virtue, always subsists.

As I abandoned myself to the charm of this delightful spot, a pilgrim said to me :

"In the ninth century, the great General Tamura-Maro offered his own home, which he tore down and re-edified in honour of Kwannon, the Buddhist Goddess of Mercy."

The man who spoke thus to me was undoubtedly simple and poor, a man of the people. His attitude was modest. Yet in his soul the most gentle and poetical Buddhist beliefs co-exist with the purely earthly sentiment, both solid and genuine, of national pride.

CHAPTER V

THE KEGON SECT

(1) The Kegon Sect. (2) Mr Ryoben Murata, bonze of the sect, explains the Kegon philosophy. The canonical texts. (3) A pilgrimage to the Todaiji, sanctuary of the sect. The Golden Hall and the Dai-Butsu. The Five Doctrines. (4) The temple of the Third Moon. In the temple of the Second Moon. A reverie beneath the stars.

1. *The Kegon Sect*

The doctrine of this sect is founded on the text designated by the name of *Kegonkyō* (Sanskrit : *Avatamasaka-Sutra*), from which the sect has taken its name. It was imported into Japan in 736 by the Chinese teacher Dôsen, who transmitted it to Ryoben, priest of the Todaiji temple of Nara, who became its propagandist. In 740, Shûmu, Emperor of Japan, entrusted the Korean priest Shuishô with the task of giving a detailed explanation of the *Kegonkyō* according to the Chinese commentaries. This explanation took place in the Hall of the Golden Bell of the Todaiji sanctuary, and lasted no less than three years. Even today one is obliged to address oneself to the learned priests of this temple if one wishes to make an orthodox study of the aforementioned sect.

According to mere statistics, the Kegon sect is not very important, but its canonical text, the *Kegonkyō*, is one of the most celebrated of Buddhism, and several other sects count it amongst their fundamental books. It will therefore be seen that the philosophical rôle of this sect is not to be disdained.

The Kegon sect counts 27 temples and monasteries, 48 abbots and priests, more than 200 perpetual subscribers, and 22,000 occasional subscribers.

2. *Mr Ryoben Murata, bonze of the sect, explains the Kegon philosophy*

Evening again in the sacred park of Nara. In the distance we hear the tolling of the Todaiji bell.

"According to the *Kegonkyō*," declared my master, "everything, be it thought or matter, is derived from one source, which is 'unconditioned state,' or absolute nature. Buddha and men are of one and the same essence. We call this common essence *Buta-Thâtata*, and we compare it to the calm ocean, whereas the world of sense may be compared to the passing waves of the rough sea. Below there is unity and identity. On the surface, the ephemeral phenomena of life."

The vibrations of the great bell struck by some pilgrim were dying away, one by one. The great peace of Buddha was descending upon the temples and penetrated our souls.

The bonze continued:

"But it is not this identity, which you might term *substantial*, of life and matter which forms the original characteristic of the Kegon conception. That which lends to the latter a special aspect and transforms it into a profound cosmological and hope-fraught vision, which may perhaps appear to you strange, improbable, and fantastic, is the development contained in the sutra itself, in our canonical text, the *Kegonkyō*."

"What I know of it," I remarked, "has left me the impression of an astounding metaphysical poem, *the* most astounding perhaps ever conceived by men."

"Yes. But one must not be content to read it merely with one's eyes. One must also read it with one's heart. It is a love poem. It celebrates the love of Buddha for all living creatures. It is based upon the following fundamental structure: the thought of Buddha reflects and repeats itself infinitely, eternally, in all parts of the world, and even in the minutest specks of dust. A law of reciprocal interpenetration of all things assures the radiation of Buddhist spirituality. In the cosmic ordering of things, every atom reflects the whole, and the whole reflects every atom. Thus in the matrix of a world formed of correspondences, reciprocal echoes and reflections, one word of Buddha repeats itself throughout myriads of worlds and prolongs its vibrations simultaneously everywhere, eternally."

The bonze stopped speaking. For a minute the sound waves of the Great Bell of Todaiji which the echo repeats interminably, broke the silence of the night. My companion smiled and said:

"Does it not seem as if sympathetic matter wishes to make the smallest atom profit by the sound we hear? Would it not seem as if all the atoms together wished to sing of the wisdom of Buddha? The reading of the *Kegonkyō* produces the same impression of universal resonance. The night is magnificent. Listen well to what I am going to say to you."

I looked at my companion; a star seemed to twinkle in each of his eyes. He then declared in a voice rendered still more musical by the euphony of Japanese syllables:

"Each one of the grains of dust forming myriads of worlds contains myriads of Buddhas, which in the past, the present and the future, eternally inculcate wisdom to men. Each particular thought of a Buddha is the whole truth (*Shin-nyo*) and is at the same time the thought of all the Buddhas. Every gesture of a Buddha towards the East or the West is repeated by all the other Buddhas. Every speck of dust is a world in which is heard the same concert propagated like a dazzling image indefinitely repeated in all the other worlds.

"Everything that one Buddha proclaims is also proclaimed by the other Buddhas in time, space and eternity throughout an incalculable number of *kalpas* or cosmic periods. And just as innumerable Buddhas inhabit each atom, and as infinite myriads of atoms form worlds, so the whole Universe, from a speck of dust or the minutest of insects to the myriads of suns, stars and planets, chants and preaches the wisdom of Buddha throughout eternity."

I looked at the star-constellated sky. How many times, gazing at the stellar immensity, had I not asked myself: "What are we? Why do all these worlds exist?"

Tonight an explanation of this mystery was offered me. The universe is a vast mechanism which the Buddhas utilise to save us from suffering. One must have visited Nara, one must have seen the mystical old park at night in the company of a bonze expounding the *Kegonkyō* in order to understand the sudden emotion which surged through me. But, I reflected, if innumerable Buddhas are present in each atom, if we are all of *Buddhist essence*, should we not conclude that man himself becomes a supernatural being?

"So we are all gods?" I asked.

"Not at all," answered the bonze prosaically, restraining my exaltation. "Buddha is merely a man like you and me."

"Yet all this sublimity?"

"Is a fact. The universe is a spiritual inter-reciprocation in which each element, even the lowest, reflects the whole light —and in which the whole reflects the minutest element. Thus all concurs to a task as immense and eternal as life itself, the object of which is to save man from suffering. The following historical anecdote will allow you to understand better what I mean. One day, the disciples of the patriarch Genju-Daishi (643-712), who taught the Kegon philosophy in China under the Tang dynasty, begged their master to explain the mystery clearly to them in simple terms, as he would to children. Genju-Daishi reflected a few moments, then disposed a number of mirrors in such a way that the last one reflected all the others, which in their turn mutually reflected each other. . . . Do you understand?"

I nodded, and was happy to listen to my companion whilst he developed further the theme of this strange doctrine.

"Buddha is reflected in every object on which his light happens to fall. The world is full of the reflection of his light. Try to understand the inter-reciprocation of the elements of the world. The whole world is contained at the extremity of one of Buddha's hairs like a crystal lens which focusses a luminous point. And the universe, with all its luminous points, is contained in this particular point, and this luminous point which reflects all the others is a universe. Again, the Buddhist universe, according to the Kegon doctrine, resembles a string of pearls in which each pearl reflects its neighbours. If one takes away a single pearl, one also takes the image of all the others.

"All the elements of the world, mean as they may be, mutually condition each other, so that the suppression or the failure of one of them disturbs the whole organism. The heart of Buddha will be unsatisfied so long as there remains one human atom to be saved, that is to say to bring into port—to Nirvâna."

"If I understand rightly, according to the Kegon doctrine, Buddhism becomes a pure metaphysics of Love and an optimistic philosophy?" I remarked.

"Yes, indeed, a metaphysics of the love of Buddha for all sentient creatures," answered my master.

"The moral and the human aspect of the Kegon concept," he continued, "is to bring hope to the living, and an easier possibility of salvation. Should one speak here of optimism? It seems to me quite clear that the Kegon philosophy is not pessimistic, but I prefer to express my thought directly rather than to quibble upon these words. We Buddhists always consider life as fatally admitting of suffering. In the *Kegonkyō*, however, we see the Buddha, by reason of his great love for humanity, trying to deliver us from this suffering. The Kegon wishes to say that there is not in the universe the smallest particle in which the beneficent activity of Buddha does not express itself. The love of Buddha for all 'sentient beings' is mentioned several times in the text; and you will read that the 'Only Honoured One in the World dispenses ineffable joy to all living creatures.' The world is suffering, but salvation is near. Man is not alone in the universe like a shipwrecked person clinging to a raft, lost in the immense ocean. The universe works with him, and contributes to save him. Human beings are surrounded by a force of sympathy of which the *Kegonkyō* has striven to express the marvellous spiritual and moral mechanism."

My master then kindly gave me the text of the *Kegon-kyō*, as well as different notes and translations, one of which was in English, by Mr Suzuki, bonze and professor at the University of Kyôto. He also added the following indications :

"The complete title of this book, *Dai-hō-Kō-butsu-Kegon-kyō* (literally : Great-square-wide-Buddha-flower-ornament-book), warns you that it contains the flower of the reason and universal wisdom of Buddha ; that is to say, of his perfect and supreme thought. It is composed very differently from the other sutras. In it Buddha does not teach his doctrine himself, although his great figure dominates the whole work, and, so to speak, illuminates each phrase, each word, with its rays. In the *Kegonkyō* Bodhisattvas teach the law either openly or symbolically in the form of Psalms addressed to the glory of Buddha. I will add that this Buddha is not the historic Buddha, Sakyamuni, but the Buddha who is merely Light and Spirit, and whose spirituality is incorporated in the universe—the Buddha who exists in that ideal world which we call ' the World of the Treasure of the Lotus.' "

"It should also be remembered that one generally considers the text of the *Kegonkyō*, which we men possess, as a mere summary (*Kya-Ku-Hon*), of an infinitely vaster original text. This one is the 'eternal text,' the *Go-Hon*, which cannot be written materially because it is nothing less than the teaching preached throughout eternity and the universe by the thousands of Buddhas filling all time and space. One also cites the *Ryen-Hon*, a very lengthy text which has remained secret, and with which only a few Indian patriarchs were acquainted in the past."

Then in the twilight, whilst the venerable old bonze was saying his rosary, I read the following passages of the *Kegonkyō*, the sacred book of the sect:

This I have heard:

When the only Honoured One of the World reached Illumination, in the forest of Uruvilva, in the Land of Maghada, the trees with their trunks, their branches and their leaves, were transformed by his miraculous virtue and became seven precious jewels, and shone brilliantly. From his Lion-Throne a bright light radiated upon the ten regions of the Universe which it illuminated in all its parts, like an immense cloud of gold.

At this moment the wisdom of the Unique Honoured One of the World appeared as deep as the ocean—as extended as space. And before its light the darkness of the world vanished, and all sentient creatures were led along the road which leads to Illumination. And the whole Universe, and all that was contained in Himself, was reflected in His Spirit with a perfect lucidity and serenity, as the starry skies are reflected in a perfectly calm sea.

Innumerable Bodhisattvas, Devas and Genii were assembled around the Unique Honoured One of the World, and inspired by his miraculous power, each celebrated His merits in a song.

The First Devaraja sang thus:

> The Tathâgata is mingled in space
> With the infinite and spiritual universe,
> Eternally calm and inaccessible to trouble
> He Himself has appeared upon the earth
> To become the dwelling where reside all things.
> He has appeared on earth
> To enforce the reign of the Good Law,
> And spiritual light knows no longer any limits,
> And by His light He dispels the passions of sentient beings
> And dispenses ineffable joy to them.

The second Devaraja sang thus:

> By the virtue of His miraculous power,
> Which surpasses human intelligence,
> Residing in the centre of the smallest of atoms,
> The Tathâgata preaches the doctrine of perfect serenity.
> Like the sun illuminating all forms,
> The Tathâgata, for the salvation of sentient beings,
> Illuminates all the forms of Karma,
> And directs them into the ways of right seeing.

The Todaiji Temple, Sanctuary of the Kegon Sect

Through the infinity of Kalpas
He extends upon us His gesture of love,
And into the jar we are bearing
He pours the rain of His Good Law.

The Third Devaraja sang thus :

Living creatures flounder in the ocean of bad passions,
And their hearts are troubled by madness and perversity,
The Tathâgata in His love wished to save them,
And teach them a holy and pure life
Which He displays like a celestial light.
In each of the rays emanating from the Tathâgata
Reside innumerable Buddhas
Who tirelessly, with constantly renewed means,
Drag the living away from Evil.

The Fourth Devaraja sang thus :

The Buddha is pure in His form and eternally calm.
His glory shines in all the worlds,
His body resembles the floating cloud,
And His inner life surpasses our understanding.
The Buddha preaches in unique terms
The Law, containing like grains of dust, His innumerable lands.
His spiritual voice can be heard near by and far off,
And each sentient creature understands it in his own manner
For each one thinks that Buddha has only said what each has understood.

The Fifth Devaraja sang thus :

Of all the joys of the world,
None equal the calm joy of the Only Saint.
The Good Law is pure and flawless ;
Within it resides the Tathâgata,
And His eyes see all things in the light of reality.
All the worlds filling the ten regions
Are reflected even at the end of one of Buddha's hairs.
In truth, the unlimited life of Buddha
Resembles Immensity.
The arrogance of the living is as high as the mountains,
But the Tathâgata will dispel it
By pouring out upon the universe the light of His love.

The Sixth Devaraja sang thus :

What can we, with our feeble intelligences,
Understand of this world ?
Buddha manifests Himself everywhere out of love for humans.

E

And His action counterbalances the misery of our condition.
The world is neither reality, nor complete nihility.
The Luminous Buddha is beyond the reach of human intelligence.

The Seventh Devaraja sang thus :

But out of love for sorrowing creatures,
He has assumed on this earth a personal form ;
He accomplished in the past innumerable acts of virtue,
Now it is the high sea, calm and pure, of vows and prayers.
The living chain themselves in darkness through their folly,
Arrogant, insensate,
They rivalise in passion in their wild race.
But Tathâgata preaches the law of calmness and serenity to them.
Each in particular and all together,
He recalls them to the holy life and ineffable joys.
The Buddha is our refuge—unequalled—incomparable :
He wards off suffering from his creatures.
Those who wish to see Him, face to face,
Will see Him, like a full moon, above the mountain.
Purity of Inner Life ! Ocean of Virtues ! Illumination !
May the Karmas of the living allow them to see that light !
When their Bodhi awakens, their impurities are effaced,
They enter into the way of Illumination.

The Eighth Devaraja sang thus :

Through the past composed of innumerable Kalpas,
Evil desires which cause birth and death
Will now disappear for always.
The Buddha teaches us the holy life,
He is wisdom and life,
Birth and death, old age and illness, suffering and sorrow,
How full of miseries is this life !
But if the living creatures reach the presence of Buddha
They suddenly find themselves in a land of purity and light !

I also noted the following psalms in which is described the
love borne by Buddha not only towards all men, but towards
all sentient creatures, and the efforts made by Buddha to free
them from suffering :

The Buddha exhausts in favour of sentient creatures
All the ways of salvation which love suggests to Him.
He visits living creatures and realises Himself in them.
He who glimpses His light
Will contemplate it until complete satisfaction.

His light knows no limits,
And illumines all the worlds in the ten directions.
The Buddha exhausts all means to raise us up to Him.
All existence is nihility,
But the Buddha is the light of sentient creatures.
His love, His compassion envelop the universe like a cloud.
The rain of the Good Law falls into the slightest atom.
The ocean of suffering is fathomless,
But Buddha empties it.
He opens the eyes of our spirit
By His love and pity.
Through Kalpas after Kalpas unaccountable
The Buddha has purified the world
And by His full wisdom
He consoled the living, innumerable as they may be.
All beings are burdened with mad passions,
Incapable of perceiving Buddha.
Even after hundreds of thousands of Kalpas
All creatures suffer, crossing cycles of births and deaths.
Now, Buddha appeared upon earth
To deliver these unfortunates.
And, engaging Himself in the way of their Karma,
Buddha uproots the suffering of the living.

I also noted the psalms in which the author of the sacred text
specifies the mystic structure of our universe composed of
interdependent atoms, in which Buddhas live and act:

The Buddha manifests His presence in each speck of dust,
His virtue acts everywhere, inspiring the Bodhisattvas,
He teaches wisdom to all by miraculous and mysterious means,
He leads all His children to the world of spiritual purity;
He resides in the essence of all things,
And His sublimely pure gaze
Reaches to the confines of the universe,
Which however is unlimited.
Like the atoms, His manifestations
Are innumerable in each atom,
And His voice reaches all living creatures equally innumerable.
His voice resounds also
In each country of Buddha
And He visits everywhere sentient beings,
Purifying them from all pollution.
The Buddha possesses in a single thought
All the Kalpas, past, present, and future,
Although they are innumerable.

And blind as the world of phenomena may be,
The vision of the Protector of the world penetrates this world.
Innumerable Buddhas are present in each grain of sand,
Liberating innumerable worlds, sublime mystery,
All have but one thought,
And all the Kalpas, past, present, and future
Only constitute one thought of Buddha.
Nothing can stay the spiritual birth of Buddha.
All the countries of Buddha, according to his own spirit,
Present infinitely diversified aspects ;
Sometimes pure, sometimes evil,
They revolve in cycles of enjoyment and suffering.
And all things pursue their evolution and are changeable.
All the lands of Buddha mutually penetrate each other and are innumerable.
They fill the whole universe and more with perfect spontaneity.
In a single land of the Buddha are comprised all the lands of the Buddhas,
And each one includes all the others in itself.
And yet each one of them is neither extended nor compressed.
The Power of Buddha is seen
Even in the slightest grain of sand,
The voice of Buddha sounds for all sentient creatures
On an ocean of universal redemption.

No, I was not mistaken. The *Kegonkyō* is indeed a Gospel, a glad tiding. It announces to mankind—or rather to all "sentient creatures"—that they are not alone in the fatal struggle against pain. Buddha is with them. There is no doubt as to the final victory, and that is why, in his heart of hearts, the Buddhist is joyful and not sad. The *Kegonkyō* chants Buddhist joy, understood thus. I continued my reading. At this moment the moon was bathing the landscape in a pale golden light.

From the face of Buddha, endowed with an infinite majesty, emanated rays of spirituality which fell in benediction upon the world like dew, and lit up the world of the Lotus Treasure. The lands of Buddha are full of treasures whose rays annihilate the suffering of life, and guide beings into the Way. The perfumed water overflows from the lake where sacred flowers shine. The sacred trees rise as through a curtain of pearls.

The moon aureoled the trees of the old park, revealing suddenly the fairy-like splendours of its rays.

Having ended his prayers, the bonze bent over the holy text and read aloud :

> How marvellous ! When the light dawns,
> The Whole Universe is Illuminated !
> Filled with joy and delight,
> Our hearts awaken to the Law !

3. *At the Todaiji Temple, the sanctuary of the Sect*

I made the pilgrimage to the Todaiji in the company of numerous pilgrims, who were for the most part peasants and Kyôto merchants. Some came from distant provinces, leaning on their staffs, wearing a straw coat and a large reed hat. I conversed with them, for I like to mingle with the gentle-mannered, humble folk of this country.

We first purify ourselves according to custom in the basin of lustral water. Then having "renewed our soul," we enter in silence into the ancient sanctuary which is the centre of the Kegon sect. There some bonzes receive us with that exquisite politeness which is the distinctive mark of Japanese education.

Our first visit is to the monumental bell which has pealed over Nara for twelve centuries. Amidst a scaffolding of gigantic beams, I perceive against the grey sky its enormous mass, resembling a colossal gold and bronze goblet which has been overturned by some giant. We draw near to it. Each pilgrim in turn strikes it once—and once only—whilst making some wish in his heart. The sound prolongs itself interminably. We stand there in silence, listening to the sonorous vibrations as they die away. Meditation. Prayers. Those in and outside the temple silently commune with each other. Perhaps at that very moment, lost amidst the shadows of the park, some solitary worshipper or a group of pilgrims are listening to the voice of the great bell which brings them a message from the Todaiji, the voice of Buddha ? Mystical exchanges take place which remind me of that strange doctrine in which all is exchange, reflection, echoes, inter-reciprocation, a spiritual mechanism destined to propagate the thought of Buddhist wisdom infinitely, throughout the universe, just as the sound waves of the bell are propagated through the air.

Later we entered in silence the hall containing the Dai-Butsu. I gaze bewildered at the immense bronze and gold Buddha, almost fifty feet high, which for twelve centuries, seated on a lotus, has offered himself to the meditation of the faithful. It may be that from an aesthetic point of view others may prefer the great Buddha of Kamakura, but I am not visiting Japan as an artist, still less as a tourist. I have come hither, a man of my time, in quest of peace, to ask others the secret of their peaceful hearts.

At Nara everything is peaceful. Here the trees and animals are the friends of man. The dead are also present. The two different religions, Shintoism and Buddhism, have been prac- tised in the same temples. The gods do not trouble philo- sophers, and philosophers do not attack the gods. Here everything is human also. Sacred dancers pass beneath the trees with camellias stuck in their hair, and not far from the temple of the Third Moon there is a tea-house where I will go later to hear songs accompanied by the samisen. Oh, the charm of these places where thought is freed from all pretension and remains ingenuous, where men do not believe they know all —do not solve all, nor exclude anything.

The Emperor who erected this gigantic statue ordered that it should be melted in bronze and gold, the bronze symbolising Shinto, the gold Buddhism. Today I wished to see that gold, to see its radiation amongst these humble pilgrims, amongst these peasants and merchants beside whom I have trudged, and with whom I have communed spiritually. These Japanese, supposed to be so reserved, have become my friends. They shared their provisions with me and did not ask me a single question. Many were gay: none tried to astonish me. All were simple, modest and kind. What had they come seeking here ? *Peace of heart.*

I bowed deeply with them before the huge statue of Him who reminded men, who need it so badly, of interior peace—the greatest of all possessions, the truest of riches, of pure gold.

Nara! Todaiji! Peace of Heart!

I questioned my master:

"The Kegon doctrine is no doubt, in your opinion, the last preached by Buddha. Must one therefore conclude that the preceding doctrines, also preached by Buddha, were merely errors?"

"Not at all. Firstly, it is inexact to say that the Kegon doctrine was the last to be preached. It was, on the contrary, conceived by Buddha at the very origin of His ministry. During the twenty-one days which followed His Illumination, Buddha meditated on the Kegon doctrine. He then perceived that the intelligence of men, being too feeble or wrongly directed, could not follow His thought to the altitudes whither it soared. He therefore divided His teaching into Five Doctrines, or *successive stages* leading to the same goal, and which were different methods proportioned to the capacities of His hearers. Each of these doctrines is Truth, but the fifth alone —the Kegon doctrine—is complete Truth.

"The first doctrine, that of the Hinayana (such as the Kusha doctrine), is designated by the characteristic name of the 'little doctrine' (*Syan*).

"The second, known as the 'initial doctrine' (*Shi*), is more radical than the first and exposes that everything is unreal. (This is the case of the Sanron doctrine.)

"The third, conformably to the method of the Middle Way rising above the two preceding ones, proclaims that all creatures are of the same absolute nature, are of Buddhistic essence, so that every man can become a Buddha. Illusory and deceiving as phenomena may be, there exists an Absolute which spiritually identifies our origin with that of Buddha, allowing us to consider ourselves as potential Buddhas, and bringing to all the possibility of salvation. This is the final doctrine (*Ju*).

"The fourth is the 'sudden doctrine' (*Ton*). Indeed, it is rather a method than a doctrine, and it operates in an independent and original way. The first three doctrines may be compared to a pendulum which, having swung to the left and to the right, fixes itself in the middle. The sudden method, or doctrine, is different. It foresees the possibility for the spirit to reach *sudden* illumination—to attain Buddhahood immediately without having to pass through a progressive teaching which was often pursued during innumerable *kalpas* or cosmic periods. It is, in fact, but a just corrective to the three preceding doctrines, the long practice of which could not be imposed upon an exceptional intelligence which reaches the goal at a single bound.

"The fifth doctrine is the complete doctrine (*En*), that of the *Kegonkyō*, or, as we express it, the *Betsukyōithijo* (the unique special vehicle).

4. *In the Temples of the Third and Second Moons*

The *San-Gwatsu-dō*, or Temple of the Third Moon, is a masterpiece of the *tempyō* epoch (729-748). Its peaceful, simple lines have not learnt the art of dissimulation. The monk Ryoben, who built it, wished neither to overawe nor to astonish. Although well calculated, its proportions are modest, and remain within the human scale of things, harmonising themselves with nature, which, as my friend the eminent art critic Ryo-Yanagui told me, "is a nature which still ignored the domination of man, and remains his confidant and friend." Before this masterpiece of simplicity, the foreign tourist is apt to exclaim, "What! Is *that* all?" and pass his way.

The *Ni-Gwatsu-dō*, or Temple of the Second Moon, is built on piles on a hill-side.

From an exterior wooden gallery, called the Gallery of Torches, where luminous processions take place each year, we contemplate Nara—its mystery and its trees. I returned here on the night of a fairy-like procession. All the stars of the sky seemed to be gathered here. In the shifting lights I seemed to catch sight of the cosmological vision of the *Kegonkyō*, in which the minutest atom reflects all the others, which in turn reflect it. I meditated long on the structure of the world conceived of as a theme for Buddhistic reverie; reproducing in myriads of infinite examples the gestures and thoughts of the Buddhas who are eternally working to save us. Once again I understood that here analysis fails. The Kegon is a mystical synthesis of great richness—art, philosophy, dreams, morals—which only confides its beneficent secret to the pure of heart who simply—very simply—are seeking for Peace.

CHAPTER VI

THE TENDAI SECT

(1) The Tendai Sect. (2) A Pilgrimage to Mount Hiei. The story of Dengyō-Daishi. Mr N. Jiwaku, bonze of the Sect, explains to me the Tendai philosophy: Universal salvation. Men, beasts, plants and things, one and all being of a common Buddhistic origin, can reach Buddhahood. The *Dharma* and the *similitude* theory. (3) Buddhist kindness. The flowers themselves can reach Buddhahood. (4) Mr Fujishima, a bonze and authorised critic of the Tendai Philosophical School, gives me some precisions concerning the idea of a common origin: the Bhûta-Tathâtâ. (5) At the popular Temple of Asakusa. (6) At the Temple of Miidera. The Five Periods, and the Parable of the Prodigal Son. The Sanjusangen-do Temple. (7) Examples of *Meditations on the Lotus of the Good Law*, the Holy Book of the Sect.

1. *The Tendai Sect*

This sect was founded in China by Tche-Tcho-ta-che, on the sacred mountain Tien T'ai, from whence it derived its name. It was introduced into Japan in 804 by the bonze Saichō, better known as Dengyō-Daishi (Grand Master of the Propagation of the Doctrine), who, having gone to China, had been instructed in the Law by the spiritual successors of Tche-Tcho, and in particular by Tao-Suei (Japanese: *Dōsui*).

Dengyō taught the new doctrine in the temple of Enryakuji, on Mount Hiei, which was soon to be covered with Buddhist temples and become one of the most celebrated sanctuaries of Japanese Buddhism, worthy of being called by the Chinese "the Japanese Tendai."

After Dengyō, who was the first patriarch of the sect in Japan, Ennin, who was also called Jikaku-Daishi, left for China in 838, and upon his return to Japan definitely constituted the sect.

74

Another priest, Enchin, founded a new branch at the monastery of Onjōji. Much later, between the years 1469 and 1487, the bonze Shinzei created in Japan another branch which bears his name.

The Tendai sect refers itself essentially to the *Lotus of the Good Law* (Japanese: *Hokkekyō*; Sanskrit: *Sadharma-pundarika-sutra*), and to some other texts of lesser importance.

The sect actually possesses more than 6000 temples, monasteries and chapels, as well as large holdings in land. It counts more than 11,300 priests, more than 900,000 perpetual subscribers, and more than one million occasional or Shinto subscribers. Its annual budget, not including the secondary branches, is 150,000 yen. The three groups have between them founded three universities, numerous schools, and more than 150 social organisations in aid of the poor, as well as children's and aged persons' welfare centres, orphanages, kindergartens, etc.

2. *A Pilgrimage to Mount Hiei*

We accomplished the pious pilgrimage to Hiei, the sacred mountain, not by the modern funicular trolley, but on foot, as is seemly, in the company of other pilgrims, and we invoked the figure of Dengyō-Daishi in his temple, the Enryakuji. I shared my bowl of rice before his stone effigy with poor Buddhists, kind, simple folk. What exquisite gentleness emanates from Buddhist pilgrimages—what contentment of heart!

"On this summit," said my Buddhist master, "in front of this immense horizon, where everything seems to harmonise, both the trees and the houses of men and of gods—both Kyôto, the city of vain agitation, and Lake Biwa, blue, pure and calm —the bonze Saichō (Dengyō-Daishi) meditated upon the mysterious books he had brought back from Mount Tendai, in China, and elaborated the doctrine. All things, all beings can become Buddhas, for they are all of the same essence: men and beasts, this singing cicadae, this blade of grass and the stone in the road. Besides, as a consequence of this universal principle, all the pre-existent philosophical doctrines are incorporated into the Tendai doctrine, which is a spiritual synthesis, just as creatures and things of different aspects find their places, without excluding each other, in this blue horizon we have before our eyes.

"I particularly wished to take you first to Mount Hiei because it is here that the thought of Saichō took its flight. It is therefore normal that our philosophical itinerary should start from here. Later we will visit the other sanctuaries of the sect.

"The bonze Saichō, Japanese founder of the sect, is better known by the name of Dengyō-Daishi (Grand Master of the Propagation of the Doctrine), which was given him by the Emperor Seïma. He was born in 767. At eighteen years of age he retired upon Mount Hiei, where he lived as a hermit. He meditated a long time seeking the most satisfactory doctrine from a religious point of view, and the occasion of founding a Buddhist Church which could be universal and officially recognised. The transfer of the seat of Government from Nara to Myako, which took place at this period, favoured the plans of Dengyō. For, although a mystic, he was also a born politician, and he took advantage of the occasion thus offered him. In 804 the Emperor sent him to China 'to pursue the quest of Truth.' Whilst there, the learned Dōsui taught him the doctrine propounded on Mount Tendai, the texts of which he brought back with him to Japan.

" This doctrine was welcomed by passionate discussions in which all priests, scholars and courtiers took part. The proclamation that every man, every creature, can become a Buddha, and that Buddhahood is therefore not merely reserved to a few extraordinary natures, lent to the teachings of Dengyō a democratic, even popular aspect, which opposed them to the more aristocratic doctrines of other sects."

"Even thus," I remarked, "Christians formerly quarrelled over such questions as grace and predestination."

"I believe so. Salvation for all or salvation for a chosen

few, such was the issue. The older sects systematically opposed the new doctrine. But the generous conception of Tendai prevailed at last.

"The principle of universal salvation has been admitted by all the great Japanese sects, under different forms. The Emperor favoured the new doctrine, the synthetic philosophy of which, engulfing like so many points of view the teachings of the other sects, served his ambition to found a State Church. The nobles welcomed the doctrine favourably, attracted by its philosophical value, and by the aesthetic and symbolic character of the Tendai cult. The people came to us simply because they instinctively felt, or understood the humanity, the accessibility, of the spiritual treasure Dengyō offered them. The Emperor richly endowed the monastery on Mount Hiei, which, from being a simple hermitage, soon became a very powerful institution.

"Dengyō died in 822 before having completely realised his dream of making Mount Hiei the unique centre of ordination and initiation of the Buddhistic mysteries. But after his death Mount Hiei was covered with thousands of temples, and although, like all human institutions, it experienced many vicissitudes—although its temples were burnt down during the civil wars, its importance in the history of Buddhism was, and remains considerable.

"Like the Kegon doctrine, the Tendai doctrine is pantheistic. It restores an absolute into the metaphysics of Buddhism: that identical Buddhistic essence in all beings and things which, in terms of doctrine, is called 'the absolute nature of Buddha,' or 'Bhûta-Tathâtâ.' In other terms, Buddha and the animated and inanimate universe are fundamentally of the same nature, of the same essence, and have a same origin. Or, in still other words, men, beasts, things, the flowers of my garden, this stone, this insect, a speck of dust, a dewdrop, the sun, the moon, the stars above our heads, the worm at our feet, one and all, without exception, can attain

Buddhahood. The Kegon sect excludes inanimate objects from this privilege. The Tendai doctrine excludes no one and nothing. It poses the principle of a universal qualification for salvation. One might say that it discerns a potential Buddha in every atom of the world."

"What! Do you mean that a butterfly, a bee, a stone can become a Buddha?"

"Yes."

"Can a criminal also become a Buddha?"

"Yes, for the world, including Buddha, is of one same essence. Although the enumeration you have just made appears so very incongruous, you have merely expressed the modalities of aspect of a nature which is fundamentally one, and which has more or less progressed in the way of perfection. When you ask me if a criminal can become a Buddha, you are questioning the moral value of the Tendai philosophy. The nature of Buddha is active, not inert, and is working incessantly for the improvement of the world—*i.e.* it is striving to draw the latter nearer to the Buddhist ideal—to perfection—to Illumination. Since each being carries within itself the absolute nature of Buddha, the most fallen of men can hope to reach Buddhahood. No exclusion, no condemnation could be pronounced. There are no damned amongst us. A great hope arises amongst they who can say: 'However miserable and corrupt we may be, we are not irremediably lost. We keep the hope and possibility of reaching one day those serene heights where one no longer suffers, of reaching deliverance.' Since we are all of the same nature, some good can be found in the lowest of us, and reciprocally there is also some evil in Buddha. The greatness of Buddhism is that *Buddha was a man*. The greatness of Tendai is that men, like all other beings and things, can reach Buddhahood. It is said that a coal and a diamond are of the same nature. With time the coal will become a diamond."

"But," I objected, "I have not read all you have just told me in the *Lotus of the Good Law*."

"One must know *how* to read our sacred books. What I have just told you is implicitly contained in the theory of the *dharmas* and the *similitudes* which is to be found in the *Lotus of the Good Law*, and of which I will try to give you a rough sketch.

"The world is a composite of three thousand *dharmas*, or fundamental elements. The spiritual, and that which appears to us as material, good and evil, all our sentient universe and our illusions, are the different aspects under which the play of these three thousand *dharmas* reveal themselves to our senses and to our mind. This universe is so constructed that although it is constituted in its infinity by these three thousand *dharmas*, a single thought, mean as it may be, contains them all. The *dharmas* form the world and are all in our thought. In his intimate commentaries called *Shikwan*, Tendai-Daishi wrote: 'Were these but a single thought these three thousand *dharmas* are contained therein. A thought may be the most timid one can imagine; it nevertheless possesses by its very nature all the *dharmas*.' This idea is called 'the system of the three thousand *dharmas* in a single thought.'

"These *dharmas* are characterised by their internal nature which we can define as follows: 'essential identity and neutrality.' All the combinations of the world—force, substance, form, cause and effect are produced by the play of these *dharmas* which were originally and similarly neutral. This idea is expressed by the *Lotus of the Good Law*, and rendered by the word 'similitude' (Sanskrit: *evam*, similar or similitude). I quote the passage: 'Here is what all *dharmas* consist of: like form—like nature—like substance—like force—like action—like cause—like effect—like agent—like play—like balance. What is the sense of the term *like*? It means *similar*; that is to say, the state in which form, nature, substance, force, action, cause, effect, agency and balance are originally inert and invariable.'

"From the fundamentally neutral nature of the *dharmas* arise the following consequences which bring us back to the theory of the Middle Way, with which you are already familiar. One can, by keeping within the Truth, consider that the three thousand *dharmas* are none other than void (*Ku*) or existence (*Ké*), or neither one nor the other (*Thû*). In his *Guketsu*, Keke-Daishi wrote : 'The word "void" seems the negation of the three thousand *dharmas*. Now it is a fact that these manifest themselves through phenomena. One may therefore prefer the word "existence." But one will adopt the term "*thû*" to express the imperceptible nature of thought which can content itself neither with being nor with void.'

"These three possible manners of considering the *dharmas* which correspond to three attitudes of our thought—negation, affirmation, or abstention—are called in Buddhist vocabulary '*the three truths*' (*Sontai*). These are not distinct categories which can be isolated the one from the other. In order to understand them, you must make an effort of spiritual synthesis. These *three truths* form, from the point of view of the Absolute, an inseparable, homogeneous amalgam. This is what the Buddhists of the Tendai sect mean when they speak of the 'inconceivable state of the three truths, *inseparably combined*.' If one wishes to reach Buddhahood, one should meditate at length upon these things."

3. *Buddhist Kindness*

"You must now," continued the bonze, "strive to understand the Tendai doctrine from the point of view of the heart. For the categories, classifications, divisions and other methods of exposition are not all. Indeed, all this metaphysics is framed only in function to a moral. Its principle, practically summed up, is the following : '*Everybody and everything can reach Buddhahood*.' If successive lives signify suffering, all creatures are now able, thanks to Tendai, to escape from it and gain the Buddhist haven. Each and all can reach Buddhahood. Try to understand with your heart all the hope and contentment this proclamation of universal deliverance brings to men, and the moral regeneration it operates in them ; and, on the other hand, the duty of love which it exacts from them."

"So this complicated metaphysics of the *dharmas* hides an obligation to love ?" I queried.

"Without any doubt. I have shown you how this pantheistic world of a similar spiritual essence to that of Buddha, at one with him, realises its forms, its forces, its causes and its effects by the play of its originally neutral elements. My object was to make you understand how the principle and mechanism which make it work oblige us to love all things as ourselves. *For if everything is of Buddhistic essence, and if the play of the dharmas realises beings and things, and amongst these perfect and evil beings, how could one reject, condemn or banish a single being, or a single thing, without attempting against the hope of universal Buddhist perfection which the world carries in itself, that is without attempting against Buddha himself?* Gold and mud are of the same essence. Our love must embrace the whole, at the risk of striving to extract the gold from it. In order to accustom our mind to this great truth, we like to quote this Tendai aphorism which always astonishes novices : 'Passion is the *sambodhi* (illumination or perfect wisdom), and the *samsarâ* (painful transmigrations) is Nirvâna.' In other words : 'contraries are identical.' Therefore in practice one should exclude nothing and nobody, but love all, and help the creature to rise towards Buddhahood—in short, one must *be good*."

We were following a path through the soft earth scattered with mole-hills. I noticed that the bonze took great care to avoid walking on the freshly-made little hillocks.

"Our little sister the mole," he observed, smiling.

Even when speaking seriously a Japanese smiles, and this fact agreeably deprives his affirmations of all dogmatism. I remembered another smiling bonze whom I saw in a temple garden go out of his way so as not to disturb some bees feeding upon a peony.

"In Japan, the respect of life and kindness to animals are of Buddhistic origin," said my master. "The Tendai philosophy, such as I have just explained it to you, has merely developed this sentiment. You will notice everywhere the effects of this kindness."

"I have already noticed it in Japanese literature," I answered. "I still remember the short poems in which Bashô, your great poet, defends the sparrow, the bee and the dragon-fly."

"Observe also Buddhist kindness in real life. The humble gesture of the housewife throwing back into the river the residue of the pail is inspired by Buddhism : there may have subsisted therein certain life-germs which should not be destroyed. At Buddhist funerals one opens the cages of captive birds, who thus regain their freedom. One even quotes the case of a bonze who, having fallen asleep out of doors, awoke to find that convolvuluses had wrapped themselves around his body during his sleep : but he preferred to die rather than destroy them. The bonze Saighyō refused to visit the minister of Go-Tokudaiji, saying, 'the heart of that lord is apparent,' because the latter had stretched strings upon his roof to chase away the birds."

"I saw that you yourself made a charming gesture just a moment ago," I remarked.

"Oh," answered the bonze, "I have no merit in acting thus, for I naturally love the animals which surround my solitude without troubling my meditations. In my garden I avoid brushing against the rushes for fear of destroying the cobwebs, so beautiful in the dew. And after a shower I take care not to crush the snails. At night, whilst working at my table, I listen with sympathy to the rats gnawing at the beams of my room. The animals are my friends."

Whilst conversing thus, we had reached a small thatched temple, lost on the mountain-side.

"Here is something that is worth more than a speech," said my master. "A bonze of my sect whom I know well."

I looked in the direction he indicated, and I observed, half hidden by a hedge, a very old bonze, with a grave, kindly expression, who was solicitously bending over some flags, sole ornaments of his tiny garden. In his right hand he held the extremity of a long handle attached to a small wooden cup, with which he scooped water out of a bucket, and poured it with infinite care over the flowers. He repeated several times this gesture, which appeared to me almost ritualistic. On catching sight of us he interrupted his task, bowed deeply before us, and exchanged a few words with my master. Then laying rapidly aside his garden tools, he begged us to enter into the temple, and, pointing to the flags, he said with a kind smile as if to excuse himself:

"*Hana mo jobutsu suru.*" (Even the flowers also become Buddhas!)

4. *Mr R. Fujishima, bonze and authorised critic of the Tendai Philosophical School, explains the Universal Essence, or Bhûta-Tathâtâ:*

"If one considers the Three Truths (*Sontai*), that is to say the *dharmas* considered as void, the *dharmas* considered as having a relative existence, and the *dharmas* considered as being neither void nor existent—these, from the point of view of the absolute, do not form a plurality such as one, two or three. But from a relative point of view, they *do* form a plurality. They are called 'the three inseparably combined forms of reality.' The Buddhas alone understand the deep reason for them.

"Let us try to give an approximate explanation by means of the following comparison. Suppose that we should make a certain effect to be produced by a determined cause in the course of a dream: for example, that we are punished for having committed a crime or rewarded for a good action. Although the fact developed in the dream appears evident and manifest, it only possesses a relative existence. Indeed, one cannot lay hold of it: there is the void. But the nature of the thought in the dream is neither void nor existent: it is therefore only an intermediate form. One can therefore say that the three forms of truth exist simultaneously and are neither unity nor plurality. As ignorant beings do not understand the reason for the three forms of truth, they mill around eternally in the Ocean of Transmigrations. What is this reason? It is the Bhûta-Tathâtâ (absolute nature), which is the nature of Buddha. One must not seek the Bhûta-Tathâtâ exclusively in, or out, of our existence. Infernal beings, ghosts, etc., are all comprised in the Bhûta-Tathâtâ, which is none other than the three thousand *dharmas*.

"One calls the Bhûta-Tathâtâ the '*true Buddha*.' From what has been said, it results that the Ten Worlds are those of the Buddhas. In the *similitudes* the *cause* represents the condition of action, the *agent* that of passion, and the *effect* that of suffering. But as these are the essence of reality, these three conditions are merely the three virtues: spiritual body (Sanskrit: *Dharma-Kaya*); wisdom (Sanskrit: *Prajna*); and deliverance (Sanskrit: *Moskha*). Or, again, they are the three bodies: spiritual body (Sanskrit: *Dharma-Kaya*); beatific body (Sanskrit: *Samboya-Kaya*); and the body of transformation (Sanskrit: *Nirvâna-Kaya*). These Three Truths being thus considered in their essential nature, producing all the aspects of the world, passion is only *sambodhi* (perfect illumination) and the *samsarâ* (transmigration) is Nirvâna.

"Whether one considers the Bhûta-Tathâtâ as the essence of all things, or inherent in all things, both it and things are identical. They are the two inseparable aspects of the same existence. The absolute Bhûta-Tathâtâ resembles the ocean in a dead calm. The relative modes are the waves whose shape is continually being changed by the wind. The Bhûta-Tathâtâ cannot be separated from the relative modes, just as the water of the ocean is inherent in its waves. (According to this conception, the sun, the moon, the earth and all the stars contain the Bhûta-Tathâtâ in themselves, as do also the flowers, grass, a drop of water or a vapour. All are the products of the Bhûta-Tathâtâ of which they are a part.) In the *Nirvâna-Sutra* Sakyamuni proclaims that all living creatures partake of the nature of Buddha—or, in other words, of the same Bhûta-Tathâtâ—just as the Tendai School teaches that even plants, mountains or rivers can become Buddhas. One can say that this system is a pantheism such as one finds in certain modern and contemporary philosophies of Europe. The Bhûta-Tathâtâ of Buddhism is, after all, almost identical with the *substance* of Spinoza, the *absolute idea* of Hegel, the *will* of Schopenhauer, and the *non-conscient* of Hartmann.

5. *At the Popular Temple of Asakusa*

Today we saunter around the old red and black temple of Asakusa, decorated with gigantic paper lanterns.

A popular crowd, a crowd of feast days, joyous and vivacious, dawdles before the painted booths, on which are pasted hand-bills bearing large black and gold Chinese characters, or around the stands piled high with *delicatessen*—fruit, playthings or charms. At one of the open-air kitchens I taste some *Shajimi*, or raw fish. I am surrounded with common folk, some in kimonos, others clothed in European style. Many of those in kimonos wear caps or straw hats, and this incongruity is not ugly because it is devoid of pretension and because kindliness subsists. I draw near to a hawker selling autumn-tinted *kakis*. No one jostles me; on the contrary, everybody makes way for me smilingly.

Flags are flying from the tops of high bamboo masts. Everywhere paper lanterns, each prettier and stranger than the others, sway gently in the breeze. All the amusements are very cheap: small movies and theatres, outside of which the prologue is played in order to attract spectators, monkey and insect vendors, photographers, jugglers, popular story-tellers, singers, wrestlers, etc. It is a fair, but devoid of all vulgarity, and where everything, on the contrary, bears the imprint of the genius of the race, of its native qualities.

In the crowd the *obis* and parasols of the women throw an artistic note. A pedlar sells cardboard animals which he makes himself: each one is a work of art. In a corner I notice

Western suits and imported objects, but multi-coloured *musumes* pass by, and the bearer of a sort of paper cupboard draws from its hiding-place a cup of *saké* which he offers me with a smile. Another asks me to buy a little bird whose speciality is to sing ceaselessly: "*Hokke-Kyō*." What? "Hokke-kyō?" The Lotus of the Good Law, the sacred book of the Tendai sect?

"Yes, yes," answers the delighted seller. "It is a little Buddhist bird."

The bonze who accompanies me smiles gently.

Let us go to the temple. One climbs a few steps and enters a hall surrounded by a portico decorated with immense paper lanterns, with paintings and ex-votos which are hung even on to the wooden rafters of the ceiling. This temple is dedicated to Kwannon, the popular Goddess of Mercy. I am struck by the absolute unconcern of the faithful. One can enter into this temple without taking off one's shoes—one can speak—children play in it. Candles are burning in numerous chapels. That of Jizō, the gentle god who is the friend of little children, and that of Binzuru, the *healer saint*, particularly attracts the crowd. Visitors buy charms from the bonzes. We are here in the midst of popular Buddhism, whose practices do not shock one because they all assume a symbolical significance. Has not Buddha taught that everyone discovers the Truth according to his own capacity, and, so to speak, to his own scale? From time to time pigeons, whose graceful flight crowns the summit of the edifice, fly inside and perch upon the rafters, whilst the autumn wind sweeps in dry leaves and dust from the street. Human beings, animals, plants, matter, all seem to fraternise here. Has this effect been deliberately sought for? Do I see here the popular expression of Tendai philosophy? Each and all can reach Buddhahood, the bird and the speck of dust. Or is it a mere coincidence? My master answers this question with a smile and a vague gesture of the hand which I interpret as meaning: "It is vain to wish to unravel in human actions the part of consciousness, of instinct, or of circumstances." Yet a rigorous doctrine would not have tolerated all this joy and all this liberty.

We visit the temple. I have wished to penetrate into the very heart of the sanctuary which is not generally accessible to visitors and which a bonze has kindly opened for me. There, in front of Kwannon, who symbolises kindness and pity for human beings, there amongst all that gold, those flowers, those precious stones and the smoke of incense, Thought suddenly soars, philosophical and grave, without ceasing to be human. I think of the *dharma* theory, of all that complicated, arduous metaphysics which, however, humbles itself before the humble. Each and all can reach Buddhahood. I believe this doctrine must have pleased the merciful Goddess and that she must have smiled with joy when she saw Buddhism evolve from its negative Indian conceptions towards the Japanese doctrines of salvation for all.

6. *At the Temple of Miidera*

At the first sound of the gong of Miidera—
Ah, says the traveller, I pursue my journey through the night.

This classical poem haunts me as we approach the temple. A little before evening, at that exquisite hour which is neither day nor night, the view at Miidera enchants us like a blue dream. Over there is Hiei-zan, the holy mountain where the shade of Dengyō-Daishi mounts guard in a mauve cloud, and further away appears a dream island, Chikubu-Shima. On the horizon pale-grey mountains are dominated by two pink summits. The traditional bell is hushed. A legend familiar to all Japanese children peoples the shadows with the ghosts of Yoshitsune and Benkei. Oh, this Buddhist peace which permeates everything! How can one give an impression of it to those who have never directly experienced it?

"I have pointed out to you," said the priest, "the eclectical, synthetic character of the Tendai doctrine. You have seen proofs of it in the temples you have visited. Here you can see statues representing the Buddhist Trinity; and elsewhere, on the altar, the statue of Amida which one expected perhaps only to see in temples belonging to other sects. The same tolerance exists concerning prayers. The faithful will murmur indifferently, '*Namu-Amida-Butsu*' (I worship thee, Amida Butsu), the formula used by the Amidist Buddhist creeds, or '*Namu-Myoho-Renge-Kyō*' (Adoration of the Book of Rectitude), which formula is characteristic of the Nichiren sect. This is the Tendai spirit: *to exclude nothing, and no one.*"

"This tolerance," I answered, "needs no explanation, since this is an essentially liberal sect. But how has the Tendai succeeded, without contradiction, in incorporating itself into the philosophical systems of the other sects? Here tolerance, or rather abstention, is no longer sufficient, and I would like to know how Tendai thought has logically been able to harmonise itself with such different points of view?"

"The answer to your question is contained in the Buddhist legend of the Prodigal Son. In it one sees how Buddha divided his teaching into five periods, like so many stages, in which to attain at last the whole truth. You will see that the philosophies you speak of do not exclude each other. Here is the legend:

"A prodigal son, who had left his parents, and who lived a wandering existence, decided one day to return to his father's house. Now, during his absence, the latter had become very wealthy. He passed his days in a palace conversing with wise men, seated in a magnificent arm-chair, his feet resting upon a gold-embroidered cushion, and surrounded by numerous servants. Dazzled by this unexpected luxury, the son did not recognise his father, and departed, thinking: 'This residence is not the one I am seeking, and is not for me.' But the father, who had recognised his son, and whose dearest wish was to welcome him home, sent two servants after him with the order to bring him back. However, when the prodigal son saw a man running after him, he thought they wished to arrest him or to kill him, and his terror was such that he lost consciousness. The good father sprinkled water on his son's face and brought him back to his senses, but did not reveal his identity."

"Why?" I asked curiously.

"This first part of the story symbolises the first period of Buddha's teaching—the Kegon period. Having given men the magnificent treasure of Kegon philosophy, Buddha saw that they did not understand it. Their feeble gaze could not contemplate so complete a light. He then decided to reveal his light progressively, and to provide successive stages of different altitudes and nature, varying according to the capacities of each one.

"I continue. The father sent to this son two poor men who, by their very poverty, inspired him with confidence. The two poor men advised the son to seek work amongst the palace servants so as to earn more money. He followed their advice. The father treated his new servant with kindness, gave him a large salary, and told him to feel at home under his roof. This is the second period. To all men is given a simple teaching free of all metaphysics, and which places particular importance on practical precepts.

"Then the father called his new servant 'my son,' and treated him as such. The son, who has not as yet recognised his father, was much touched by the kindness of his employer. Although he lived in a hut situated outside the palace, considering himself unworthy of living within the palace itself, he gradually became accustomed to his new surroundings and wished to settle there.

"This is the third period. Man begins to understand the deep wisdom contained in the Mahayâna, but does not consider himself worthy of reaching the summits. Believing himself incapable of such an achievement, he does not yet enter into the spiritual way which Buddha, in his mercy, has prepared for him. Nevertheless, in his heart he longs to do so.

"Then the father, who had fallen ill, called for his son and, still not revealing him the truth, begged him to accept the direction of his immense fortune in his stead. The son acquitted himself of this task with the most scrupulous honesty, not knowing that all those treasures would belong to him some day. He continued to live in his poor hut. This part of the story represents the fourth period: one becomes a Bodhisattva, but not a Buddha, because one has not yet attained complete illumination.

"At last, feeling his end approaching, and having witnessed a great change in the heart of his son, the father assembled all the members of the family and said to them: 'This is my son who disappeared fifty years ago, and whom I have found at last. I bequeath him all my possessions.' Then the son abandoned the straw hut and took possession of the wonderful palace.

"That is the fifth period, that of the *Lotus of the Good Law* (*Hokkekyō*), the period of the final and complete doctrine. The true object of Buddha's coming into the world was to preach the *Lotus of the Good Law*."

I entered the Sanjusangen-do to muse upon these entirely merciful conceptions.

This temple of the "33,333" images of Kwannon, Goddess of Mercy and of Human Pity, was built in the third year of Chokwan (1165), was destroyed by fire in 1249, and rebuilt in the second year of Bunei (1265). Exteriorily it presents the rather disconcerting aspect of a long barn. How disappointing it is when seen after so many other temples, such as the Myo-ho-in, with its simple, noble lines, the Yogen-in, the Shoren-in, the curious Rokakudo, with its numerous super-imposed roofs, the Jakko-in, a silent, peaceful retreat, the exquisite little temple of Katata, built on piles and bathing in azure, as well as many others whether sumptuous or modest! However, my disappointment vanished when I crossed the threshold of the Sanjusangen-do. The interior is a miracle! The gallery of golden Kwannon fascinates and amazes one. According to the legend, when Kwannon descended to the nether regions, in quest of some unfortunate soul she might save, the damned, on seeing her, forgot their torments. Mercy seems indeed to irradiate upon all the world from the *one thousand and one* statues contained in the great hall—*one* huge one in the centre, and *five hundred* smaller ones on either side—for its legendary and popular name is very misleading. A touching thought of universal compassion emanates from all these golden figures. One of us murmurs gently the words of Buddha contained in *The Lotus of the Good Law*, " Here is an end of all the unhappiness of the world." How charming, naïve or magnificent are all these figures! The soft light shed by the candles creates a dream-like atmosphere in which all these golden wooden statues seem to pulsate with life, whilst a narrator, attached to the temple, chants explanations.

7. *Meditations on the texts of* The Lotus of the Good Law, *sacred book of the Sect*

Every evening the excellent bonze, some Japanese friends and myself used to meet in one of the apartments of the temple, in order to sip the traditional cup of tea whilst listening to the reading of the sacred text, *The Lotus of the Good Law*.

By the open *shōji* I gazed dreamily at the sky scattered with fleecy white clouds. I meditated long upon the pages of this admirable book so rich in thought and curious expressions, and which is truly a glittering synthesis of Eastern wisdom. Some flower petals, borne upon the breeze, were wafted across the blue square of the window.

I will merely indicate here the manner in which we used to meditate under the direction of the priest. One of the most frequent themes chosen was the Tendai idea that all creatures will be saved. Kneeling upon the mat, we used to concentrate our thought upon the following text:

And I, Bhagavat, who am delivered of the Three Worlds, I hold myself solitary and calm, and I contemplate the Three Worlds, which contain all creatures, all of which are my children.

And I show them their distress, for I know the means of saving them.

And I display ability in the choice of the methods which will allow me to save them, and I speak to each in his own tongue. And knowing the miseries of the world, I show each one the particular means of reaching Nirvâna—and yet there is only one way.

And to those children who have sought refuge near me, and who eagerly desire perfect understanding, to all those who are to me as my own children, I teach by parables the unique vehicle of Buddha. '*Understand me*, I say unto them, *and you will all reach light, eternal peace, calm and Nirvâna.*'

The Tathâgata treats all creatures equally, and not unequally, when their conversion is at stake. He is like the rays of the sun and of the moon which shine for all alike, for the virtuous man as for the wicked, for that which is elevated as for that which is vile, for that which smells good as for that which smells bad. Everywhere these rays fall indistinctly on all people.

Then as the Buddhist religion likes to touch the hearts and to enchant the eyes, the reading of another page brought us that metaphysical ecstasy in which the delighted soul surpasses the human state.

Hardly had Bhagavat exposed the subject of his parables demonstrating the Law, than a heavy shower of Mandarâva and of Mahâmandarâva blossoms fell from the sky. The hundred thousand myriads of Buddhas in the hundred thousand myriads of Universes, seated on thrones under trees of diamond, were all covered with flowers.

Sandal powder fell next, perfuming the atmosphere. In the air, timbrels, struck by no hands, gave forth delicious sounds. Thousands of streamers of marvellous stuffs fell to the ground. Garlands, collars, pearl chaplets, precious gems, immense and resplendent diamonds were suspended in mid-air at all points of the horizon. Hundreds of thousands of diamond vases containing suave essences advanced from all sides of their own volition. And above the Tathâgata, Bodhisattvas supported interminable lines of parasols made of gems, which rose to the firmament. And the whole world re-echoed with praise and with music.

Flowers, wafted in by the breeze, fell into the room through the open *shōji*. I used some of them to mark the pages of the holy book.[1]

[1] *The Lotus of the Good Law* has been translated into French by Burnouf (*Le Lotus de la Bonne Loi*), Maisoneuve ed. See Appendix.

CHAPTER VII

THE SHINGON SECT

(1) The Shingon Sect. (2) A pilgrimage to the monastery of
Koya-San. The marvellous and legendary life of Kōbō-Daishi.
(3) Before the pond of White Lotus. An introductory lesson on the
Ten Spiritual Degrees. (4) Mr Shinzai Hayashi, bonze of the sect,
explains to me the mystical principles of Shingon. The Universe,
the essence of which is Mahâvairocana-Buddha, or the Great
Illuminator, presents two aspects: the exoteric and the esoteric.
Shingon communes with the secret truth. In the mysterious shade
of the great cryptomerias: the revelation of the Three Mysteries.
(5) Mr Takaoka, bonze of the Shingon Sect, and professor at the
University of Koya-San, proposes to us a concentrated formula of the
Shingon philosophy. (6) How to read and to practise the *mandara*, or
mystical diagrams. The World of Two Parts. (7) Does the *mandara*
possess magic properties? Explanations are given us by Mr Masaharu
Anesaki, bonze and professor at the Imperial University of Tôkyô.
(8) At the Shingon Temples: the Toji and the Daigoji. (9) Extract
from the *Si-do-in-dzu*, or Seals of the Four Rites, according to the
commentaries of the bonze Horiu Toki, Superior of the Temple of
Mitaniji.

1. *The Shingon Sect*

This sect, whose name signifies *True Word*, was founded in
Japan in 806 by the Japanese bonze Kūkai, better known under
his posthumous title of Kōbō-Daishi—the most celebrated
saint of Japan. In 804 Kōbō-Daishi went to China, where he
received the Shingon esoteric doctrine from the Chinese priest
Houei-Kouo, whose disciple he became. It is said that the
latter had received it from an Indian seer who held it from
Nagarjuna, who, in turn, had received it from the wise
Vajrasattva, whom Buddha himself had chosen to inherit
the Law.

The principal canonical texts of the sect are the *Dai-ni-shi-*

kyō and the *Kon-go-chō-kyō* (Sanskrit: *Mahâvairocanâbhisam-bodhi* and *Vajrasekhara sutras*), to which must be added the works of Kōbō-Daishi. The cult usually comprises essentially symbolical, mystical or magical practices.

The sect numbers more than 6000 temples, monasteries or chapels, the chief of which are the Koya-San, the Daigoji and the Toji. It possesses 3000 abbots, 4700 priests, 2,600,000 perpetual subscribers, and 8,800,000 occasional or Shinto subscribers. All these grouped together have founded more than 180 social organisations and several schools.

2. *A pilgrimage to the monastery of Koya-San. The marvellous and legendary life of Kōbō-Daishi*

Still in the company of Buddhist pilgrims I have scaled with difficulty but with a contented heart the height of Koya-San, the sacred mountain on which the great saint, Kōbō-Daishi, founded the most celebrated monastery of the Shingon sect. In order to meditate better we had taken the longest way, that of Yoshino, which passes through the rocks and woods in which mountain torrents sing. The roots of giant crypto-merias often served us as steps. In the dark forest the stagnant humidity formed a light mist which enveloped us like a dream. Pale golden shafts filtered through the black trunks like rays announcing a luminous, if still hidden truth. As we advanced, the peace of these holy precincts invaded us, and seemed little by little to purify our souls. We had conversed along the way, but now we were silent. After the deep shadows, light again took possession of the landscape. A small chapel marks the first stage of purification. The little bridge one crosses seems to introduce the visitor into a new and pure life. Temples and different edifices appear disseminated here and there. We have reached our goal.

One of the priests receives us very kindly, and gives me a few explanations. He tells me "that the temple was founded in 816 A.D. by Kōbō-Daishi."

Kōbō-Daishi! How many times have I heard this name piously uttered by my road companions! This holy mountain covered with deep woods and temples, this sect celebrated for strange and magnificent magical ceremonies—for its incantations and its symbols—awaken a certain hesitation in my heart. Shall I understand these mysteries? The charming and warm welcome of the priests whom I cannot sufficiently thank here, the affectionate solicitude of my own companions—poor pilgrims who never ceased showing me the greatest indulgence and help—encouraged me to persevere in my intention of initiating myself to this mysterious doctrine. Following the advice of a priest, I accepted to stop at the monastery the time I would deem necessary for my studies and for the realisation of my spiritual aspirations.

There is no inn at the Koya-San, but the priests receive the pilgrims. I was given a room in one of the apartments of a temple. Certain temples, like the Shōjo-shin-in, the Henjo-ko-in and a few others, are especially arranged to receive guests. Slightly fatigued by the journey, I took a rest. The traditional tub of hot water was ready for me. I tasted the herb soup and the bowl of rice which a monk brought me, and which were both delicious. No meat nor fish, of course. Several pilgrims who had become my friends took tea with me. Then my Buddhist master told me the legendary story of Kōbō-Daishi.

"Who does not know this story? Kōbō-Daishi was born in 774, of a noble family. It is said that he was born in the attitude of prayer, his hands joined together. He was a prodigious man, supernatural, mystic, philosopher, artist (you will see his works in many temples), scientist (he imagined our *hiragana,* or system of phonetic writing), magician, whose genius could dominate the elements and change the course of things. A number of fabulous facts are attributed to him. Everyone has heard of the struggles he had so many times to sustain against evil spirits during his novitiate. One day, at Cape Murato, dragons issuing from the waves strove to trouble his meditations. The saint immediately dispersed them by reciting magical formulas, and projecting upon them the rays of the evening star which, descending from the sky, had placed itself upon his lips. Another time, as he was praying in a temple, which he had built himself, the demons came to torment him; but the saint enclosed himself in a magic circle into which his all-powerful will prevented them from entering.

"It is indisputable that Kōbō-Daishi was a genial, universal saint. The '*mandaras*,' those mystical diagrams of which he is the author, and which symbolise the spiritual and visible Universe, the totality of things, seem to have been but a projection of his mind, microcosm of the world.

"Destined originally for an official career, he studied at the university, where the starting-point of his spiritual journey was Confucianism. But the latter, which is a code of morals and traditional propriety, could not satisfy him. He was possessed with the desire of discovering the profound esoteric sense of the thoughts of Buddha, and of the mystery which surrounds us, hidden beneath the outward aspect of Buddhist texts and the world. Having neither teacher nor adviser, he next studied the Chinese philosopher, La-Tse, who had been conscious of the ineffable depths of life and thoughts.

"The central idea of Kōbō-Daishi is born of a genial and luminous intuition, confirmed by his immense knowledge, namely, that everything possesses an exterior and an interior, an *exoteric* and an *esoteric* aspect—a truth which proclaims itself and a *secret* truth—and that the thought of Buddha himself had voluntarily submitted to this law. *The elect are those who accede to the esoterism of this world.* But how can one lead all men towards this goal? Intellectual power does not suffice to do this. Now the Shingon sect wishes to save all men. It is here that our practices operate, and allow, thanks to certain concrete acts, the mystery of the world to penetrate into all hearts.

"At twenty-four years of age, after long meditations, Kōbō-Daishi reached Illumination by a revelation of Buddha, one day that he was contemplating the ocean. In 793 he was admitted to the priesthood. In 804 he left for China, where he became the disciple of the sage Eka, who transmitted to him the secret truths which form the Shingon doctrine. Having returned to Japan, he settled at the Toji, and a few years later, encouraged by the Emperor Heizei, he founded the Shingon sect and the monastery of Koya-San. He enjoyed an immense popularity. The celebration of rites, their philosophical and aesthetic character, greatly attracted the Court and the thinkers of his time. On the other hand, people found, and still find, certain real satisfactions of the heart in the Shingon temples, and from direct communion with the Buddhist truths which appropriate practices allow them to attain.

"In 825, having finished his earthly work, Kōbō-Daishi assumed the attitude of ecstasy, and insisted upon being buried alive. The pilgrims assembled here will tell you that he is not dead, but that he still lives in his grave, and is awaiting silently to leave it that Miroku, the future Buddha, should appear upon earth."

3. *Before the pond of the white lotus. An introductory lesson on the Ten Spiritual Degrees*

We were admiring the white lotus floating on a little pond.

"I will first initiate you," said my teacher, "to the Ten Degrees of Spiritual Elevation as they were defined by Kōbō-Daishi in the book I am holding, and which was written by him. The lotus of this pond will furnish me with the necessary comparisons."

"What is the title of the book?" I asked.

"*The Jewel Key, or the Storehouse of Mysteries.*"

"I am listening."

"The first degree is characterised by the expression *Shō-tei-yo-shin* (The thought of the Goat in another existence). The goat symbolises man, who is still in a bestial state of existence. At this degree man obeys only his lowest instincts: his belly and his sex. Will he ever rise to a superior degree? *Comparison:* look at this pond. Long before blooming and pushing its flower to the surface of the water, the lotus is hidden in its germ, under the slime and the mud. Will it ever emerge?

"*Second Degree:* Gu-dō-shi-sai-shin (The thought of the adolescent), who does not as yet understand, but respects the commandments. Light has not yet penetrated the being. Alone a few signs reveal that a soul is about to be born. One conforms oneself to the rules, without as yet understanding their spiritual import. This is the stage of the adepts of Confucianism. One murmurs formulas, one makes certain gestures, one abstains from others. Yet what a progress it is on the former state: conventional morality prepares the *milieu* in which the spirit is about to develop. One observes the five Buddhist precepts: not to destroy life, not to take that which is not a gift, to refrain from unlawful sexual intercourse (an ignoble thing), not to lie, not to drink intoxicating liquors. One observes, according to Confucius, the Five Cardinal Virtues (pity, justice, politeness, wisdom and prudence), and the Five Relationships (lord and vassal, parents and children, husband and wife, brother and sister, friends). *Comparison:* the moment preceding dawn. Look below the muddy water of the pond, at these frail green stems, future supports of the splendid flower. They are as yet but delicate weeds, but they already awaken a hope.

"*Third Degree:* Ei-dō-mu-in-shin (Thought of the child delivered from his terrors). The creature escapes indeed from the three evil states (hell, ghostly state of the dead, state of all impure animals). A soul is born, characterised by its innocence, its detachment, intoxicated by its own emptiness. It has reached a summit and does no more harm, but it does not as yet perceive the light. This is the state of the Taoists and of the Brahmans, who stop and fix themselves in their own personal visions. *Comparison:* tormented by the inner surge of sap, the lotus stem rises towards the light. Will it halt on the way?

"*Fourth Degree: Yui-un-mu-ga-shin* (Conscience of the aggregates devoid of self). A mind is born seeking the truth. It will find as yet only a glimmering of it, but its ascension towards the light has begun. The doctrine of the Kusha sect resumes this thought. The proud 'self,' cause of a thousand illusions, and itself but an illusion, disappears like a cloud before the first rays of dawn. The glimmer continues to grow. *Comparison:* the lotus stem pushes its bud, enveloped with leaves, to the surface of the pond. At the first kisses of the sun, the bud will burst its sheath and the flower will appear.

"*Fifth Degree: Bastu-go-in-shū-shin* (The thought of exterminating the seed and the causes of passions). This is the degree reached by the *Pratyekabuddha* (individual Buddhas). The wise men have extirpated from their hearts all passions, all desires. By meditating upon the causes of passion, they have once again found illusion. Life and the world are but the dreams of a dream. *Comparison:* the flowers, the leaves, the clouds are reflected upon the mirror of the water. These images have no substance. They are merely illusions. Draw nearer and look."

We both bent over the pond, pushing aside the reeds, so as to see better. The bonze drew my attention to a lotus just emerging from the water and declared gravely:

"Look! A white lotus has ascended *above the mirror of illusion.*"

"*Sixth Degree: Ta-en-daï-jō-shin* (Thought of the Great Vehicle for the salvation of others). Yet thought exists in this world of illusions. It alone exists, and from it all emanates. You will recognise here the Hosso doctrine. On the quality of my thought will depend the aspect of my life. My thought will be of an inferior order, and my life will be inferior, and I will therefore not become a Buddha if, though possessing the secret of freedom, I did not make others profit by it. Would Buddha be Buddha if he had not brought salvation to men drowning in the limitless Ocean of Pain? Therefore the thought which is desirous of progressing must liberate others. *Comparison*: sometimes parasitic plants wind themselves around the lotus stems; grouped in a sheath these free themselves and pursue their ascension towards the sun.

"*Seventh Degree*: *Ka-ku-shi-gu-sho-shin* (Thought conscious of the negative). This is the stage of the Sanron sect. Meditating on the eight following negative terms: birth, non-dissolution, non-going, non-coming, non-identity, non-diversity, non-existence, and non-nihility, thought liberates itself from vulgar points of view and reaches the colourless and undefinable summits of the Middle Way. *Comparison*: the lotus has ascended above the surface. If it is not reality, neither is it a vain image reflected upon the surface of the water. It is neither reality nor non-reality: its nature is undefinable.

"*Eighth Degree*: *Thi-dō-mu-i-shin* (Thought of a universal and real way of salvation). We have reached the stage of the Tendai doctrine: the original identity (the Universe being Buddhist in essence, offers to all the possibility of salvation). *Comparison*: all the lotuses will eventually ascend towards the light. The pond will be covered with lotuses.

"*Ninth Degree*: *Goku-mu-ji-shō-shin* (Absolute thought of nature in itself). We have reached the stage of the Kegon sect—the extreme point of exoteric thought. *Comparison*: the lotuses are beautiful, blossoming in the sun. What could one imagine more beautiful, or more perfect? Yet I wish to awaken in you the longing for a still more sublime vision."

The bonze relapsed into silence for a few minutes.

I gazed at the lotus pond of the old temple. It is only in Japan that I learned to understand the mysterious and deep charm of the lotus. There the lotus is not merely a flower like another. Too much thought is concentrated about it. The purity of its petals, their tints at dawn and at sundown, the perfect shape of its corolla, its diurnal and nocturnal life—everything about it possesses a symbolical or mystical value.

When one watches its growth, its blooming as we had just done, the soul seems to rise in quest of light, and when, in the silence and on the clear water, the lotus bursts open with a sharp, dry sound, which is almost an appeal, one has the impression of receiving a sudden revelation of the mystery of things which lives in its golden heart.

The bonze resumed:

"The *Tenth Degree* is called *Hi-mitsu-shō-gon-shin* (Thought embellished by the mystery). What mystery? Well, is not everything a mystery? The universe, the Buddhist texts, are mysteries: one *must rediscover their inner light, their perpetual potentiality and dynamism* which are also ours, or, in other words, the *Dai-nichi-nyō-rai* (Sanskrit: *Mahâvairocana*), *i.e.* the Great Illuminator, or Buddha himself, considered as a metaphysical principle which is at the same time the essence, life and centre of things, and of which everything, *absolutely everything*, even the smallest speck of dust, is an expression. Blind indeed is he to whom the lotus is a mere joy for the eyes! Blind is he who, having examined as we have done the different stages of its growth, has only retained a rational explanation thereof! *It is necessary to understand the world from the inside. We have the same heart as Buddha, and this lotus has the same heart as us.*"

4. *Mr Shinzai Hayashi, bonze of the sect, explains to me the principal mysteries of Shingon*

We had just visited in the Kongo-Buji an extraordinary treasure consisting of a collection of eight thousand scrolls of Buddhistic writings. The remembrance of their gold and silver characters remained long before my eyes. The sight of such a treasure of art and thought again filled me with that feeling of discouragement which I had already experienced and which is, perhaps, common to all novices in Buddhism. Of what use trying to persevere? A whole human life would not be sufficient to study those texts. Of what use could be to me a doctrine, the depth of which I perceive but which far surpasses me, and which I will never completely understand?

My teacher read me the beginning of the *Jewel Key of the Mysteries,* which completed my confusion.

"Infinite is the number of yellow silk scrolls—infinite is their number. There are thousands and thousands of them. Some contain the exterior doctrine. Others the Buddhistic doctrines. Obscure are the ways which open before the novice. And one becomes discouraged at reading so much, at writing so much. Of what use is it? The depth of being has never been reached and always remains inaccessible. Each one reasons and reasons again in the darkness without a light. Unconscious of their folly, all creatures are blind, and pass, unseeing, through the three reigns of existence. They are born and die, and yet they still remain blind. What do these eternal rebirths bring to them? Nothing. The Blind are not conscious of the Light.

"We return to darkness, come back again and return once more. And Death retains its mysteries. Who will lift the veil of this shadow in which the living are drowning?"

Shortly afterwards I sauntered with my master in an alley shaded by magnificent cryptomerias, which winds its ways amongst the graves and stelae of the celebrated cemetery of Koya-San. I know no trees more impressive than these cryptomerias. They are gigantic beings, which, with their shifting shadows and their monstrous roots rising from the earth, conjure up before one's eyes human or fantastic forms. They are half plants, half giants. The mist of this rainy morning shed a ghostly aspect upon all things. Shades of Atsumori and of Kumagai, of Asano avenged by his faithful Rōnins, shades of Bashô the poet and of many celebrated Daimyōs, whose monuments are scattered about the Field of the Dead, did you hover around me, a pilgrim and a stranger? You were all Japanese and Buddhists, and the Japanese soul is made of your substance. But could I—corrupt heart that I am—

come from the furthermost Europe—could I, without risk, draw near to the golden altars of their sacred shrines? Accustomed to the logical thought of my race, and to trenchant and practical syllogisms, by what newly-acquired super-faculty could I understand a doctrine which sanctifies Mystery equally with Spirit, whilst restituting the gold hidden in its depths and before which reason is dazzled?

My master said to me:

"Just like the Tendai doctrine, the Shingon sect poses a universal principle, *i.e.* that all creatures and all things have a common origin, made of the same spiritual essence as Buddha himself. To define this Principle we use the word *Dai-nichi-nyō-rai*, or the Sanskrit term *Mahâvairocana* (The Great Illuminator), which designates, as I have already told you, Buddha himself considered as a metaphysical entity, and as universal essence. Nothing exists but by *Mahâvairocana*. One can even say that the world is but the play of his light, more or less focussed or diffused. We know, however, that this pantheistic conception of the universe is not special to our sect.

"I have already alluded to that which distinguishes and differentiates this sect from all others, *i.e.* that Shingon insists upon considering two aspects of the universe; the apparent and the occult, the exterior and the interior—hence an exoteric doctrine (*Ken-Kyō*) and an esoteric doctrine (*Mitsu-Kyō*). All the sects content themselves with exoteric explanations. All except the Shingon sect, which goes further still and opens up for us esoteric vistas in which the profound thought of Buddha resides in its absolute purity, and which give us access to fundamental reality. A Buddhist text, one of those golden scrolls we have just been examining, can be understood in two different ways, according as one considers its apparent and immediate sense, or its hidden and deeper sense. Those initiated to the Shingon sect study the second sense and declare that to understand completely the esoteric sense of this world is to be Buddha.

"The other sects content themselves with superficial interpretations. *We* believe that the whole universe must be deciphered according to our methods. The living, central truth, the heart of things, are secret realities which account for the mysticism of our practices. Since all beings and all things are of the same essence, and since logical reasonings, discussions and dialectics only scratch the bark of things, one should, by thought and other means, by acts of mystical value, by the practice of our symbols, of our incantations and of our formulas, strive to feel and to understand the cosmic life and become conscious of our intimate and universal communion. We are not foreign elements created by an exterior force and thrown into the cosmos. We *are* the cosmos, and the cosmos *is* ourselves."

I said to my master :

"Men communicate between themselves because they think and speak. But how can man and things communicate or commune with each other ? To understand the esoteric sense of the world it would be necessary for the latter to speak to us, or to give us a sign ?"

"Precisely. The world speaks to him who knows how to hear it. We have now reached the point to which I wished to bring you. I must now reveal to you one of the essential conceptions of the Shingon doctrine which is taught under the name of *The Three Mysteries*. It can be resumed thus :

"Each thing possesses Body, Thought, Speech."

"Like men and the Buddha himself ?" I inquired.

"Absolutely."

"In that case these cryptomerias under the shade of which we are discussing . . . ?"

". . . possess Body, Thought, Speech, and these constitute what we call *The Three Mysteries*. The speech of these trees is, for example, the melody of their foliage shaken by the wind. Listen to it. . . ."

The giant trees sang in the wind. Boughs creaked. The more I listened, the more I perceived the thousand murmurings and whisperings of their prodigious branches. It was like a concert which sounded, first faintly, then rising to drop again. How many myriads of atoms took part in these mysterious vibrations? Why did Nature emit these weird sounds? Why do these trees sing thus in the wind?

"Mystery of speech," said the priest. "The world thinks and speaks to us. But can we authenticate the source, the absolute, from whence these mystical communications reach us? Or again, if the inner self of all things is identical with my own self, and if for this reason I can understand what the cryptomerias think—just as I can apprehend in its very depth the thought of Buddha—or, better still, *myself be* the thought of Buddha and the thought of the cryptomerias—to what deep cause would I owe this privilege?

"Here is the explanation. We believe in the permanence of the Three Bodies of Buddha—the *Dharma-Kayâ*, or spiritual body; the *Sambhoya-Kayâ*, or body of beatitude; and the *Nirmâna-Kayâ*, or body of transformation. It is the *Dharma-Kayâ*, the spiritual body, mystical substrata of the deep, direct, absolute, understanding which the Buddha possesses of the world, which expresses itself everywhere in nature under a thousand different forms, and to which we are listening at this very moment.

"In the doctrines of the other sects the *Dharma-Kayâ* is referred to as being without form or speech. The Shingon doctrine, on the contrary—and this is essential—teaches that the *Dharma-Kayâ* possesses both form and speech. If you listen attentively, it will speak to you, providing you know how to reserve an interior sanctuary for it in your inner self, and how to conform yourself to our rules of spiritual exercise. Purity of heart is one of the first conditions for this. Is it possible that, sensitive as you are, you have never perceived the inner echo of its voice? Have you never been tempted by the need to fathom the depths that are in you? Let it be well understood that I am not urging you to accomplish a simple psychological exercise of introspection. I am inviting you to an act of a totally different nature, and which it is difficult to express—*to a deep mystical evasion from the psychic layers which ordinary thought still reaches*—to an ultra-intuitive aspiration towards the comprehension of the mystery, in the mystery, and by the mystery, in the light of Buddhist faith."

The wind soughed more loudly in the cryptomerias. Never before had I understood in so direct a way how much the Westerner, systematically stemming his mystical values within himself, shuts himself off from many curious views of the world.

The bonze remarked to me :

"Universal mechanisation, coming to us from the West, has made man a blind and dumb automaton, and not a complete mind. Whatever may be the benefits of positive science, spiritual power, which is still more important, must defend its rights and retain its place. Bathe yourself here in a mystical atmosphere. . . . Does what I say to you strike you as absurd ?"

I protested energetically and in all sincerity.

"But," I admitted, "when we say that the cryptomerias are speaking, I presume we are merely expressing a poetical comparison ?"

"Not at all : rather a mystical reality. Do not postulate that what I am telling you is impossible, and that a positive explanation of it would suffice to demonstrate its inanity. The domain of current sciences is necessarily exoteric, as these do not answer questions of a metaphysical order, nor reply to the human aspiration towards an absolute point of view. You do not contest that things possess a body, yet you refuse them thought and speech. What a singular *parti pris* ! Each body lives by a thought of which it is but the material expression, or which seems so to us, and each thought expresses itself in words, in sounds, in gestures. Silence does not exist, but the *'mental murmur'* subsists, which explains why beings can sometimes understand each other by silence itself. He who will perfectly understand the *Three Mysteries*—Mystery of Body, Mystery of Thought, Mystery of Speech—will reach Buddhahood. One must meditate and study long before understanding them. One must first liberate one's soul from the mean prejudice which erects a barrier between supposedly inanimate objects and living beings. The ignorant creates categories where the Spiritually Enlightened sees none."

A long silence followed these explanations. The wind sang softly in the lofty summits of the cryptomerias. "Thought is everywhere," continued the bonze. "It directs unfailingly the stars through space, and regulates those interior exchanges contained in the smallest speck of dust. The harmony of the cosmos and the structure of the atom, the final causes, the blossoming of the lotus which, sprouting in the mud, emerges towards the sun—all reveal a Thought, or rather reveal that *All is Thought*. Similarly, speech is omnipresent: in order to express itself, the *Dharma-Kayâ* is not obliged to borrow exclusively the language of mortals.

"Sometimes," he added dreamily, " closing my eyes, I listen by the seashore to the Ocean speaking. Or, like today, to the voices of the great, centenarian trees, or to those of the streams of Mount Koya. Sometimes, at night, in a temple garden, I listen to what the insects and the rustling leaves are saying. Then I open my eyes and I see the branches swinging to and fro and the passing clouds or the dust of the road swirling away. . . . Body, Thought, Speech are everywhere. Now are you beginning to understand the Three Mysteries?"

That day we pursued in silence our walk amongst the sacred woods, and our visit to the temples of Koya-San. The world,

I reflected, is heavy with mystery, but most men forbid themselves to think of it. In the West, Mysticism is considered foolish, and silence is impolite.

I passed again in front of the *Go-Byo*, or the grave of Kōbō-Daishi, and I remembered that, according to popular belief, the saint will awaken when the future Buddha will appear upon the earth. Little by little I felt unknown mystical values awaken within me. I was not dreaming. My lucid thought was seeking in all good faith to understand other men, other consciences, other reasons. Had I been dreaming, the little bronze statue of Kōbō-Daishi at the foot of the steps leading to the Mandoro would have recalled me to reality by its intense and true expression, by its fixed and contemplative thought.

In the impressive shadows of the Mandoro—the Hall of Ten Thousand Lamps—of which only a few are lit, a multitude of thoughts besiege me. And it is thus that I remember the gentle legend of the place, according to which a lamp offered one day by a poor woman shines more brightly than all the others. Another example of Buddhist compassion. Then I reflect that all this hall could be illuminated, fairy-like, with its ten thousand fires : a complete illumination is contained potentially within its dark flames. It lives upon a secret, like the universe, according to Shingon.

Then my teacher in Buddhism recited to me the following stanzas by Kōbō-Daishi :

The Buddhas in the innumerable Buddhist Kingdoms
Are none other than the Only Buddha in the depth of our soul ;
And the golden lotus, as numerous as the drops of water on the ocean,
Are our Body.
In each of the holy characters myriads of figures are contained.
In each product of the brush, chisel or metal
Is manifested the vitality of the universe,
In which myriads of real entities of virtue are present.
And thereby each is called to the understanding
Of his own glorious personality, even in his own physical being.

5. Mr Takaoka, bonze of the Shingon Sect, professor at the Koya-San University, gives us a concentrated formula of Shingon philosophy

"All the activities of the world—the forms, sounds, colours, seasons—are but varied aspects of the essence of the universe. *The self which is in man and things expresses itself from the exterior. All the activities of the world are but the radiation of the 'self.' One should study and meditate deeply the law of the Three Worlds, these Three Mysteries, and strive to understand what is meant by causality. One should then conform the rhythm of our life to cosmic guidance which signifies the fulfilment of one's social, human and national duty.*

6. How to read and use the "Mandara" or mystical images

In one of the temples of Koya-San are kept the "*mandaras*" composed by Kōbō-Daishi. My master gives me certain explanations as to the sense and scope of these graphic symbols, the use of which is traditional in the Shingon sect.

"Firstly," he said, "what is a *mandara* or a *himitsu-mandara* (secret *mandara*)? It is a symbolical diagram consisting of two parts intended to express the universe—unity and multiplicity, essence and forms, the essential and dynamic centre of which is Mahâvairocana, the Great Illuminator—and to favour intense speculation, the awakening and activity of mystical forces corresponding to the figures, symbols, signs which enter into its composition. The exhaustive practice of *mandaras*, so important in the cult of our sect, reveals at the same time a whole philosophy of the universe of which they simplify the plan and structure, and offers man the possibility of evoking, by means of thought, the living active presence of Buddha, or of one of his emanations.

"These diagrams, which sometimes, as in the case of those of Kōbō-Daishi, constitute true works of art, are in principle composed as follows:

"Of the two parts which compose them, the one symbolises

the ideal aspect of universal life, the other its dynamic manifestations. The first is called *Kon-go-Kai* (Sanskrit: *Vajra-
Datū*, literally 'elements of diamond,' *i.e.* the world of in-
destructible forces). The Great Illuminator, Mahâvairocana
Buddha, is represented seated in the centre of the *mandara* in a
meditative attitude. His head is aureoled by a white disc, and
he is surrounded by his saints, and by other white aureoled
emanations seated on lotuses. The central square containing
this picture is framed by eight other squares which contain
other figures and symbols. This represents one of the aspects
of the cosmos: the ideal and potential world.

"The second part—the dynamic universe and its manifestations—is called *Tāi-zo-kaï* (Sanskrit: *Garbha-Datū*, or primitive element). In the centre, emerging from the eight petals
of an open lotus, representing the heart of the world, stands
the Great Illuminator aureoled with a red disc. The red
symbolises activity and dynamism. He is surrounded by
divinities and symbols—representations of all the different
forms of life which exist only by his life and his love.

"Certain *mandaras*, true works of art, are composed of a
multitude of golden Sanskrit letters, traced on a dark silk
background, which unrolls itself like a kakemono. These are
the *Shuji-mandara*. The two surfaces of a *Shuji-mandara* also
symbolise 'the worlds of diamond' and the 'primitive world,'
and the letters traced thereon have certain secret relations with
the divinities. The Great Illuminator is symbolised by the
Sanskrit letter *A* traced upon an open lotus."

"The *mandara*," I remarked, "remind me of certain ideas of
Pythagoras, who distinguished the *Cosmos*, or place of regulated uniform life, from the *Ouranos*, or place of the mobile
'becoming.' It is an image of the world."

"It is much more than that, or, if one wishes to use the term
'Image,' it is the image of a mirror which reflects the light and
heat of the sun, although not being itself either heat or sun.
By the communion of our faith with the essential principle
symbolised by the *mandara*, by virtue of prayers and incanta-

tions, by appeals to Buddha, it is the very power of Buddha himself which is present and acts."

"It is therefore an object of magic?"

"What do you call magic? If by this term you mean a fetich, you are absolutely wrong. An answered prayer is not a magical formula. The *mandara* is an element of our mystical ritual, the practice of which restores all their living forces to the effects of our unity, of our fundamental identity with Mahâvairocana Buddha.

"Evoked by our prayers, Buddha realises his presence amongst us. But the exhaustive practice of the *mandara* is a science which cannot be learnt in one day.

"The most learned amongst the Shingon priests discover in these drawings, mirrors of the world, the most extreme subtleties, the secret solution of the most complicated metaphysical or religious problems, and the indication of universal correspondences or affinities. From the *Kon-go-kaï* proceeds that wisdom which leads to universal salvation; from the *Taï-zo-kaï* that wisdom which works for the salvation of others. In the *Kon-go-kaï* reside the five sciences—the science of the evolution of things (*Hokaï-taï-shō-thi*); the science of the mirror (*Daï-en-kyō-thi*), reflecting the elements of the world; the science of equality (*Byō-dō-shō-thi*), which considers things as they are without attempting to classify them or to subordinate them the one to the other; the science of the just look (*Myō-kwan-zatsuthi*), which, differing from the preceding one, distinguishes between right and wrong, thereby founding a moral law; and, lastly, the science of duty (*Jō-shō-sa-thi*), that is to say, the salvation of oneself and of others.

"To each of these sciences corresponds mystically in the other part of the *mandara*, or *Taï-zo-kaï*, one of the six great elements of the universe (*Roku-Dai*), *i.e.* ether, earth, fire, water and air. The sixth element, which is 'understanding,' is included in the first part of the *mandara*, in the world of Indestructibles.

"One should not forget, however, that in ideal and active

reality, all is One. It is only on the analytical plane that the world can be taken apart thus, and that the affinities special to certain of these elements manifest themselves, and may be inscribed in a diagram. It is our mind which must reconstitute the synthesis. The *mandara* is the material expression of this synthesis and the opportunity for our mind to come into intimate contact with the forces of life."

7. *Does the mandara possess magic qualities? Mr Masaharu Anezaki, bonze and professor at the Imperial University of Tôkyô,[1] answers this question*

"The graphic representations of the two cycles is called the *mandara*, and constitutes the central point of the ceremonies of the Shingon cult and of several mysteries. The composition of the *mandara* proceeds in part from mystical speculation, and also for a great part from ritual customs, according to which personages and symbols were disposed under a ceremonial canopy, in order to evoke corresponding faculties.

"Each of these representations is supposed to possess a certain power which is the essential function of the divinity or of the symbol and which is, at the same time, inherent in each of us.

"Thus, according to Kōbō-Daishi, worship is nothing more than a realisation, through the effects of the mystic ritual, of the inherent unity and the potential communion existing between the divinity which is worshipped and the worshipper.

"Seen in this light, religion is the suggestion of that fundamental unity, of the harmonious union of our faith with the persuasive 'elevating power' (Sanskrit : *adhisthana*) of the Great Illuminator.

"*From this union results the fact that every act of adoration possesses the virtue of evoking, and of literally causing to appear,*

[1] A very scholarly bonze and professor who gave several lectures on Buddhism at the Collège de France, in Paris. For all references as to the works of this author, see our annotated Bibliography at the end of this volume.

*in answer to its appeal, the mysterious power of the cosmic Lord,
or of any one of His manifestations.*

"Thus it is that religious acts are accomplished through all
the modes of our corporal, oral or mental activity.

"The sitting attitude of meditation, the gesture of the joined
hands, are combined, according to prescribed rules, with the
judicious use of symbols and of instruments, such as the lotus
flower, different weapons and symbolic thunderbolts, etc.,
which not only figure in the celebrations of the mysteries,
but also play a determined part by incorporating the movements of the cosmos into our own life.

"The oral exercises, such as the repetition of the names of
Buddha of mystical formulas and sacred texts, are a part, a
translation, of the cosmic word which the Great Illuminator
expresses perpetually and everywhere.

"Shingon Buddhism insists particularly upon the efficacy of
mystical formulas for the evocation of divine powers. This
is a characteristic feature of this branch of Buddhism, which
derives its origin from the Hindu belief in the mysterious virtue
of hymns and formulas

"Thus interpreted and handled, the symbols and mysteries
can assume an almost infinite variety, and the domain of their
application is limitless.

"The mysterious powers can be subdued by a simple movement of the fingers, by the recitation of a formula. Likewise
a very grand and pompous ceremony may be celebrated with
the same object of evoking the divine mysteries."

8. *The Shingon Temples, the Toji and the Daigoji*

At the Toji temple, founded in the eighth century, and
rebuilt in the seventeenth, one of the important centres of the
Shingon sect, I was little moved by the legend which declares
that Kōbō-Daishi straightened the pagoda by the sole effect
of his prayers. So many miracles add nothing to the virtues
of the great saint. His glory will subsist because his was a

really stupendous and complete mind, enamoured of science, art and mysticism, as were our scientists of the Renaissance, for whom the problems of the world comprised not only mathematics but also mystery and magic. But, on the other hand, I was infinitely touched by the simple and severe aspect of the edifice, with its red pillars and rafters, and its white walls. This simple hall produces a very deep impression. A secret thought still lingers here and pulsates with the same rhythm as the temple, which only assumes a certain animation once a month when Kōbō-Daishi, who lived here, is celebrated. It resumes its meditation the rest of the time until spring, when adorable processions of women—the *Tayu-no-dochu*—bring back to it youth and flowers.

These alternatives of shadow and light, of life and death, seem copied on the movement of the world, on its mystery. Many of the art treasures contained in the temple are the artistic realisations of the thought of Kōbō-Daishi himself. Some amongst them, such as that kakemono on which the genius of the Saint painted in powerful colours twelve dreaming gods seated on lotuses, abruptly transported our thought to the sphere of high speculations, and introduced it at once to the heart of the mystic doctrine.

Of the Daigoji temple, founded in 904, and which was restored later by the piety of Hideyoshi, I preserve an autumnal remembrance of its delicious garden, full of flowers, in the shade of which I dreamed of the Three Mysteries, and of the image of the pagoda in which I erected in thought the Ten Spiritual Degrees.

The enchantment begotten of visits to Shingon temples is indescribable. One should visit in springtime the Ninnoji, hidden amongst its flowers, and in the autumn one should not fail to see the Shingokokuji, situated on Mount Takao, all decked with red maples.

But it is especially the marvellous visions of the ceremonies of the Shingon cult which survive in my memory—a whole art of evocative, symbolic attitudes and gestures, practised in appropriate shadows and colours, through which the burning incense mounts in blue spirals. At the sound of the gongs, so strangely moving, the soul is filled with a sort of vertigo. One has the impression of discovering within oneself a disregarded sixth sense—the sense of mystery. I remember a procession of bonzes in the courtyard of a temple. They advanced grave and impressive along a pathway of mats which the rising sun tinted with gold and pink. The priests advanced chanting, clothed in brocaded silks. Several upheld, at the end of staffs, a scarlet canopy. Before them marched children crowned with gilt metallic ornaments which sparkled in the sunlight. Their painted faces, lips reddened and eyes artificially blackened, completed my impression of a cleverly composed picture which some magician had animated with a rhythmic life.

I also assisted several times at the evening services in the temples, bathed in mauve shadows. Between the red-lacquered columns and the panels decorated with Chinese lettering and streamers of yellow silk embellished with Chinese characters hanging from the ceiling, I caught sight of the officiating priest. He was perched on a sort of stool, covered with a stole, and he chanted in a monotonous voice whilst pouring perfumes into different perfume-burners. Crouched behind him, their *geta* placed in front of them, the priests resembled waxen statues. One would have said that the murmur of the prayers and of the responses came from some unreal distance. Occasionally the officiating priest made some queer, rapid gestures with his hands or fingers. I was told that the signification of these gestures is consigned in secret manuals, of which the *Si-do-in-dzu* (*see page* 116) is one of the most elementary.

This silent language, these ceremonies veiled in incense, the discreet explanations which were given me, as if one consented to indicate to me the entrance of the temple without deigning, however, to reveal any of its inner sanctuaries, carried my soul from mystery to mystery. I had the impression that night was passing, giving place to a glimmering of a divine softness; but that I, at least, would never see the crude and definitive daylight.

9. *Extracts from the Si-do-in-dzu, or Seals of the Four Rites, according to the Commentaries of Horiu Toki, Superior of the Temple of Mitaniji*

Buddhism is divided into two great schools called *Kengniô* or 'exoteric doctrine,' and *Mikiô* or 'esoteric doctrine.'

The *Kengniô* school teaches the theory of the doctrine, but does not teach which acts one should accomplish, or the degree of wisdom one should acquire, in order to attain Buddhahood. The *Mikiô* school alone teaches the acts which produce 'the incarnation of the Bôdai (Sanskrit : *Bodhi*). The Acts of Incarnation constitute the teaching of the *San-Mitsu*.'

What is the *San-Mitsu* ?

The *San-Mitsu*, or the Three Mysteries, consists in three different kinds of acts :

1. Acts of *Kuan-Néen*, 'meditation,' *i.e.* meditation on the *raison d'être* of the great Buddhist laws.

2. Acts of *Sĭn-gon*, 'true word,' *i.e.* a scrupulously exact recitation of the words of the *dhâranis*, the Sanskrit formulas endowed with unlimited powers.

3. Acts of *Si-In*, 'hand-seal,' consisting of making *mûdra* or Seals (cabalistic or mystical signs) with the fingers in order to acquire, in this life, the quality of Buddha.

Therefore the acts by which a priest becomes an incarnation of Buddha consist in accomplishing these Three Mysteries. We will, however, consider here only the third, that of the Seals.

In order to be initiated into these Mysteries it is, before all, necessary to have proven one's fidelity to the Buddhist religion, and one's unwavering faith in Buddha. Otherwise both initiated and initiator incur the chastisement reserved by Buddha for the violators of mysteries.

But, you will ask, are we not transgressing this Buddhistic law if we explain the theory of the Seals ? No. We commit no transgression. Scholars do not study Buddhism to turn it into derision. They wish to instruct themselves in order to learn the law of Buddha in all its depth. We will not therefore violate any law of our religion by giving this explanatory commentary on the Mystery of the Seals in order to instruct men devoted to Science and respectful of Buddha.

Nevertheless, we must make the following observation: Buddhism is, before all, a moral law. Therefore he who would practise the rite according to observations contained in a book, without submitting himself to the meditation of Buddhist laws, would commit an insensate act. This is a very important advice.

The *Kegonkyō* says: '*One is all,*' meaning that a simple formula may have an immense virtue. Our commentary explains each formula. When we say that a Seal may contain an immense virtue, we mean that when the officiating priest has accomplished the Seal, after having duly meditated as is prescribed, its miraculous powers appear simultaneously. Each Seal is explained separately.

For the celebration of the Rite of the Mysterious Laws it is necessary that all the elements of the rite, such as the site, the edifice, the altar, the cardinal points, the choice of a day, the vestments, the priest's food, the objects of worship, the offerings, the decorations of the hall, be complete and in conformity to rule. Besides all these material formalities it is indispensable that the officiating priest should have perfect faith in his religion. Then only can the miraculous effects resulting from the accomplishment of the Rite of the Mysterious Laws be produced. One should not imagine, therefore, that one can accomplish the Rites of the Mysterious Laws by merely knowing the signification of the Seals.

Another observation: a Seal may vary in signification according to the circumstances in which one forms it. For example, the Seal of the *Butsu-Chō* (the Seal of Buddha's forehead) is the same as that of *Shin-chimu-chō* (Seal to render the heart without birth), which is made on the heart in order to meditate upon the principle of 'non-birth' and 'non-destruction.' Many others are in the same case because the sense of a Seal varies according to the words which are pronounced by the officiating priest and the meditation to which he abandons himself.

The word *In* (Seal) is taken in the sense of 'sign of a well-founded resolution,' like the Seal which is placed on a solemn contract. The Seal is therefore merely a material formula which affirms one's resolution to become a Buddha.

In the theory of the Seals the right hand symbolises the 'World of Buddhas,' and the left hand 'the World of Men.'

Each finger has a particular value.
The thumb signifies 'infinite space, void or ether.'
The index signifies the element, 'air or wind.'
The middle finger is the element 'fire.'
The fourth finger represents the element 'water.'
The little finger represents 'the earth.'

SEALS OF TAIDZŌKAÏ

The *Taidzōkaï*, or 'World of Form,' is the counterpart of the Kon-go-Kaï, or the 'World of Law.' The creatures inhabiting it have reached the state of Buddhahood, but return to this world out of charity in order to save other men. They are the 'equals of the Buddhas' and are 'one' with them.

The first part of the book treats of the Seals which the officiating priest executes according to certain rules when he accomplishes the particular rites before the *Mandara* of Taidzōkaï.

KADJI-I

The Purification of Clothes.

The priest makes the first Seal before entering the temple, in order to 'purify the clothes of the law,' or sacerdotal ornaments. To this effect he must hold the vestments in his left hand and form the Seal with his right hand: this consists in closing the fist, the thumb being imprisoned under four bent fingers. This gesture is called the 'lotus fist,' and symbolises the bud of this flower. Just as the lotus flower which grows in the mud elevates itself above the mud so as not to be defiled by it, so the priest must purify his ornaments defiled by the touch of men.

NIU BUTSU SAMMAYA

To enter into the Sammaya of Buddha.

This gesture is accomplished by applying against each other the tips of the fingers of the two outstretched hands so as to leave a small space between the hands, the two thumbs being bent and resting against the base of the index. This Seal, called *Chō-Butsu-funi* (Buddhas and men are One), indicates that the officiating priest has entered into the Sammaya of Buddha, *i.e.* that he has attained the perfection belonging to the fundamental law.

HOKAI-CHŌ

Seal of the Production of the World of Law; also called Kayen-Chō, Seal of the Production of Flame.

According to an ancient translation brought back from India, and adopted by Buddhism, the Body of Fire is triangular. So the Seal of Hokai-Chō consists in forming a triangle by joining the tips of the two extended forefingers, the other fingers remaining closed. It symbolises the production of Fire, which must destroy all that is impure in the World of Law, and render the world sacred and saintly.

TEN-HO-RIN

The Revolving Wheel of the Law.

The Revolving Wheel of the Law is the preaching of Buddhist dogmas. The word 'Law' is used here in the sense of 'Law of Buddhism,' and the word 'Wheel' is used figuratively. Indeed, the strength and power of predication breaks and destroys all bad thoughts and erroneous or malicious judgments, 'like an iron wheel crushes that over which it passes.' The expression 'turn and turn again the Wheel of the Law' signifies 'to preach,' so that by forming the Seal of the Revolving Wheel of the Law, whilst pronouncing very exactly the *dharâni* and perfectly accomplishing the rite, the priest really preaches thus as he wishes to.

The Seal consists in joining the backs of both hands by interlocking the fingers, the tips of both thumbs touching each other.

KENJO-BINAYAKIA

The Chasing of Binayakia.

Binayakia, a Sanskrit word having the sense of 'obstacle,' is the name of a very powerful divinity who takes pleasure in accumulating obstacles. He is the elephant-headed Ganesh of Brahmanism, so skilful in assuming varied forms. This god is very badly disposed towards those men who follow the ways of Buddhism, and in consequence the officiating priest must chase him away before beginning the celebration of the ceremony. The Seal is composed of two *Kongō fists* formed by the hands being joined by the 'fingers of the wind,' the thumbs being imprisoned under the three last fingers, which are bent double. This Seal produces a 'violent wind,' which obliges the god to run away.

HI-KO

The Putting on of Armour.

Hi signifies 'to cover,' and *Kō* signifies 'armour.' The god of obstacles being driven away, the priest dons his armour to become invulnerable. That is why this Seal assumes the form of a helmet.

It is formed by joining the hands, the last two fingers being bent and covered by the thumbs. The tips of the extended middle fingers touch each other, and the forefingers are applied to the back of the middle fingers.

There is also another explanation for this Seal. The fourth and fifth fingers, bent towards the palms, represent the 'body of the officiating priest,' and the thumbs covering them symbolise 'void.' That means that 'the void exists around the body of the priest.' The lifted middle finger represents 'two great flames fanned by the wind,' which is symbolised by the forefingers. This Seal signifies that the body of the officiating priest is protected by the void and by an ardent flame, which renders it inaccessible and chases away the demons which are obstacles to the following of the ways of Buddha.

ZEN-IN

The Fastening on of the Armour.

This Seal is the complement of the preceding one. The two gestures which compose it are merely the decomposition of the *Hi-Kō*.

The priest makes believe that he is fastening on his armour with strings. After having undone the preceding Seal, he lifts, first, the indexes, the other three fingers and thumbs of each hand being bent, and turns them three times around one another whilst pronouncing the Sanskrit formula: '*On Ton.*' *On* means 'awaken,' and *Ton* signifies 'to fix on faith.' Then he makes the gesture of tying strings and repeats it several times on different parts of his body, such as, for example, on his navel, his legs, his chest, neck, forehead, etc.

TO BUTSU ZEN SAN-GHE KÉ

Confession before Buddha and Recitation of the Ké Formula.

Having donned his armour, the priest presents himself before Buddha and confesses his sins.

The word *San* is an abbreviation of the Sanskrit *Sanma*, which signifies 'to regret, to confess one's faults.' The term *Sanghe* is a combination of the Sanskrit *san*, and the Chinese *ghe*, fault. The *Ké* formula is quoted in the *Juhachi-Dō* rite.

This Seal is called the *Kongō-gō-chō*, or 'junction of the *vajra* hands.' It is made by placing before one's chest the two joined hands, the tips of the fingers being interlocked, and it symbolises 'the priest concentrating upon a fixed idea.'

DJO-SAN-GO

Purification of the Three Things.

This Seal is also called *Mi bé renghé gachō*, 'joining of unflowered lotus hands.' It is formed by applying the palms of the wide-open hands one against the other, so as to leave a little space between them. The fingers are joined at the tips, with the exception of the two forefingers, which remain slightly apart. This figure is named the Lotus Bud.

To execute this gesture to the accompaniment of the recitation of a *dhârani*, one must purify all the acts of Body, Thought and Speech. That is why it is called the Three Things. It is given the shape of the Lotus Bud because this flower is always pure, although born in slime.

KADJI-KO-SUI

Purification of the Perfumed Water.

The object of this Seal is to consecrate the perfumed water placed on the altar, by means of a *dōkō* which the priest holds in his closed fists. The word *Kadji* means 'to render a thing sacred and holy by the power of the Mysterious Laws.'

CHO-DJO

Purification by Aspersion.

The *Cho-Djo* rite consists in making in all directions, with the help of a small wand of white wood, called *sandjō*, aspersions of consecrated water in order to purify all that might be defiled in the temple, both living beings and objects.

KADJI-KU-MOTSU

Purification of Offerings.

This is the same Seal as the *Kadji-Ko-Sui*, applied by means of a special *dhârani* to the purification and consecration of the offerings placed on the altar.

HAKU-CHO

Clapping the Hands.

This Seal has two objects. It is an instrument of praise and serves also to frighten or awaken creatures. The priest claps his hands in order to frighten away the demons or malicious spirits who may be hovering over the offerings. As its name indicates, it consists in striking the left hand with the right.

TAN ZI

To throw (noisily) the Finger.

Here we find another form of the idea expressed in the preceding Seal. The fist being closed, one bends the forefinger compressing it with the thumb, and distends it abruptly, as if to give a fillip. The freed thumb then presses itself against the forefinger, which double movement produces a slight noise. However weak this sound may be, it has the same effect as clapping hands.

KO KU

The taking away of Impurities.

After having chased the demons away from the offerings, one must take away the impurities they have left thereon. A first general purification has been made by the accomplishment of the *Kadji-ku-motsu* rite. The second has for effect to purify the offerings in each one of their elements.

To execute this Seal the officiating priest bends the fourth finger and the thumb in such a way that they touch one another. He then forms with the three other fingers the figure of the three-pointed lance or trident. Both hands make the same sign simultaneously. The right hand remains hanging alongside the right thigh, and it is the left hand which, with the help of the recitation of the *Kadji* formula—'means of becoming holy'—clears the offerings of the impurities left on them.

CHO-DJO

Purification.

The impurities of the offerings being effaced, one confers upon them a still more perfect purity by sprinkling them with consecrated water.

In order to do this, the two hands make the gesture of the *Kongō* fist. Whilst his left hand rests upon his left thigh, the priest takes the *San-djō* with his right hand, plunges it into the water and sprinkles the offerings.

KO TAKU

Bright Light.

The offerings having been purified and consecrated, one must still confer upon them the quality of 'shining with a perfect light.' To this effect the officiating priest forms with both his hands the Seal of the three-pointed lance. He 'takes up the lance of the left hand with the lance of the right hand,' that is to say, he touches his left arm with his right hand, and with this 'three-pointed lance' he confers a magic brightness upon the offerings. The object of the rite is to satisfy the Buddhas by giving to the offering the quality of 'shining with an agreeable contour,' by means of the power of the brandishing of the three-pointed lance.

MASHI GHE BAKU

To rub the Hands and interlock the Fingers.

The offerings being prepared, the priest reads the *Hiō Haku*, or 'explanation of the object of the ceremony.' Before reading, he rubs each of his hands with the back of the other, and then forms the Seal of the Interlocking of Fingers. The rubbing of the hands signifies harmony, the interlocking of the fingers forms a round figure which is that of the full moon, which indicates that the spirit of the officiating priest is not interiorily defiled, but 'is as full of purity as the full moon.' Having his heart perfectly pure, the priest explains to the Buddhas the reasons motivating the rite he has just accomplished.

KU-YO-MON

Offering Speech.

After the reading of the *Hiō Haku*, an offering formula is read. During this reading the priest holds in his left hand a chaplet, a *dōkō*, and an incense burner with handle, according to the exactions of the rite, which requires that one should hold the incense burner whilst celebrating the praise of the Buddhas, and announcing the offerings made to them. This rite signifies that the incense is the messenger which bears to the Buddhas the true intention of the officiating priest. As for the chaplet and the *dōkō*, they have no particular signification in this case. The priest holds them continually. He only puts the *dōkō* down when it is necessary for his hands to be free to form the Seals. On the drawing, the incense burner is replaced by a lotus flower, symbol of unrivalled perfume.

CHO RAI

The Reciting of Compliments.

The names of the Buddhas are respectfully uttered (formula of invocation), and they are thanked for their kind intervention. In this case the Seal consists simply in holding the *dōkō* in the joined hands, according to the rite of the joining of the *vajra* hands.

KIO GAHU

Awakening.

Wishing to invite all Buddhas to take part in the ceremony, the priest must 'awaken' them, *i.e.* call their attention.

This Seal consists in bending the middle and fourth fingers of each hand over the thumb, lifting the forefingers and drawing the hands apart by interlocking the little fingers, symbolising thus the greatness and solidity of the earth, to which the firmness of the priest's faith is compared. One next revolves the tips of the two indexes three times. By virtue of this Seal, the Buddhas of all the infinite worlds are 'awakened.'

SARAI HOBEN

Means (of becoming Buddha) by the Salutation (of the Buddhas).

There are nine means or different acts which lead to the state of Buddha: acts of adoration, respect, confession, etc. These are the *Ways of Perfection*.

To respectfully salute the Buddha the priest forms the Seal called *San-kō-chō*, which expresses the firm resolution of never retreating. Indeed, when a person remains firm in his resolution of obtaining the *Maha Bodhi*—'Great Understanding'—he manifests by this his intention of honouring all Buddhas.

This Seal is made by directing the palm of the wide-open left hand towards the earth, and applying the back of the right hand on to the back of the left hand, so that the right thumb crosses the little finger of the left hand and vice versa. The three other fingers of each hand form two *san-kōs*.

SHITSU-ZAI HOBEN

Means (of becoming Buddha) by the Destruction of Wicked Actions.

This is a real confession with perfect contrition. The priest confesses his sins and prays that they may be 'annihilated'—that is not only that they should be forgiven, but that there should remain absolutely nothing of them—so that the effects which would fatally result from them be destroyed, and that the sins themselves can no longer reproduce themselves.

This Seal called *Dai-yé-tō*, 'Sword of Great Intelligence,' is executed by the two open hands with uplifted fingers. The thumb is made to join the bent forefinger; then the two hands are drawn together by crossing the tips of the three fingers of 'earth, water and fire.' This gesture is the symbolical figure of the mystical sword. At the same time the priest enters into meditation as to the best ways of destroying sin.

CHAPTER VIII

THE ZEN SECT

(1) The Zen Sect. (2) The Kinkakuji or Golden Temple. According to Mr Guessan Kanaï, bonze of the sect, the personal and original Zen philosophy is inexpressible. It was born of a smile of Buddha before a lotus. We must therefore understand it intuitively. Let us each discover in ourselves the Buddha which exists in us. (3) A pilgrimage to the Zen monastery of Obaku-San. Mr K. Noyori, a former monk of the monastery, explains the principal aspects of a Zenist soul. The life and the discipline of the monks. The *Zendo* or Hall of Meditation. (4) Zen, an intuitive method of a pure and liberated life. Explanations given by Mr Teitaro Suzuki, professor of Zen Buddhism at the Buddhist College of Otani (Kyôto). The secret virtue. Chinese, the mystical language. Declarations of Mr Kaiten Nukariya, professor at the *Kei-o-gi-jiku* University, and at the Buddhist College of the Zen Sect in Tôkyô. The sacred writings are without importance. Man partakes of the "nature of Buddha." Mr G. Hosaka, bonze and professor at the Zen Faculty of *Komazawa-Daigaku* at Kyôto, tells us that all men being the children of Buddha, *are* Buddha. Paradise is to be found on this earth. (5) The theory of *Satori*, or enlightenment, which arouses in the soul of the Zenist the revelation of a new vision of life. (6) Characteristic extracts from the *Zenso-mondo*, dialogues of Zenist bonzes, collected by Shundo Tsuchiya. (7) The Zen Temples—the Myoshinji, the Nanzenshi, the Tofukuji, the Kenshoji and the Enkakuji. Okuyama. A pilgrimage to the grave of the poet Bashô, a Zen Buddhist.

1. *The Zen Sect*

This sect, whose name is an abbreviation of Zenna, a transcription of the Sanskrit word *dhyana*, which means "contemplation," counts amongst its Hindu patriarchs the celebrated sage Bodhidharma, who remained nine years in meditation, seated cross-legged, his face turned towards a wall. Bodhidharma lived in the sixth century A.D.

In Japan the sect comprises three groups: Rinzai, Sōtō

and Obaku, the principles and methods of which are identical, and which only differ by their history.

The first group was illustrated in China by the celebrated priest Rinzai, who is held by Zenists to be the founder of the sect. This group was founded in Japan in 1191 by the Japanese monk Eisaï, who had gone to China to instruct himself.

The second branch, Sōtō, was founded in Japan by Dōgen (1200-1253), who spent four years in China, where he was the disciple of the greatest Chinese Zenists. He is one of the outstanding figures of Japanese Zenism.

The third branch, Obaku, was founded in Japan about 1653 by a Chinese monk named Igen, who became superior of the monastery of Obaku-San, of which we will speak later.

The Zen sect is very original. Its methods of teaching are oral and intuitive, and it claims no canonical book and no texts.

The three groups of the sect—Rinzai, Sōtō and Obaku—count more than 20,000 temples, monasteries and chapels; more than 7800 abbots, 36,000 priests, 8,000,000 perpetual members and 800,000 occasional or Shinto members. It possesses a great deal of landed property. Its annual budget exceeds 5,000,000 yen. The Sōtō branch counts by far the greatest part of the above-quoted figures.

2. *The Kinkakuji, or Temple of Gold. Mr Guessan Kanaï, bonze of the sect, tells me that the Zen philosophy is inexpressible*

We have reached the Temple of Gold, the celebrated Kinkakuji, standing before its lotus-covered lake dotted with picturesque islands. A bonze of the Zen sect, who watches over this treasure, welcomes us with the exquisite and ceremonious politeness of Old Japan.

What retreat could be more propitious than this one for dreamers, for Inkyō? [1]

---

[1] He who retires from active life and who abandons the direction of his house.

Although this wooden pavilion which the Shogun Ashikaga Yoshimitsu built in 1397 in order to live there as a Zenist monk, is gilded from its base to its summit, and even to the phœnix perched on its pinnacle, it appears neither insolent nor parvenu. It is true that it has acquired the patina of age. Yet, if one imagines it as it was when new, the same impression of good taste and modesty subsists. The edifice does not wish to crush the delightful scenery surrounding it, but merely to live near it humbly and in harmony with it. Its proportions, its delicate structure, the play of its shadows and lights, are all calculated with this object in view. It has voluntarily left the place of honour to the lotus pond, to the islands, to the pines. Zenist purity of heart exacts the submission of human work to nature. To spoil the carpet of floating lotuses would be just as sacrilegious as to destroy the pavilion itself. I admire the indulgence of the kind priest who welcomes me. Is my heart sufficiently pure to allow me to be received here?

We gaze for a moment, from the wooden gallery, at that perfection—the Garden of the Kinkakuji. Occasionally the surface of the lake ripples, revealing hidden lives therein: carps. Their shadows pass swiftly and the lotuses move slightly.

In the interior of the temple, where the walls, the columns, the very flooring are all golden, statuettes by Unkei [1] welcome us. On the ceiling the angels of Kano Masanobu,[2] which are, alas, very effaced by time, seem at our approach to have hidden themselves amongst the clouds. The remembrance of Yoshimitsu is everywhere present. Here is the place where he used to take his tea whilst conversing with his intimate friend Séami Motokiyo, the dilettante and one of the founders of No plays (1363-1444). From here he used to contemplate the

---

[1] A celebrated sculptor of Buddhist images who lived in the eighteenth century.

[2] The first of the celebrated Kano family of painters, founder of the famous school of painting. Sixteenth century.

The Kinkakuji or " Gold Pavilion," Kyôto

flowers, the moon. He lived amidst beauty, like all Japanese Zenists, for contemplation and aesthetics cannot be disassociated under the Nipponese sky. I am shown some magnificent kakemonos, and I greatly admire those of Cho-Densu, representing the Three Lights: Confucius, Buddha and Lao-Tze.

"The Zen doctrine," remarks my master, "owes much to the Chinese philosopher, Lao-Tze. This great intuitionalist understood that meditation in the very heart of nature, in the woods or on the banks of a lotus pond like this one, helps us more efficaciously to rediscover in ourselves our true fundamental nature, and to develop its spiritual potentialities, than all systematic teachings and texts. Nature discovers herself. So does the Zenist."

The kind priest who receives us so charmingly will not allow us to depart before he has offered us tea, served according to the highly refined rules of the *Cha-no-yu*, or classical tea ceremonial. Silently we enter the thatched hut hid in the garden: within, all is simple and pure, but carefully calculated to produce an impression of delicacy and sobriety. Alone a secular cultivation of sensibility has enabled the Japanese soul to create for itself superior pleasures with such elementary means. I watch with delight the ritualistic gestures and listen to the sweet singing of the water in the kettle.

As we leave the enchanting hut in the garden, my master explains to me:

"Do not be surprised that we should have given so much importance to tea and have spoken so little of philosophy.

"Certain aesthetic conceptions, such as the tea ceremony, are intimately related to Zen thought. A similar philosophy unites them. Formerly the monks of our sect, after having picked the perfumed tea-leaves before a statue of Bodhidharma, used to drink the divine beverage in a single bowl to the accompaniment of ritualistic gestures. From this sacramental formalism sprang the tea ceremony of which the Zen sect has

I   129

elaborated a complete ritual, and the practice of which was popularised amongst the Japanese élite from the fifteenth century onwards. One must have a very sensitive mind to understand it. Under the Tangs the tea ceremony was supposed to reflect cosmic harmonies. Under the Sungs one saw in it rather an intuitive method, and it is thus that Taoism and Zenism are related to the art of tea in view of the realism of personal perfection. 'Tea,' said the Chinese Wangyucheng, 'produces *a direct appeal to my soul*.' I should like you also to feel this direct appeal this evening at the hour when the lotus buds close for the night," added my master gently.

"But," I said, "will you not explain the Zen doctrine ?"

Night was falling. A pale moon waxed in the sky and waned in the water of the lake. My master reflected a moment, then he recited very slowly the following poem by Dōgen :

> Midnight.
> The air is calm. Serenity.
> The water is like a mirror.
> The moon—light in the air—light in the water, is everywhere,
> Pure, oh pure—transparent—a boat sails by.

He waited a moment, then asked me :

"Did you understand ?"

"Must I understand that the soul of a Zen Buddhist is as pure, serene and transparent as the landscape you have just described ?"

"Still more : detached from everything. Free. The things of this world leave no trace upon it. Listen to this other poem :

> The bamboo shadows flit over the steps
> But leave no dust.
> The light of the moon penetrates to the bottom of the water,
> But leaves therein no trace."

"Those poems are indeed charming," I remarked, "but at the risk of appearing prosaic, I insist that you should give me a precise explanation of the Zen doctrine. For you never speak to me of that doctrine."

The priest smiled and replied:

"*It is inexpressible.*"

We had stopped on the edge of the lake. Toads croaked near us. It is only in Japan that I understood how melodious and moving the song of the toads can be, rising in the night. The Japanese do not share our contempt for these amphibians.

The priest continued:

"Nature does better than explain. It suggests personal comprehension in us. That alone is Truth. One day the wise Gensha was asked to explain the Zen doctrine. Just as he was about to speak a bird passed in the sky uttering a little cry. 'Oh,' cried Gensha, 'see that little bird preaching the essence of the doctrine and proclaiming the supreme Truth.' And he stopped speaking."

"So the doctrine is inexpressible?" I asked. "Must I therefore renounce to understand it?"

"To understand it, no. But to have it explained to you, yes. Listen; I will tell you its origin. One day Buddha took a lotus in his hand. He looked at it and smiled, saying nothing. None of his disciples understood what that smile meant, except one of them, his favourite pupil, who looked at his Master and smiled also. *Each in silence had understood the other.* Do not ask what that smile meant. No one could tell you. I have the same opinion of explanations as that which a Chinese sage expressed concerning translations: 'They are brocades which one looks at from the wrong side. The threads, the colours are the same, but the essential is no longer there.' The Zenist thought transmits itself without the help of texts or words. That is why it is called 'The doctrine of Thought transmitted by Thought.'

"Seek in yourself your own authenticity by an intuitive, personal, original and incommunicable effort. *Each of us carries in himself his own Buddha.* You must find it. Discover it. It awaits you. . . . And, having found it, smile at it."

3. *The monastery of Obaku-San. Mr K. Noyori, former monk
of the monastery, explains the principal aspect of the Zenist
soul. The life and discipline of the monks. The Hall of
Meditation*

On a fine October morning we were following the
mountain path leading through the pines to the Zen
monastery of Obaku-San, near Uji. As we approached the
sanctuary the atmosphere became purer and our hearts
calmer.

My companion said to me:
"And now, abandon all remembrance of the world."

The great peace of Buddha lay upon the hills. At our feet
the landscape faded gradually away. A blue mist hung in the
valleys, torn here and there by the black outline of a pine, or
the grey crest of a rock. It dogged our steps and we seemed
to emerge from it as out of a cloud.

I tasted the joy of feeling my soul purify itself. I was
ashamed of possessing a travelling-bag and of carrying some
money with me! I would have wished to be poor. There
took place within me a phenomena which resembled a spiritual
decantation. I believe that the impurities of my life, of my
body, of my thought fell to the bottom of the valley, down
there in the mist—and my lightened and liberated soul
appeared to me colour of mother-of-pearl. I had had the same
impression whilst accomplishing the ascension of Mount
Fuji with other pilgrims.

At last we reach the monastery, surrounded by a great
wall.

We cross the doorway surmounted by a double roof and
flanked to the right and to the left with wooden sculptures.
A central alley leads to a temple also surmounted by a double
roof: this is the *Tennodo* which shelters a Miroku Bosatsu, or

Future Buddha, and Shi-Tenno, one of the Four Guardians of the World. A little before this temple, to the right, a small and very simple edifice contains a basin of lustral water. We accomplish our ablutions according to custom. The pure fresh water reflects our happy faces. I had never believed until now that one could free oneself of all pride and worry merely by crossing the threshold of a Buddhist monastery. That little hut of lustral water, so simple and so modest in which we wash ourselves so prosaically, marks indeed a halting-place of the soul.

To be pure and to become still more so, then to conceive the possibility of becoming purer still, and to endeavour to be so, such is in truth the first spiritual exercise of the Buddhist. Then only do mundane pleasures, ambition, glory, the need of consideration and so many other platitudes, of which our aspirations are composed, appear terribly empty and ridiculous, whilst Buddha appears very great. Before the mirror of lustral water framed in stone the creature I was, and which I put off, is merely a derisory phantom behind me. Here one forgets. Here one creates oneself anew. Indeed, there is no system, no theory. I do not seek to understand. I merely try to discover once again the soul of my childhood, according to the Zen method.

My master said to me :

"Purity and simplicity are, I believe, the racial character-istics of the Japanese. Nature is pure and simple, and we adore nature. Zen has formed itself at the school of nature and not by text-books. That is why contemplation is its very basis. Have you noticed how the most simple things are moving in nature ? Have you noticed how the pebbles of the road are polished and pure after the rain ? True works of art ! And the flowers ? No word can describe them. One can only murmur an 'Ah!' of admiration. A Japanese writer and bonze has said that 'one should understand the ah! of things!' By its deep understanding of nature, Zen has won the Japanese soul which, in its turn, has reacted upon it with its love of nature and its need of expressing its aesthetics. If you understand and love the simple straw hut of Kinkakuji, reserved for the tea ceremony, and this simple little pavilion of lustral water, you are taking your first steps in the way of Zen. . . . Later you will be obliged to make a personal and intuitive effort to 'put off' your soul completely. The latter must appear to you quite naked and sincere. Let us disdain the texts over which the other sects exert themselves. The demon of pretension and of reasoning reason is hid therein! How well I understand the master Yaku-San, who, when asked to dissert in the Hall of Meditations, declared: '*The sutras are explained by scholars specialised in sutras. I believe in Silence. Am I not a Zen monk?*'

"Even if our knowledge was immense, we should still have to render first homage to simplicity and purity of soul. A Zenist master once said: '*One must elevate oneself to the aureole of the Buddha Vairocana, and yet know how to become again so humble that one would willingly bow down before an infant.*'"

Some monks receive us most graciously and make us visit the monastery. After the first temple, one follows the central alley, and, after climbing a few steps, one penetrates into the principal temple, the Hondo, surmounted by a triple roof, where a gold Buddha is seated on a throne, escorted by Anan and Kasho. On the altars are placed some tablets bearing inscriptions in golden letters: the autograph of an emperor. I bow respectfully before the radiant effigy. These successive temples represent different spiritual halting-places. Profound psychologists have conceived their arrangement. At each halting-place the soul makes a new progress towards the summit.

"This monastery," remarks a monk, "was founded by the Chinese monk Ingen, and the thirteen first patriarchs who succeeded Ingen were all Chinese. From the fourteenth to the twenty-first they were alternately Chinese and Japanese. But even today we still observe in the daily service the rites and the pronunciation of the Mings. Our rules have remained unchanged since the foundation."

Outside of the central alley, in the Hatto, sixty thousand blocks of wood, minutely engraved, preserve for all eternity the Chinese version of the Buddhist canon.

"But texts have no importance," declares my master. "All is within ourselves."

I admire the monastery garden, its harmony and the free and personal fancy of its lines and plans, its flat stone pathways, its foliage.

At the end of the garden towards the left is the Hall of Meditations, a characteristic institution of Zen monasteries of which I will speak later, and the residence of the Superior. To the right are the dormitories, a succession of bare cells. A Zen monk possesses nothing. I have passed many nights in Japanese monasteries, and I have never failed to notice the miracle of epuration and of spiritual renovation which freely consented poverty produces in us. How great man is when he has sufficient will-power to be poor!

"Poverty," said my master, "is the material condition of moral independence, and of the development of the intuitive qualities. A strong inner life should be freed from all that obstructs or distracts men. Money, possessions, honours, ambitions, ready-made formulas, habits, personal interests, how many things hide our own secret value—or, as we say, our 'Buddha value'—from our own eyes. For we all possess fundamentally the same nature as Buddha. What we lack is to be conscious of it, and to favour its complete expansion in ourselves by means of absolute detachment, complete freedom of mind—poverty. The monks which you see here have for all possessions a few belongings which they each shut up in a box: a change of gown—a bowl. They deem that is already too much. When they travel they sling their box around their neck. But in exchange for their poverty they acquire inner joy and peace of heart. Our masters have expressed these ideas very poetically.

"The sage Mumon used to say :

> In springtime, flowers. In autumn, the Moon.
> In summer, the refreshing breeze. In winter, the snow.
> Need I anything else ?
> Every hour is a joy for me.

"And the scholar Shuan declared :

> I am seated quietly.
> The smoke of the incense ascends. . . .
> Inner joy. The world and its riches are forgotten.
> The spirit alone subsists and lives,
> And nothing can touch my serenity."

"Since I wish to practise Zen," I remark, "I will take care to preserve the serenity of my soul, and with this object in view, live in poverty."

"You will, at first. But later you must even forget that care. You will have to live detached from all, *detached even from your own detachment.* One should live in poverty, but without even noticing that one is poor. Then only is one in a state of perfect poverty. In fact, all the sentiments of the Zenist must reach the state of perfection—of *non-acquisition*, as we call it—where interests, goal and explanations have no longer any sense. The Zenist escapes from the relative modes in which ordinary man lives. Here are some practical reflections by Zenist sages on this point.

"The master Yogi lived in a house, the pierced roof of which let the snow leak through. He consoled himself by reflecting that the ancient sages had only the shade of a tree as shelter. But this thought does not reach Zenist perfection, for it admits of the consciousness of the state in which one finds oneself. Here is an exchange of poems between two Chinese Zenists which will explain my thought better.

"The sage Kyogen, aspiring to perfect poverty, used to say:

> Formerly my poverty was not complete.
> A small imperfection still subsisted in it.
> Very small, like the hole of a gimlet.
> Now that has disappeared. My poverty
> Is today a real poverty.

"To this the wise Kobokugen answered:

> That sage is not really poor
> Who perceives a flaw in his poverty.
> He who is still conscious that he possesses nothing
> Is merely the guardian of his own poverty.
> I, of late, am truly poor,
> Because I no longer notice that I am poor.

"The goal is to discover our 'Buddha nature,' and to reach purity of soul and Buddhahood intuitively, without calculation.

"I have insisted rather at length on the love of nature and of poverty, two characteristics of Zen. Others are work and energy, for meditation, such as the sect understands it, is not an empty, edulcorated reverie, but leads to a personal mysticism which expresses itself in acts. A Zenist will be contemplative, intuitive, a poet, and aesthete, and also a man of generous action, or a Samurai. These *états d'âme* do not exclude each other. On the contrary, they harmonise with each other because they all proceed equally from a pure and disinterested heart, from a liberated conscience which has discovered within itself, like a hidden treasure, its 'Buddha nature.'"

After a little pause my master continued:

"I will now describe for you the life of a monk at the monastery of Obaku-San. On awakening at four a.m. there is manual work to be done. The monks hasten to their household duties. They wash the floors, dig, hoe and rake the garden and kitchen garden, which is full of salads, cucumbers and vegetable marrows. One of our patriarchs, Hyakujô, considered manual labour one of the chief occupations of the monks. One recalls the following anecdote concerning him: one day his disciples, who had compassion for his old age, hid

away his gardening tools. Hyakujô refused to eat, saying:
'*No work, no food!*' This formula has remained active amongst
us. As soon as they quit meditating our monks are active,
either when they are begging alms out of doors or when they
bring their spiritual help to the faithful, sometimes in very
distant places, or else in the interior of the monastery, whose
Halls of Meditation or temples are kept spotlessly clean and
in a state of absolute purity, of which you can form an idea.
One could tell a hundred anecdotes concerning the Zen monks
at work. Here are a few:

"One day a monk said to his teacher, Jinshu, who was
cleaning the floor: 'What! Does a speck of dust dare enter
this sacred place?' And Jinshu, who continued his task with
renewed ardour, declared simply: 'Here is another one.'

"One day, whilst digging in the garden, a monk cut a worm
in two. He asked Shiko, his teacher: 'In which of the two
sections does the nature of Buddha reside?' Without answering, Shiko showed him first one fragment of the worm, then
the other, and lastly the distance which separated the two.
As one can see, for a Zenist monk work is an occasion to
think."

"But," I asked, "how can one conciliate the rule of work
with the attitude of the celebrated Hindu sage, Bodhidharma,
one of your ancient patriarchs, who remained nine years in
meditation and who was even nicknamed 'the Brahman
contemplator of the wall?'"

"Zen, born in India, has been formed in China, and the
Chinese are laborious," he answered. "The Japanese, who
are both poetic and positive, discovered in it a source of pure
poetry, of disinterestedness, and imbued it with something of
their own practical and active character. Our mysticism, our
methods of meditation are verified in our acts, and create man
anew by helping him to discover his true nature. The same
foundation of Buddhist purity allows the Zenist to become a
monk, a poet or a knight, to acquire an enterprising and
acceptant soul, because the secret of these different states is

absolute detachment and intuitive originality. Zen is not the metaphysics of an exhausted mind, it is a vigorous activity of the soul.

"Seen under this aspect, Zen is a knighthood.

"Why did the Samurais, those intrepid and energetic knights, adopt Zen preferably to the doctrines of the other sects, so that one can even say that Zen was the religion of the Samurai? Because they found in it a law of absolute disinterestedness which was related to *Bushido*, their code of chivalry —to a discipline analogous to their own, and to the same contempt of riches and of death. Zen monks and Samurais endure all vicissitudes without complaining. They ignore self-interest, shameful actions, sordid calculations. To them especially can the old Japanese proverb be applied : '*The falcon dies rather than touch the grain.*' The man who is conscious of his Buddha nature does embarrass himself with either meanness or fear. Here is an anecdote bearing upon this point. The monastery which was directed by our master Seigen, who came to Japan from China in 1280 to propagate the Zen doctrine, was one day invaded by barbarians who threatened to behead the Superior. Calm and smiling the great Zenist said to his aggressors :

> Neither the sky nor the earth is my shelter.
> Body and soul are illusion.
> Your sword, like a lightning flash,
> Is about to cut . . . the spring breeze !

"A Samurai could not have expressed himself better. The bandits retreated full of admiration.

"The methods of Zen education are inspired by a sentiment of virility and admit of a rather disconcerting bluntness. Zen is indeed a *réveillé* and not a lullaby. The shock before which one remains impassive is a trial to the soul, and can shatter the conventional lies with which it surrounds itself and which only too often stifle in it both its intuitive purity and its true capacities.

"One has often spoken of the violent blow a teacher of Zen

delivered silently full in the face of the warrior Tokiyori, who was seeking to initiate himself. Although an ardent fighter, Tokiyori suffered the assault with a smile. There was no doubt that Tokiyori possessed an understanding soul, but it remained to be proven whether he possessed an *acceptant* one. Often also the brutal gesture aims at liberating us. A novice had come several times to consult his master. The latter sent him away each time after striking him on the face, and saying: 'Withdraw thy spirit from the subterranean shade!' One day the novice ran towards his master and confessed to him sincerely, and without any artifice, a natural and pure emotion he had just experienced, such as that which we sometimes experience at night before the Moon. And the master cried out delightedly: 'I knew that I would meet thee!'

"Zen is an intuitive search for Buddha, or, as you would say, for the divine, the liberated man. . . ."

At this moment some monks passed by. They were walking in a single file, each holding a bowl of lacquered wood, and were going towards the refectory.

"I will continue my description of the life of the monks of the Zen monastery of Obaku-San," said my master. "At six a.m. they partake of the *assukemono* (frugal meal). At half-past six, prayer and meditation follow in the great temple. An hour later the Superior retires to his own residence whilst the other monks, gathering in groups in the smaller temples, continue to pray and to meditate. Certain monks, designated for this task, leave the monastery at 8 a.m. to go a-begging or to say prayers in the houses of private citizens who have sent for them. At midday a few strokes of the gong call the monks to lunch. They file towards the refectory in a procession, each carrying his bowl. Before eating, the monk meditates according to the rules. He takes out of his bowl seven grains of rice, which he offers to the invisible spirits, whilst mentally invoking them. All eat in silence. The food is always the same and consists of a soup made of *soya*, rice and barley, followed occasionally by some *tôfu* (bean paste), and vegetables out of the kitchen garden. Meat, fish and eggs are never served. Tea is the only drink allowed. Each monk washes his bowl himself. Then the monks receive special instructions concerning the afternoon's activities, which vary according to their seniority (for they are divided into three classes) and to their spiritual value. They are instructed as to the occupations they must follow, such as spiritual exercises and meditations, studies and manual work. In the evening at 6 p.m. they are allowed to take a little food, but only what is necessary to sustain their strength.

"Lastly, at 7 p.m., whilst the monks of the second and third class are at prayer in the temples, the monks of the first class assemble silently in the Hall of Meditation.

"The Hall of Meditation, or Zendo, is characteristic of the Zen sanctuaries. It is a large room in which the monks, seated in the attitude of contemplation, meditate upon those philosophical or religious subjects which have been proposed to them (*Koan*). The Superior occupies a central place. For example, the following questions may be asked: '*What is self?*'—'*What is individual religion?*'—'*What is the pure doctrine of Buddha?*'—'*What is the fundamental nature of man?*' Each monk present expounds his opinion. He is only asked to express himself with an absolute sincerity of heart. There is no discussion to speak of. One seeks neither to vanquish nor to convince. Nothing is more moving than the spectacle of these consciousnesses in search of Truth, with no other concern than that of discovering it. *Zen only seeks the light which man can find in himself.* It tolerates no hindrance to this seeking. The great master Ummon used to say: '*Clear every obstacle out of your way.*' When the monks have spoken, the Superior gives his opinion in his turn.

"Often the words pronounced are laconic, enigmatical and incomprehensible to the uninitiated. For the monks do not seek to incorporate into their minds ready-made reasonings, but to provoke an intuitive and personal effort. Then the monks enter into meditation, and silence settles down upon the Hall with the shades of night.

"Do you wish to know how to meditate? Here is the advice Dōgen has given on the subject:

'Seat yourself cross-legged, the right foot resting against the left thigh, and the left foot against the right thigh. Clothe yourself in a dress and girdle, but be careful not to tie them too tightly and to maintain symmetry. Then place the palm of the right hand upwards on the calf of the left leg, and the back of the left hand in the palm of the right hand, the tips of the thumbs touching each other. Hold the body upright, leaning neither to the right nor to the left, neither backward nor forward, the ears touching the shoulders, the nose bent towards the navel. Apply the tongue against the roof of the mouth and join the teeth together. Keep your eyes open and breathe normally through the nostrils. Exhale your breath deeply; then, after having verified the rectitude of your position, balance your body to the right and to the left, and abandon yourself to the contemplation of that which surpasses the intelligence.'

"The assembling in the Zendo takes place every evening, but one week a month the monks devote themselves exclusively, night and day, to meditation. This is the 'Sesshin' (concentration of spirit). These special *séances* open to the sound of the 'Mokugyo,' a sort of wooden drum, whose deep and sonorous vibrations you have certainly often heard in temples and monasteries. Mystical recitations take place, then readings borrowed generally from the works of much appreciated masters such as the *Rinzairoku* (Souvenir of Rinzai) and the *Hekiganroku* (Souvenir of the Green Rock). These works consist of collections of themes for spiritual exercises and meditations, the sense of which generally remains obscure for the uninitiated, but which becomes singularly illumined for the monk who has already studied several years, and who possesses special aptitudes for intuitive life."

Whilst pronouncing these last words my master gave me a copy of the *Rinzairoku*, recommending me to read it when I wished, and also an English translation by Mr T. Suzuki, bonze and professor of Zen, which one will read below, and which consists of an exhortation addressed by *Rinzai*, the founder of the sect, to his disciples. I read it one evening by the light of a paper lantern, and I read it again to assure myself that I was not the dupe of some mirage, so scandalous and incomprehensible did the terms in which it was couched appear to me at first.

O you disciples who aspire after truth, if you wish to obtain an orthodox knowledge of Zen, take care not to deceive yourselves. Tolerate no obstacle, neither interior nor exterior, to the soaring of your spirit. If on your way you meet Buddha, kill him! If you meet the Patriarchs, kill them! If you meet the Saints, kill them all without any hesitation! That is the only way of reaching salvation.

Do not allow yourselves to be entangled in any arguments whatsoever. Place yourselves above them and remain free. So many men come to me pretending to be the disciples of Truth, who are not even freed from the vanity of a goal, of a prejudice which dominates them. Therefore when I see these men I strike them down. Such a one has confidence in his arms? I cut them off. Another counts on his eloquence? I make him hush. Yet another believes in his foresight? I blind him.

I have never seen one who was completely free—who was *the unique*. Most of them have filled their minds very uselessly with the farces of the old masters. What have I to give them? Nothing! I try to remedy their evil by delivering them from their slavery.

O you, disciple of truth, strive to make yourself independent of all objects. Here is my thought. Since five or ten years I have vainly awaited a free soul. None has come to me. I can say that I have only seen the phantoms of beings, contemptible gnomes haunting the woods or the bamboo groves, pernicious spirits of the desert who nibble at stacks of filth. O you with the eyes of moles, why do you waste all the pious donations of the devout? Do you believe yourself worthy of being called a monk of the Zen doctrine if you possess such an erroneous idea of it? I tell you: No Buddha! No teaching! No discipline! No demonstrations! What are you ceaselessly seeking in the house of your neighbour, O you with the eyes of moles? Do you not understand that you are placing another head over your own? What do you therefore lack in yourself? That which you are using at this very moment differs not from that of which Buddha is made. But you do not believe me and you seek elsewhere. Renounce this error! There is no exterior truth. And now you attach yourself to the literal sense of my words so that it is much preferable that we should end this discourse, and that you should be nothing at all.

I remained awake long after my companions were sleeping, and by the light of my lantern I meditated upon the enigmatical exhortation.

"If you meet Buddha, kill him!"

At last its meaning became clear to me. This is what Rinzai meant to say: let he who aspires to the light of Zen shake off and discard all borrowed values—scholastic formulae, prejudices and modes with which he encumbered himself and which blind him, even were they to be presented to him under the features of Buddha. All that you have not found yourself, in your inner consciousness, by a personal and intuitive act, is but a vestment of hypocrisy with which you clothe your conscience. It is not Buddha. First liberate your spirit. Open your eyes, O moles! *Buddha is within you!*

4. *The intuitive Zen method of a pure and liberated life*

Mr C. Teitaro Suzuki,[1] *professor of Zen Buddhism at the Buddhist College of Otani* (*Kyôto*), *expresses himself as follows:*

"The Zen ideal, which invites us to a simplified life, is contained essentially in the aptitude of remaining master of oneself, and of practising what are called the 'secret virtues.' These characterise the moral discipline of Zen. This term signifies to do good without seeking a reward, *neither from others nor from oneself, through a sense of interior satisfaction.* The Christians express an analogous sentiment when they say

[1] Mr Suzuki has acquired a world-wide reputation by his science and his works. See Bibliography at the end of this volume.

'Thy will be done.' For example, a child is drowning. I throw myself into the water and save it. That is all. I think absolutely no more about it. I pass by and do not return. Nature acts thus. A cloud passes by, then the sky becomes blue again. *There is no merit in that.* This is what Zen calls 'the act without merit.' It is compared to the act of a man who fills a well with snow.

"Zen does not wish, like Christians, that man should pass his time in prayers and in mortifications for the absolution of his sins. A Zen monk has no wish to be absolved from his sins, for this desire would be selfish, and a Zen monk is liberated from all selfishness. He longs to save the world from the weight of *its* sins, but he cares nothing for his own, for he knows that they are not inherent to his nature. He is the type of man of whom it can be said, '*that he cries as if he did not cry, that he rejoices as if he did not rejoice, that he uses the things of this world as if he did not use them.*'

"When the Christ says : '*Let not thy left hand know what thy right hand doeth*,' this is conformable to the secret virtue of Buddhism. But when He adds, '*My Father which seeth in secret will reward you openly*'—Buddhism and Christianity deviate from each other. As long as you believe that somebody—be it God or the devil—has witnessed your good action, Zen says to you : 'You do not belong to us. That is not "an act without merit." That act has left traces and marks. The perfect vestment is seamless. We expect nothing, neither from our own consciences nor from God.'

"The Zen ideal is to be 'the wind that passes, and to whose voice we listen without being able to say from whence it cometh, or whither it goeth.' The Chinese philosopher, Lie-Tzu, has described thus this state of the soul : 'I allowed my soul to meditate according to its will. I no longer distinguished what belonged to me or what did not belong to me, my gains or my losses, or if Lao-Shang was my master or if Pa-Kao was my friend. I was essentially transformed. At that instant the senses identify themselves, the mind becomes concentrated.

The eye becomes like an ear, the ear like a nose, the nose like a mouth. Forms dissolve, bones and flesh are diluted. Where was I? Whither were my footsteps leading me? I went, indifferent as the breeze, towards the East or the West, like the leaf detached from the branch. Was I carried by the wind, or was it I who carried the wind?'

"All the aspirations of the heart have flown away. All the vain thoughts which obstructed the course of vital activity have disappeared. The wise remain empty and poor. As they are poor they know how to admire the spring flowers and the autumn moon. The Zen method has for object to reach the state of 'non-acquisition,' to use a technical term. The fundamental idea is to make man poor, humble, perfectly purified. Knowledge is but a superficial gain; it is but 'vanity and captures the wind,' and tends to make men arrogant. The mind must purify itself of the accumulation of centuries. Then it appears bare, empty, naked, free and sincere. It then recovers its original strength. And that also is joy . . . joy from which nothing can be taken away, and to which nothing can be added. . . . Doubtless all mystics seek a similar goal, but in Christianity the faithful are still *too conscious of a God.*

"Zen wishes to efface all trace of consciousness in a divinity. . . . That is why it goes so far as to say : '*Do not tarry where Buddha is, and pass by very quickly where he is not.*'

"I believe the Chinese language to be the vehicle most appropriate to Zen thought. The monosyllabic character of Chinese confers to it a compact and vigorous aspect. A single one of its words contains multiple significations. This is perhaps a disadvantage from the point of view of precision, but in our case it is an advantage, and Zen has known how to make use of it. The mystery of a word, its very vagueness, becomes a powerful instrument for the Zenist master—not that he wishes to be either obscure or deceiving, but because under these conditions the carefully chosen monosyllable which falls from his lips acquires a full sense which is sometimes charged with the whole of Zen thought.

"The Zen teacher is always laconic. He strives to express his ideas by the shortest word possible, and to strike directly at the goal. Here development is not tolerated. Now the Chinese language is admirably suited to this intuitive kind of expression. Its chief qualities are concision and force: each syllable is a word and sometimes a whole sentence. A sequence of words without verb or connection often suffices to express a complex thought. Chinese literature abounds in incisive epigrams and replete aphorisms. The words are heavy, without relation to each other. Assembled, they remind one of uncemented splinters of wood. The Chinese phrase is not an organism: each link of the chain possesses a particular and independent life of its own. But, as each syllable is pronounced, the total impression is formidable. Chinese is the mystical language *par excellence*.

"A few scholars have maintained that the Zen philosophy is not contained in primitive Buddhism and that Buddha was not its author. This is to deny that a religion must prove its vitality by adapting itself to the genius of the people who adopt it, otherwise it is condemned to disappear. Zenists have never ceased to proclaim, even in China, that they transmitted the *spirit* and not the *writing* of Buddha. From this we can conclude that they are independent of the original Buddhist doctrines, and that they were obliged to incorporate personal expressions and modes of thought into their philosophy. The Zenist weaves for himself an inner tissue, just as the silkworm weaves its own cocoon. The tissue is perfect, seamless, and out of it the wise man can cut a really celestial work."

Mr K. Nukariya, professor of the Kei-o-gi-jiku University and of the Buddhist College of the Zen Sect in Tôkyô, speaks as follows:

"The universe is the Holy Writ of Zen. Text-books are but scraps of paper. Zen is placed on the highest spiritual plane which Shakamuni himself has reached. Its ideal can only be realised by him who succeeds in rising to this plane. To give a complete statement of it by means of words exceeds the power of Gautama himself. This is the reason why the author of the *Lankavara-sutra* insists upon the fact that Shakamuni, during the forty-nine years of his long career as a preacher, does not say a word about it and that one reads exactly the same warning in the *Mahaprajnaparamita-sutra*. The Scripture is neither more nor less than the finger indicating the direction of Buddha's aureole. When we have found this aureole, and when it has shed its light upon us, this invitatory gesture has no longer any use. And just as this gesture possesses no light in itself, just so the Buddhistic Scriptures have no sacred character. They are the current money which represents real spiritual riches. That money may consist of gold, shells or cow dung, it never has more than a fictitious value. Alone that which it represents possesses real value. Then do not bother us with your wooden swords! Do not watch the post against which a running hare crashed and died of a broken head! Do not wait for another hare, for one will not always come! Do not mark on your boat the place where your sword fell into the sea! The boat always continues to advance. All that is vain. The canonical Scriptures are windows through which we observe the great scene of spiritual nature. To take contact with the latter, one must jump out of the window. Only the flies buzz eternally against the window-panes! He who spends his life studying the Scriptures, argumenting, reasoning and splitting hairs, is exactly like those flies: good for nothing than to buzz technical words devoid of sense. It is in this spirit that Rinzai said: '*The twelve chapters of the Buddhist canon are worth no more than a scrap of paper.*'

"Man is in himself neither good nor evil. Man is 'nature of Buddha.' By this term we Buddhists mean a latent spirit which exists in us, not naturally developed but capable when it develops and realises itself of leading us to Illumination. This belief explains why, according to Zen, man can be considered neither good nor evil, in the sense usually attributed to these expressions. He is provided with a fundamental nature which is the same for all: 'a nature of Buddha.' A good person (in the vulgar sense) differs from an evil person (in the vulgar sense), not by this fundamental nature—his '*Buddha nature*'—but by the development which the latter reaches in his works. Although all men possess this fundamental nature, of one same quality, their different stages of development do not grant them an equal latitude to express it in their conduct. One can compare the Buddha nature to the sun, and the individual mind to the sky. The illuminated mind is a beautiful sky in which everything is bathed in sunlight. It often happens that a thief or a murderer is a kind father and a good husband. At home he becomes once again an honest man. The sun of his Buddha nature illumines him in his home. Outside of it, the dark clouds of evil burst upon him.

"Listen to what Nature says to us.

"You will listen to the sermon of Nature with the eyes of your spirit, the eyes of your heart and of your soul. You will never understand it by intelligence, logic or metaphysics. To understand it one must *feel*, not define; *observe*, not calculate; *sympathise*, not analyse. You will have to take hold of it fully, not criticise it; not explain it, but *feel* it; not abstract it, but seize it. You must go directly to the soul of things, piercing through their material bark, thanks to the light of your intuition. A Japanese Zenist has said: '*The fall of dead leaves and the blooming of flowers reveal to us the holiness of the law of Buddha.*'

"You who are seeking purity and peace, go to Nature. She will give you more than you ask of her. You who desire strength and perseverance, go to Nature. She will train you and strengthen you. You who aspire towards an ideal, go to Nature. She will help you to realise it. You who are seeking Illumination, go to Nature. She will never fail to grant it to you."

Mr G. Hosaka, bonze and professor of the Faculty of the Zen Sect of Komazawa-Daigaku, near Kyôto, expounded the following principle: "All of them being children of Buddha, men are Buddhas. Paradise is our Earth."

"Buddha is essential, unique, universal existence," continued Mr Hosaka. "The divinities of the different Buddhist sects are so many Buddhist expressions, differentiated by local or geographical influences and by popular customs. *In reality, Buddha is All.* The non-Buddhist religions present the counterpart, the non-Buddha. *I believe with all my faith in Buddha and his universal nature.* I would like to convert the whole world to our human and grand ideal. I applaud your initiative. Ask our bonzes to give you all the explanations necessary. Send Frenchmen here to study our faith on the spot, and may the day dawn when Frenchmen will in their turn become bonzes.

"From a static point of view, Buddha, as I have just said, is *One*—is *All*. The world of Nature, the world of sentiments, are nothing else than aspects of the body of Buddha. Each thing is in fact but a particle of this body. Buddha is the essence of the world, of life. What is meant by the word *Paradise*? Paradise is the world itself—we are in it since it is here that the essence of Buddha is to be found. There is no future life. There is nothing exterior to be hoped for. The life of Buddha is the life of all creatures—men, beasts and plants. Death is but the return to the universal Buddha. We are like the children of Buddha, consubstantial with him—Buddha being Truth, Kindness, Beauty.

"Sciences, philosophies, morals, arts, letters—all civilisation exist in him, and by him.

"From a dynamic point of view Buddha is constantly in action, and his activity is continually ameliorating the world. Eternal and progressive creation pursues itself continually throughout the universe. Life transforms itself into thousands and thousands of aspects which themselves evolve, and the world forms itself and progresses constantly. Since we are all children of Buddha, we are all equals or brothers. There is no distinction between men. Buddhism is not the religion of a race, it is the true and luminous vision of all, and that vision reveals to us that we are all of the same essence, including the animals and all living creatures. In centralising this conception of the human mind, Buddhism remains foreign to all prejudices of race, caste, class or frontier.

"Man, being a child of Buddha, depository of a sublime ideal, what will be the principle of his action, of his duty? Shall he strive by long practice to become a Buddha? Not at all. *You are Buddha,* and therefore there is no question of *becoming* Buddha, but of *acting* as Buddha. *It is not Man who becomes Buddha, but Buddha who has become humanity.* Man has therefore only to fulfil his active rôle of Buddhahood to realise the essence of Buddha which is in him according to his qualities and his capacities. To do his work as a man is to participate with his whole being to Buddhistic creation. We must do our man's work. Some say that life is but a passing froth. I do not believe this at all. *Life is the active expression of Buddha at work.*

"Here I reach my conclusion. Yes, all of us men, we who are Buddhas, *are builders of the world according to Buddha.* Far from us of addressing a prayer to Buddha, or of asking him anything. We do not beg any help, being ourselves. We partake, as associates, in the edification of the Buddhistic world. No vocation is finer than ours. I do not fear death. I complain of no suffering. I partake of death and of suffering with joy, for they are merely travails endured for the universal and Buddhistic creation. We have our part to play, which is to elevate, to embellish life, to make the world. If our morals are those of the middle mean, far from extreme passions, tolerant, kindly and gentle, that is because these sentiments are necessary for the *constructor.* Nothing durable is erected by the passions or by extreme doctrines. For example, we believe in the equality of all creatures—children of Buddha. But we respect those inequalities which are natural. Varieties and differentiations are riches included in creative evolution. Those extremist occidental doctrines which deny these varieties are disastrous. Unification is degrading and sterile. To resume: the relation of subjects to masters (mutual help), of masters to disciples (moral culture), are not particular to Zen. That which is Zen is the conviction *that we are all children of Buddha*. We have nothing to ask for in our prayers, we do not fear Death. Ourselves Buddhas, we are building the world.

5. *Theory of the Satori, or Enlightenment which provokes in the soul of the Zenist the revelation of a new vision of life and of the world, explained by Mr T. Suzuki* [1]

"The essence of Zen Buddhism consists in the acquisition of a new point of view on Life and on all things in general. By this I mean that if we wish to penetrate into the intimate life of Zen, we must abandon those habits of thought which govern our daily life, we must try and see whether there is not another way of judging things or if our ordinary way of living is always sufficient to satisfy our religious needs. If we feel that we are not satisfied by our encounter with this life, if our ordinary way of living deprives us of our liberty in its most holy sense, we must strive to find elsewhere a better way which will lead us towards a sense of achievement and satisfaction. Zen proposes to lead us to it, and assures us of a new point of view seen from which life appears under a still unconsidered aspect. This acquisition presents itself as the greatest mental cataclysm one can imagine, and which it is possible to undergo in the course of life. It is not an easy task, but rather a sort of rude baptism. To reach the goal we must pass through storms, earthquakes, landslides and splintering rocks.

"This acquisition of a new point of view in our relations

[1] See page 229 in our annotated Biography, the short analysis of the masterly work by this author, *Essays in Zen Buddhism*.

towards life and the world is commonly called *satori* (Chinese: *Wu*) by students of the Zen doctrine. Other expressions are also used, each having its special value to designate that psychological phenomenon. There is no Zen without *satori*. It is the alpha and omega of Zen Buddhism. Zen deprived of *satori* would be like a sun deprived of light and heat.

"*Satori* can be defined as follows: '*An intuitive glance into the very nature of things,*' in opposition to the intelligent and logical comprehension of the latter. Practically it signifies '*the revelation of a new world*'—until now unperceived in the confusion of our dualistic mind. We can say that through *satori* all that surrounds us is seen under a completely unexpected angle of perception. For those who have won *satori* the world is no longer the old world it ordinarily was, even with its impetuous torrents and devouring fires—no, it is never the same any more. Logically, all its oppositions and all its contrasts are united and placed in harmony in a consistent and organic whole. It is a mystery and a miracle, but according to Zenist teachers such a miracle takes place every day. Moreover, *satori* can only be really understood when we have experienced it personally.

"Perhaps we can compare it with more or less exactitude to the impression we experience when we have found the solution to a mathematical problem, or when we have made a great discovery, or when a means of salvation appears to us in the midst of the most intricate and despairing complications. In a word, when one suddenly cries out 'Eureka! Eureka!' But this explanation holds only for the subjective or emotive explanation of *satori*.

"Intellectually *satori* concerns the integrality of the life of each one of us. For what Zen proposes to achieve in each one of us is a moral *revolution*, a *revalorisation* of the spiritual vision of life. If one solves a mathematical problem, the solution affects in no way the life of the seeker. But *satori* is a sort of new life, and the Zenist makes his whole life over. When *satori* is real (for there are many shams), its effects on moral and spiritual life provoke in us a complete revolution capable of elevating our soul, and of purifying us, as well as exacting much of us morally.

"The Zen masters always try to put to profit apparently ordinary facts, so as to lead the souls of their disciples in a way until then quite unperceived. It is just as if, pushing back a hidden bolt, a torrent of new experiences should burst through the opening. It is like the striking of the hours of the clock. When the time is past, the clock strikes and the percussion of sound is widely dispersed. It seems as if the soul could be compared to this mechanism. When a certain moment arrives, a cloud screen is rolled away and an absolutely new spectacle presents itself to our gaze, changing the whole tone of our own life. This mental 'shock' is what is meant by *satori*. Nothing is more important than this method. We must admit that there is something in Zen which defies all explanation, and that no master, however clever he may be in psychological analysis, can ever teach his disciples. *Satori* cannot be reached by logical reasoning, but once one possesses the key to it, everything appears to bare itself before you, and the whole world takes on a different aspect. The change is recognised by all the *Initiated*.

"All Zen can do to help the dawning of *satori* is to indicate the way and to leave the rest to the personal experience of each. . . . By following this indication we can reach the goal alone without the help of anyone. All the masters, the science and the ability in the world will be of no avail to the disciple if he is not fully and interiorily ready to receive this new birth. We can't oblige a horse to drink against its will. To lay hold of final truth one must depend upon oneself. Just as the flower blooms by the fact of the necessities of its inner nature, so this glance into our own nature can only be the result of our own inner life. Zen is personal and subjective.

"I have said that Zen renounces to explain itself in intellectual terms, that it does not waste its time in argumentation, but is content to propose or to indicate, not that it wishes to be vague, but because that is really all that it can do for us. It does everything to help us to reach understanding, but it cannot do so by reasoning. Thus the teachers, whose kindness of heart cannot be doubted, are obliged to await the moment when their pupils' souls are at last ripe for the final success. When these circumstances are realised, the occasion to take a glimpse at the truth of Zen will be found everywhere. One can seize it in the audition of a sound, in an unintelligible remark, by looking at the blooming of a flower, or in the way one meets an ordinary incident of daily life, such as the falling of a stone, the rolling of a screen, the waving of a fan. The most modest facts are then seen to be conditions sufficient to awaken intimate sense, and their effect upon the soul surpasses all one could expect : it is the spark of the ignited fuse, or the explosions which shake the very foundations of the earth. And all the causes of *satori* are to be found in the soul. That is why, when the hour strikes, everything that was dozing bursts forth like a volcanic eruption, or projects the light of a vivid flash of lightning. Zen calls this phenomenon : ' *The return to one's own home*,' and says to its disciples : 'At last you have found yourselves. Nothing had been hidden from you from the beginning. You alone shut your eyes to the truth. In Zen there is nothing to explain, nothing to teach, nothing that can accrue your knowledge. Your riches come from yourself. Borrowed feathers never grow.'

"The realisation of *satori* marks a decisive stage in your life. Let us examine the nature and *nuances* of *satori*. To merit the name of *satori* the inner revolution must be sufficiently complete for the subject to be really and sincerely conscious that a true baptism has taken place in his mind. The intensity of the sensation is in ratio to the effort accomplished by the candidate to *satori*. For in *satori* there are different degrees of intensity which reveal the nature of our moral activity. The possessor of a mild *satori* will not experience the same spiritual revolution as a Rinzai or a Bukko, for instance. Zen is an affair of character, not of intelligence. A brilliant intelligence will be unable to unravel all the secrets of Zen, but a strong soul will drink deeply at its inexhaustible fountain. I do not know if intelligence is merely superficial and touches only the border of a man's personality; but the fact is that *the will is the man himself* and that Zen appeals to this will. When a man becomes conscious of his inner mechanism, the blossoming of *satori* and the understanding of Zen follow as a matter of course. As the Zenists say, 'the serpent has changed itself into a dragon,' or, to take a more picturesque comparison, a vulgar dog, a miserable mongrel wagging its tail to obtain more food and caresses, and, unmercifully teased by the street urchins, has become a superb lion with a golden mane, whose roars frighten to death all weak-minded persons.

"Certain masters have expressed in the form of poems known as *Gé* (*gâthâ*) what they perceived or experienced at the instant when their mind's eye was opened. Their verses are called *Tôki-no-gé*. By reading them one can form a just conclusion as to the nature and purpose of *satori*, so deeply appreciated by the disciples of Zen. The contents of these *Gé*[1] are so varied and diverse, at least if one merely considers their superficial sense, that it would be vain to compare them. Those which simply describe sensations defy analysis, and the critic will only appreciate them if he has experienced these same sensations in his own inner life. They will, however, help the beginner to understand Buddhist mysticism.

"Seppo (822-908), whose eyes were opened whilst he was rolling up a screen, composed the following poem:

> How abused was I, how abused in truth,
> Roll up the screen, come, look out upon the world,
> What religion dost thou believe in ? you ask.
> I lift my *hossu*[2] and smite your mouth.

---

[1] Buddhist poem in verse.
[2] Stick surmounted by a tuft of hair—the symbol of religious authority, and borne only by bonzes of high rank.

"Yengo (1063-1135) was one of the greatest Zen masters during the Sung dynasty and author of a Zen text-book known as the *Hekiganroku*.[1]

"Will the reader, however, discover the deeper sense of Zen contained in this poem?

> A happy event in the life of a romantic young man.
> Alone his betrothed is allowed to know it.

"Yenju of Yōmeiji (904-975), who belongs to the School of Hogen, is the author of a book entitled *Shûkyôroku* (Remembrance of the True Mirror). He composed it one day on hearing a mass of fuel falling to the ground.

> Has something fallen? Is it nothing else?
> To the right and to the left there is nothing terrestrial.
> Rivers, mountains and the great earth
> In them everything reveals the great Dharmârâja.

"The first of the two following poems is by *Yôdainen* (973-1020), the great statesman under the Sung dynasty. And the second is by *Iku*, of Toryô, by whom Yogi (1024-1072), founder of the Yogi section of the School of Rinzai, was ordained monk:

> An octagonal millstone is hurled through space.
> A golden-coloured lion is transformed into a mongrel.
> If you yourself wish to hide in the Northern star
> Turn around and cross your hands behind the Southern Star.

> I possess a jewel dazzling with light.
> It was long buried beneath earthly sorrow.
> This morning having shaken off its veil of dust,
> It has once again found its radiance
> Illuminating the rivers, and mountains, and ten thousand other things.

"I chose these poems to show how greatly they differ in form, and that it is impossible to obtain an intelligible explanation of '*satori*' simply by comparing or analysing them. Without doubt, one will discover in some of them the sensation of a new revelation; but, in order to ascertain what this

---

[1] Celebrated book of the Rinzai School, brought to Japan from China by Dōgen, founder of Japanese Zen.

revelation is, in itself, it is necessary to acquire a certain sum of personal experience. In every case, however, all the masters bear witness to the fact that there exists in Zen something known by the name of *satori* which transports one into a new world filled with astounding values. The old manner of considering the world is abandoned, and the latter acquires a new signification. This is what explains that the masters should declare that they were first deceived, then that their former understanding was thrown into oblivion, whilst others confess that until then they had been insensible to the beauty of the refreshing breeze or of the dazzling jewel.

"If we observe merely the objective side of *satori* we do not advance much in the fathoming of that mystery which is called 'the opening of the eye to the Truth of Zen.' We have seen that the master makes a few remarks, and if these be sufficiently opportune, the disciple reaches a sudden realisation, and sees clearly into the mystery of the world. It would seem as if everything depends on the disposition, the state of mind, and the psychic preparation in which the disciple finds himself at that particular moment. And we might be tempted to believe that Zen Truth is due to mere chance. But when we hear that it took Nangaku *eight* long years to answer the question, '*Who is it who is walking towards me?*' we understand that he must have undergone much mental anguish, and that he must have endured many tribulations before reaching the final solution and being able to declare: '*Even when one affirms that there is something here, one omits the whole.*'

"Let us now consider the deep psychological aspect of *satori*, that inner mechanism which provokes the opening of the door of the eternal secrets of the human soul. To do this we will quote the very words uttered by those masters who, at the moment of the blossoming of their *satori*, applied themselves to a profound introspective examination.

"Kôhô (1238-1285), one of the great masters who lived under the Sung dynasty, worked passionately at the questions which his teacher proposed to him. One day the latter asked

him : '*What is it that enables you to transport your lifeless body?*'
The poor fellow was greatly embarrassed by this question.
He knew that his master was pitiless, and that to discontent
him would be to court a severe punishment. He meditated.
One night, in the middle of his sleep, he remembered that in
former days, when he was under the direction of another
master, the latter had proposed to him to discover the final
signification of the axiom : '*All things become one again.*' This
problem kept him awake several nights. Whilst he was in
this state of acute mental tension, he remembered the words of
Goso-Hoyen (1104) on the first patriarch of Zen :

> One hundred years, thirty-six thousand mornings,
> This same old comrade moves for always.

"This phrase dispelled Kôhô's doubts and he was able to
answer the question : 'What is it that bears your lifeless
body ?' From that moment he became a new man.

"In his *Goroku* (Reported Words) he has left us the description of his spiritual struggles :

Formerly when I was at Sokei (he writes), and before a month
had passed since my return to the Hall of Meditations, at that place,
one night as I was sound asleep, I found myself suddenly fixing
my attention on the question : '*All things return into One—but
where does this last thing return?*' My attention was fixed so intently
on this point that I forgot to eat, that I no longer distinguished the
East from the West, nor morning from evening. Whether I laid the
cloth or placed the bowls, whether I cooked or rested, whether I
spoke or remained silent, my whole existence was enveloped in
this thought : '*Where does this thing return to?*' No thought penetrated my mind any longer. No, even had I wished to tear out a
particle of thought I could not do it, if it was not in correlation
with this central thought. One would have said that my sole
thought was screwed down or stuck. I tried to shake it out of
myself, but it refused to budge. Although I was living in a con-
gregation, I felt as though I was quite alone with myself. From
morning till night, and from night till morning, my feelings were
so transparent, so tranquil, so majestuous above all things. My
thought absolutely pure and without an atom of dust, my only
thought embraced eternity. The outer world was so calm, I was

so forgetful of the existence of other people. I passed my days and my nights thus, like a simple-minded person, like a man deprived of intelligence. Then one day I entered a temple with other monks, reciting the sutras, and I lifted my head thinking of the verses of Goso. A sudden awakening took place in me, and the signification of the phrase: '*Who bears your lifeless body?*'—the question Kuozan, my old master, had asked me of yore—burst luminous upon me. I experienced an extraordinary emotion. It seemed to me as if limitless space had burst asunder, and as if the whole world was levelled. I forgot myself. I forgot the world. I was like a mirror which reflected another world. I tried several *ko-an* (problems) in my mind and I found them perfectly clear. I was no longer deceived after the accomplishment of this wonderful work of *prajna* (transcendent wisdom).

"Hakuin (1683-1768) has also recorded in writing his first experience in Zen. In his book entitled *Orategama* we read the following description:

When I was twenty-four years old I lived at the monastery of Yegan, at Echigo, and applied myself assiduously to the solving of *Ko-an* (opinions, problems). I slept neither day nor night. I forgot to eat and to rest, *when suddenly there took place in my mind an intensive concentration of thought.* I shivered as if I were on a field of ice extending for thousands of miles. I perceived in my inner self a sensation of extreme transparency. There was no forward movement and no sliding backwards. I was like a being deprived of reason, of intelligence. Nothing existed for me except the solution of the proposed problem. Although I attended the lectures and discourses of my master, they seemed to me to come from a distant Hall, many yards from where I was. Sometimes I had the sensation of flying through the air. I remained in that state for several days. Then one evening the tolling of a temple bell overthrew my mental balance. It was like the bursting of a basin full of ice, or the fall of a house made of jade. When I awoke, it seemed to me as if I myself was Ganto (828-887), the old master, and as if, in spite of the lapse of time which had passed, the latter had lost nothing of his personality. Whatever my doubts and indecisions may have been, they all appeared to me like a piece of melting ice. I cried: 'How marvellous! How marvellous! There is no longer any birth or death! There is no longer any supreme understanding (*Bôdhi*) to pursue. All the thousand and seven past and present complications are no longer worth worrying about!

"The case of Bukko (1226-1286) was still more astounding than that of Hakuin. He has left us a detailed account of it:

When I was seventeen I resolved to study Buddhism. I expected to finish this study in the space of a year, but did not succeed in doing so. Another year passed without my making much progress, and the three succeeding years found me having still made no progress.

One night as I was seated I kept my eyes wide open. And suddenly the sound of a blow struck upon the table in front of the room of the superior monk reached my ear, and immediately revealed to me 'original man' in all his integrity. The vision which had appeared to me when I shut my eyes had quite disappeared. I left my seat in haste and ran into the garden in the moonlight. I reached a garden belonging to a house called Ganki, where, in looking up at the sky, I burst into peals of laughter. 'O how great is Dharmakâya! O how can he be so great, so immense for eternity!'

My joy knew no bounds. I could no longer sit quietly in the Hall of Meditation. I went off aimlessly amongst the mountains, walking here and there. I thought of the sun and moon which in one day cross four thousand million miles in depth. 'My present abode is in China,' I thought, 'and it is said that the district of Yang is the centre of the earth. If this is so, this place is two thousand million miles distant from the place where the sun rises. Yet how is it that its rays immediately light upon my face as soon as they are born?' I thought also: 'The rays of my eyes must travel as swiftly as those of the sun. Are not my eyes, my spirit, themselves Dharmakâya?' Meditating thus, I felt all the bonds which had bound me for so many years become suddenly loosened and drop from me. For how many incalculable years had I been seated in an ant-hole? Today, in the hollow of my hairs, reside all the Buddhas of the ten quarters. I thought again: 'Even if I did not accomplish a greater satori, I am now my own master.'

And Bukko composed the following verses:

All at once I completely shattered the cave of Ghosts.
Look! Here is where one can see the front face of the monster Nata,
Both my ears were deaf, and my tongue was tied,
Should you touch it, whilst playing, the proud stars will appear."

These few examples will suffice to give an idea of the mental circumstances which accompany the accomplishment of *satori*. Naturally these examples are specially chosen and are even rather exaggerated. All *satoris* are not preceded by such extraordinary phenomena of concentration. But one can always observe a processus more or less similar to these in the souls of the monks aspiring to the truths of Zen. The soul then appears so cleanly swept, so clear, that there does not remain in it a speck of dust, nor a trace of thought. When all mental movements cease, the consciousness of an effort to preserve an idea disappears. This is because, as the disciples of Zen declare, intelligence is so completely possessed by the object of its thought, that even the notion of identity is lost. In the same way, when a mirror reflects the features of another person, the subject has the impression of living in a transparent and luminous palace of crystal.

"With Zen your whole vision of the world is renewed, but you remain normal as usual. You have merely acquired something new. All your mental faculties work now on a different scheme of which you possess the key. They are more satisfying, more peaceful, more full of joy than ever. Spring flowers appear more beautiful, the mountain torrent fresher and more transparent. A subjective revolution which brings about this state of things cannot be called abnormal. Since life is more attractive, and since its radiation, in yourself, is as vast as the Universe itself, one must conclude that *satori* is both healthy and dignified. Our ordinary life is slavery: *satori* is the first step towards liberty."

6. *Characteristic Extracts from the* Zenso-Mondo

(Dialogues between Zenist Bonzes)

One day the celebrated scholar Yosui Matsui asked a Zen bonze :
'What is Zen ? Where is Zen ?'
'Zen is on your head,' answered the bonze.

'I understand,' replied the scholar, 'you wish to speak of the roof of the house: shelter is the symbol of human charity.'

'No, I do not mean the roof. Rise higher.'

'Perhaps you mean the crow perching on the roof? Chinese tradition says indeed: "Even a mere crow practises the law of Love towards his father."'

'No. Higher still.'

'In that case you mean the sky. The old sages counsel us to first understand the sky.'

'No. Higher still.'

'Higher than the sky? I do not understand. Pray explain yourself clearly.'

'If you do not understand the "higher still," then look towards the "lower still."'

'I believe I understand. You mean that Zen is similar to that green mat which we tread underfoot. The more we tread on it, the more shiny and luminous it becomes, and the more one appreciates it. Thus it is with Zen; the more one studies Zen, the wiser one becomes.'

'No. It is not that. Lower still.'

'Under the floor there is air. Are you speaking of space?'

'No. Lower still.'

'Then you must mean the earth?'

'Lower still.'

'Lower than the earth? I do not understand. Pray explain yourself clearly.'

'Do you know this ancient saying. "The sky is high . . . endless. The earth is deep . . . endless?"'

One day the famous bonze Takuan presented himself at the palace of the great Lord Tajimanokami, who had the reputation of being a first-class swordsman, and declared:

'I absolutely wish to see Lord Tajimanokami.'

A servant, seeing that the bonze was clothed in rags, asked him:

'Why do you wish to see our lord?'

'To fence with him.'

'Be off, wretched beggar,' cried the indignant servant.

But the lord who had had heard this dialogue cried to his servant:

'Let this insolent bonze come in. I am going to kill him.'

The valet then said ironically to the bonze:

'Mr Bonze, you have a very queer idea. You have surely come here to lose your head.'

'I thank you,' replied the bonze. 'May your lord take my head.'

The lord arrived armed with a sword. Takuan followed him very quickly into the fencing-room.

'What,' cried the lord, 'do you dare measure yourself against me?'

'Yes. Pray excuse me for the trouble I am giving you.'

'Don't be astonished if I kill you.'

'Oh,' said the bonze smiling, 'I always await death.'

'You do not care for life?'

'I do not understand your question. What life? What do you mean? I am attached to nothing. I am poor and free.'

'Well, you will have wished it. Let us begin our duel.'

'May I first ask you a question? You are known to be the greatest fencer in Japan. Suppose that you had to deal with two enemies at the same time, what would you do?'

'I'd kill them.'

'And if they were four?'

'I'd kill the four.'

'And if they were ten?'

'Be they ten or a hundred, I'd kill them all.'

The bonze began to laugh and said:

'I am very disappointed. I thought you were a master swordsman, whereas you are but a fool or a coward. You believe you kill all these men, but you don't kill them at all.'

'I, a coward?'

'That angers you. What a queer idea. I have not learnt the art of fencing, but if ten thousand people were to attack me I could defend myself as easily as I blow these specks of dust off the surface of this table.'

'Do you possess a magic sword?'

'Yes, I do. It is called *Rojinken*.'

'What is that?'

'If you wish to know, recite this poem this evening in the moonlight:

> What is life?
> Noise—wind soughing in the branches of a pine,
> Which an artist drew on a Chinese lacquer . . .'

When the bonze Guannô, who was reputed for the purity of his heart, was travelling, he asked one night for hospitality in a certain house.

Now as luck would have it, this house was a house of pleasure.

But, of course, the bonze had no inkling of the fact. Hardly had he begun to pray, kneeling on the mats of the room, than a very beautiful young woman drew near and began to smile at him ingratiatingly, whilst making all kinds of advances. Although Guannô was but a young man, his heart was invincibly pure. He therefore cried out indignantly:

'Call the master of the house.'

The manager of the establishment soon appeared.

'This woman,' said the bonze, 'is indulging in a thousand follies before me. Kindly chase her away.'

'This woman, Mr Bonze, wishes to become your wife for the night. Does she not please you?'

'Where am I, please?'

'In a house of pleasure.'

The manager withdrew. The bonze began to reflect upon the incident. Night was falling fast. Shadows engulfed all things.

'What mysterious causes led me here?' the bonze asked himself. 'The chain of causes, of the reason determining our acts, is infinite. Our intelligence cannot understand everything. What must I do? Preach the law everywhere. . . . Woman, tell me is it right that woman should obey man?'

'Yes,' answered the courtesan.

'How many women are in this house?'

'Seven.'

'Tell them to come here, all seven of them. How much shall I pay them?'

'Seven women cost three *ryos* and two *bu*.'

'Very well. Bid them come.'

When the women were assembled the bonze said to them:

'A mysterious cause has led me here. This woman has said that it is right that woman should obey man. Therefore I order you to listen to me.'

So saying, the bonze drew out of a box he constantly carried tied to his belt, a small image of Jizô Bosatsu. Then he poured incense into his incense burner, and the smoke of the incense soon purified the room. He then prayed fervently, interrupting his prayer with exhortations to live according to the law of Buddha, in purity and calmness of heart. He prayed and preached in this manner until dawn. At first the women laughed at him. Then little by little they were gained by the charm of his doctrine and by the light of truth, and when the sun rose, all the women of the establishment, as well as the servants, the manager and the clients—

in fact all the people who had spent the night under the same roof as the bonze—were listening respectfully to him as he preached the liberating doctrine of Zen.

During the epoch of wars, all the Samurais accomplished spiritual exercises according to Zen. One day a great warrior named Shingen went to a Zen temple and asked the following questions of a very young bonze he met there.

'Where are Paradise and Hell ?'

'*Kuso wo Kurae*' (Go and eat dung), answered the bonze.

Shingen pounced upon him and wrung his wrists.

'That is Hell,' said the little bonze.

'And this,' demanded the warrior brandishing a sword, 'is this death or paradise ?'

'The object itself is death.'

'Where is paradise ?' inquired the warrior.

'Look and see.'

'Will you tell me ?'

'I cannot.'

'I will kill you.'

'Life is beyond the notion of frailty.'

And the little bonze went his way very calmly without even throwing a glance behind him.

One day the bonze Igonzenshi received a visit from a man who said to him :

'I have doubts. Can you enlighten me ?'

'Certainly,' replied Igonzenshi, 'but I am very busy just at present. Return this evening.'

When evening came, the man returned. Many other visitors were assembled around the bonze. When Igonzenshi caught sight of the man he had seen that morning, he threw himself upon him, and strangling him brutally, he cried :

'You have doubts, have you ? *Now* do you understand ?'

The commentator gives the following explanation of this anecdote. 'A shock : be oneself, *first be oneself.*'

A celebrated bonze of the Soto sect called Tenchu, who lived in Shimada, was known for his severity and for the abrupt methods he followed in controversies. But he was adored by peasants and simple folk.

One day, Hakuin, the celebrated sage and priest, passing before the temple in which Tenchu was officiating, said to the bearer of his palanquin:

'Is this where the bonze Tenchu lives?'

'Yes,' answered the bearer.

'Well, when thou seest him, do not fail to tell him that on passing before his temple a bonze said: "Does that fool, that idiot of a Tenchu, still live?"'

The bearer, indignant at hearing how his fare spoke of the venerable Tenchu, immediately rushed to find the latter to tell him what he had just heard.

But Tenchu appeared delighted, for he asked with a smile:

'No doubt was it Hakuin who spoke thus?'

'Why,' said the bearer, 'are you not angered by his insolent remarks?'

Then to his amazement Tenchu, who appeared ever more delighted, walked away murmuring:

'It is a great compliment, a very great compliment.'

One day an old gentleman of eighty years said to the bonze Ryokan:

'I fear I have reached the end of my life. Will you please say some prayers for me so that I may live longer?'

'How many years do you want to live?' asked Ryokan.

'Until I am one hundred years old.'

'Only? Well you are not very exacting.'

'Well, then, let us say one hundred and fifty years old.'

'Only one hundred and fifty years? That's not much.'

'Well, if you wish it, let us say three hundred years.'

'It's little, very little. For long as your life may be, it will never be more than a point compared to the infinity of time or to the infinity of space. Three hundred years? What's that? The instant of a dream. Why not ask for eternal life?'

'Can one pray in that sense?'

'Why, certainly one can.'

And the commentator adds: 'All that Buddha has said is a law of eternity.'

One day a man of the people said to the bonze Ikkyu:

'Mr Bonze, will you please write for me some maxims of the highest wisdom?'

Ikkyu immediately took his brush and wrote the word *Go-yo-jin* (attention).

'Is that all?' asked the man. 'Will you not add something more?'
Ikkyu then wrote twice running:
'Go-yo-jin.'
'Well,' remarked the man rather irritably, 'I really don't see much depth or subtilty in what you have just written.'
Then Ikkyu wrote the same word three times running.
Half angered the man demanded:
'What does that word "attention" mean, after all?'
And Ikkyu answered gently:
'Attention means . . . attention.'
And he recited the following poem:

> When your heart sighs for tomorrow
> So as to see the cherry tree in bloom;
> Do you know if a sudden storm
> Will not destroy all the flowers this very night?

A Zen bonze called Gensa one day asked Shinno-Daishi:
'It is said that all the objects of the universe are but reflections of the heart. Can you explain this mystery to me?'
'You would not understand it,' answered Shinno-Daishi.
'Yet . . . ?'
'What is this object?' asked Shinno-Daishi, showing him a chair.
'It is a chair.'
'A chair? Yes. One says that. I perceive that you have a stunted intellect, and do not understand the deep reason for the Three Spiritual Worlds.'
'Yet this object is what is called a chair,' insisted Gensa. 'Don't you see its different parts made of bamboo and of wood?'
'Yes, you are right.'
'Well, then . . . ?'
'The mind of man likes the shadows.'
'Explain yourself.'
'That's all.'
'I beg you to explain yourself.'
'Well, you can say "chair," just as you could say any other word. The exterior aspect of an object is error, and whatever the aspect, it does not aggravate the error.'
'I do not understand very well.'
'The essence is "heart of the world."'

Although he was then only five years old, the child who was later to become Nishzumi-Mokusan, a celebrated bonze of the

Zen sect, asked his mother one day as they were visiting a temple:

'What beings go to Hell?'

His mother answered:

'Bad, naughty, disobedient children like you.'

'And you,' asked the child, 'where do you go?'

'Well, as I love the wicked child you are, I will follow you to Hell, being bound by my maternal love.'

'I who am naughty, will go to Hell, and you who love me and who are good, will also go to Hell. In that case, *who* goes to Paradise?'

'If you became a great bonze, you would go to Paradise, and in that case you could carry your poor mother along with you in your wake.'

'I want to become a great bonze.'

'Alas, how could you, you who are so original, so personal, who only wish to follow your own sweet will. Where would you find the patience necessary to study and to meditate? Indeed,' said his mother, laughing, 'I think that even if you became a bonze you would yet find a way of driving all your relations to Hell.'

Comment: 'Heart of Zen, what care I about Hell for myself? But I wish to save my mother.' And the child did eventually become a celebrated bonze of the Zen sect.

One day a scholar asked the bonze Kaufu:

'Describe your soul to me.'

'My soul is infinite. I have swallowed the universe.'

'If you had swallowed the universe,' retorted the scholar, 'you would be able to throw it up by your mouth. Pray do so.'

The bonze remained calm and smiling, but did not answer. His thought appeared to be elsewhere, very far away.

'Well,' continued the scholar, 'do you insult me by refusing to answer me? Do you know who I am?'

A gentle murmur issued from the lips of the ecstatic bonze:

'An idiot.'

The next day the scholar returned and asked the bonze:

'Kindly give me an explanation. I am continually hearing Zen bonzes speak of a place where man is no longer the prisoner of the notion of good, or of the notion of evil.'

The bonze reflected.

'Does such a place really exist?' insisted the scholar.

'Certainly.'

'Then, where is it?'

'At the point where the white cloud seems to come out of the mountain to disappear immediately.'

One bright, soft spring day the bonze Remoku visited the bonze Sekito in his temple, and said to him:

'Certain Zen scholars pretend that the law is inexplicable by means of words. Is this quite certain?'

'It is certain,' answered Sekito.

'Nevertheless, you who are considered the greatest scholar of the Zen world . . .'

'Pardon me, it is *you*, and not I, who are considered thus.'

'Yet even if the law is inexplicable,' continued Remoku, 'you can certainly speak of it to me and make me understand it. I am listening to you.'

Sekito did not answer, and both remained seated, facing each other, during one whole day. The next day Remoku returned, hoping to obtain some enlightenment. But Sekito, who was still seated cross-legged, did not even open his mouth.

The Remoku went off, persuaded that Sekito did not possess the science that was attributed to him. But as he walked away, he heard the voice of Sekito calling out to him:

'Death is nigh. There is not an instant to lose in speaking foolishness. Therefore let us be silent and meditate until our death.'

Remoku bent his head, duly rebuked, and went off meditating deeply.

When the bonze Daigu inhabited the temple of Nanzenshi, a certain servant girl, who had been condemned to death for having disobeyed her master, came to ask him for shelter and protection. The excellent priest welcomed the poor woman and, in order to save her life, he even authorised her to live in the temple. This incident was immediately seized upon by his detractors, who accused him of living a life of debauchery, and the Superior of the Mother Temple of Mihonshinji inflicted a blame upon him and even laid him under an interdict. Extremely affected by this injustice, Daigu resolved to go to Mihonshinji in order to justify himself. As he was crossing a mountain the man who was leading his horse began to sing naïvely:

'*Like the mountain rain our heart opens itself to the light when not occupied by worries.*'

The bonze understood suddenly. He turned his horse and returned home.

Comment: All that one does, all that one says, proceeds from fatal causes. He is a fool who rebels against it. Innocence will be recompensed one day, but time is necessary for this. Let us allow time to pass. And indeed, seven years later, everybody rendered justice to the virtue of the good bonze Daigu of the Nanzenshi temple.

At Kamakura, in the temple of Enkakuji, used to live the bonze Seïsotsu, who was a very wise man. One day a great scholar coming from Hasé undertook to expound his scientific knowledge to the bonze, and in order to do this, made many demonstrations and a great show of his knowledge and competence.

The bonze ended by saying to him:

'Is that all?'

'Not quite,' answered the scholar, who was about to begin a new discourse.

Whilst they were both walking side by side in the temple grounds, a little insect passed in front of them, returning to its hole, carrying a few twigs.

The bonze said to the scholar:

'You resemble this little insect. You are hoarding all your life.'

The scholar was deeply struck by this remark. Later he understood that true light was to be found elsewhere than where he had sought it until then. So he sat down, cross-legged, and devoted his life to meditation.

One night some disciples visited the bonze Seiju, who lived in solitude amongst the mountains. As the bonze had left his hut for a few minutes, and would no doubt soon return, one of the disciples said:

'Here is a fine occasion to surprise our master and to see clearly into his heart.'

It was then decided that one of the disciples should hide in a dark corner of the forest and spring upon the master as soon as he saw him, whilst asking him abruptly a question. He would then see if the master, being unprepared, could answer it. This was done. As soon as the disciple saw the master, he caught him by the throat and cried out:

'What are we, here on earth?'

The master answered smiling:

'I do not understand, either.'

Disconcerted, the disciple then asked:

'Then who will instruct us?'

'I do not understand,' answered Seiju, 'and you, do *you* understand?'

Comment: To say 'I do not understand' does not mean that one understands nothing. *Truth is felt,* but cannot be expressed.

Buddha was hardly born when he pointed to the sky and to the earth, saying:

'I am the most intelligent of children. Amongst all the thousands of children who are born every day I am he who has understood.'

He became wise amongst the wisest.

One day the bonze Zenshio asked Ummon, the great Zenist bonze:

'Is it true that from his youth up Buddha was very different from other men?'

'Yes,' answered Ummon, 'he was very different from the others. He was very queer and did the most extravagant things.'

'How is that?'

'Assuredly he was a megalomaniac. He divided the law into thousands of parts. He even proposed thirty-four thousand. If I had been near him I would have killed him.'

'Oh! What are you saying?' cried the horrified bonze.

'Yes,' continued Ummon, 'I would have killed him and thrown his body to the wild beasts.'

'Oh!' said the bonze Zenshio, astounded, 'why do you utter such abominations?'

'Because it is on account of Buddha that all beings suffer.'

'But he has poured such kindness, such grace upon the world!'

'In truth, he is constantly tormenting us.'

The two bonzes began discussing passionately, then came to blows. Still fighting they fell to the ground in the temple garden. A young disciple ran towards them and doused the fighters with fresh, clear water. Then Ummon began to ring the temple bell and said to his adversary:

'Well, have you heard? Do you understand this sound?'

But Zenshio dragged out the tongue of the bell and said:

'No. One hears nothing at all.'

'Well, answered Ummon, it never depends upon another person whether one hears or not—it depends upon oneself.'

One day a disciple asked the bonze Eka:

'Why did Dharma come from India? Why did he come from such a distant land?'

Eka said to him:

'Do you see this tree? What is it?'

'It is an oak.'

'Yes and no. It is an oak and it is Dharma.'

'No, it is only a tree,' affirmed the disciple.

'Child, do you not understand? Look well at this tree, with all your strength, and you will end by seeing that it possesses all the features of Dharma.'

The young bonze looked fixedly as he was bidden, but he never saw anything else but a tree. Yet, upon reflection, he understood how vain his questions were—for the essential, the real, is what one thinks with fervour.

Ryokan was a celebrated Zen bonze, indifferent to riches and to honours. His heart was as pure as an autumn sky.

One day a thief introduced himself into his hut but found only a few chipped tea bowls. The thief went off wondering how such a celebrated man could live in such dire poverty.

'Thief! Thief! Come back,' cried Ryokan.

'What do you want of me?' asked the thief suspiciously.

'Since you entered my hut to take something, you must not go away with empty hands. Here, take the coat I am wearing.'

The thief took the ragged garment and saw that it was covered with lice. Rather alarmed, he asked:

'What are these little insects?'

'They are lice,' answered Ryokan, 'creatures living by the charity of Buddha. You are exactly like these lice. There, take my coat and be off with you.'

The thief left, very astonished at what he had just heard. The bonze watched him go, and then addressed a secret prayer to Buddha.

Through the open window a pure shaft of moonlight entered into the poor little cottage.

The bonze sang:

> The thief has robbed me,
> But the pure moonlight
> Remains with me still. . . .

Having reached the age of sixty, a bonze realised that his spirit had never been able to grasp the truth. He presented himself at the temple of Daitsuin, at Totomi, and asked the celebrated scholar Hakuin to accept him as disciple and to teach him that Truth that was for ever escaping him. The bonze lived six years in this temple, which was smaller than his own, devoting himself to spiritual exercises and to meditation. Yet he still did not understand and he tearfully confided to Hakuin:

'In spite of all my studies, I still do not understand.'

Hakuin replied:

'Continue to meditate, and if in three years you have not understood, I will give you my head.'

The bonze meditated three years. He then returned to Hakuin and said:

'I still do not understand.'

'I am not going to cut off my head immediately to give it to you!' retorted Hakuin. 'Continue to meditate for three more years.'

At the end of this time, as light had not yet dawned in him, the bonze in despair resolved to return home and to kill himself. As he was walking towards his temple, he crossed a mountain pass called the *Satta*. Gorges and deep precipices offered themselves to his gaze. The place seemed a propitious one in which to commit suicide, and he prepared to throw himself into the abyss. Suddenly he saw a ray of light filtering through mauve clouds. Then he understood the Zen thought in all its deepness, and his soul was illumined by an indescribable joy.

In his youth, he who was to become the bonze Chinrô undertook on one day, during an absence of his master, to fish a carp in the temple pond. When the master returned, all the young disciples bowed before him; all except Chinrô, who, being very embarrassed by the basket in which the carp was struggling, was only able to cover it with a piece of silk stuff. But suddenly the carp leapt out of the basket and fell at the master's feet.

All the young disciples paled with emotion. The master asked:

'Who has dared take this fish?'

Chinrô answered very calmly:

'See! emotion is in every heart because of this carp. The carp of worry and of discord has slipped of itself into the hearts of men.'

'Where did it come from?' asked the master.

'From up there, from the ceiling.'

The master considered his disciple with interest and said:

'And which way shall it depart?'

'Why send it back to the stagnant pond? asked Chinrô. Life is nothing. Is not death to be preferred for this carp as for all creatures?'

The master smiled.

One day the wise Keiu Nakamura asked the bonze Kenso to expound to him the *Hokkekyô* (*The Lotus of the Good Law*). The bonze acquitted himself perfectly of this task, and even gave many supplementary details to Nakamura.

The latter remarked to him witheringly:

'Why, I thought that Zen bonzes disdained texts, theories and systems of logical explanations?'

'Zen,' returned the bonze, 'does not consist in knowing nothing, but in the belief that *to know* is outside of all texts, of all documents. You did not tell me you wanted *to know*, but only that you wished an explanation of the text.'

The bonze Taikuan, having gathered at his dwelling scholars, jurists and writers, ordered his young disciple to fill a cup to the brim with hot water. Then he said to the assembly:

'Is it possible to fill this cup any more?'

'It is impossible,' answered all present, 'for otherwise it would spill over.'

'So are your minds filled to the brim with science, theories and systems,' replied the bonze. 'Zen and science are two different things.'

'What is Zen?' asked his wise auditors.

'It is,' answered the bonze, 'to have the heart and soul of a little child.'

Looking at the sea dotted with boats, the bonze Kanguen asked his disciple Daichi:

'Could you stop the progress of these boats from your room?'

The young disciple closed the shôji.

'Nevertheless you could not have stopped these boats had you been deprived of your hands.'

The young disciple then closed his eyes.

One day a certain bonze asked Sozan Daishi:

'What is the most precious thing in the world?'

'Anything, a carrion, the head of a dead cat,' replied Sozan Daishi.

'Why?'

'Because it cannot be evaluated.'

Comment: A diamond which is worth 300,000 yen is only valued in human money. It is believed precious because, humanly speaking, it is worth a lot. What is that which is precious in itself?

The bonze Tokuan-Tokuo had lost his daughter and was crying bitterly. A bonze of the Shinshu sect said to him:

'It is not wise to cry—so why cry?'

The Zen bonze answered him:

'Foolishness! I cry because I wish to cry.'

A Shinshu bonze who was officiating at the funeral of a young girl exhorted her parents not to cry.

'Why cry?' he asked. 'Your daughter is in Paradise.'

'Yes,' answered the parents, 'such is truly the teaching of Buddha. But we cannot help crying because we loved our daughter.'

The following year the bonze lost his son and cried bitterly. His relations exhorted him not to cry, saying:

'One must not cry! One must not cry! Of what use is it to cry?'

Then the poor man withdrew to a solitary spot far from his friends and cried all the same.[1]

7. *The Zen Temples*

The Myoshinji.

In the Zen temples of Myoshinji, founded in the fourteenth century, the Emperor Hanazona reserved for his use a retreat full of art and silence which is, however, imbued with a very personal sentiment. Within a courtyard of golden sand grow secular old pines, one of which even dates from the foundation of the temple, and which immediately invite one's soul to meditation. Whilst reflecting in their shade the mind frees itself of all the vanities which occupy it, and of the common-

[1] These extracts from the *Zenso-Mondo* were translated from the Japanese by Kuni Matsuo and E. Steinilber-Oberlin.

places which crush it. How many foreign, inert acquisitions obscure one's true nature, one's "Buddha nature," and which one should cast off before presenting oneself at the threshold of a Zen temple? This is perhaps the effort which is asked of you by the great dragon, the masterpiece of Tan-Yu-Morinobu which occupies the whole ceiling of the Hondo.[1] It seems to wish to ask us a question: Who are you? Do you even know who you are?

In the Kyôdô, the eight Tennin carved in wood by Chuen have an extraordinarily energetic expression. Thus I pass from meditation under the old pines, to the enigmatical dragon and thence to a reminder of energy. Nature, philosophy, action: the whole of the Zen doctrine. In the temples, apartments, in the Hall of the Bell, in the Hall of the Drum, everywhere I see either works of art or the working up of that other art which consists in awakening one's thought and restoring it to one deepened by the aspect of planes, spaces and lines.

A Zen temple is not a dead building nor even a mere place of meditation. It is an instrument of spiritual, individual and original exaltation. It reacts upon us and we must know how to use it. Why do the paintings of Kano Motonobu stir me particularly? Because their creator lived in this place as a fervent Buddhist. The sincerity of his soul materialised itself here. Amongst these paintings some, in vivid colours, are of Chinese importation. Others are Japanese landscapes in black, grey or white strokes. I like to think that Chinese influence and Japanese taste formed the souls of the Zenist bonzes who surround me. Farther on, a new surprise stirs our mystic depths. The *Kaisandô*, or Hall of the Founder, is completely black: black stones, black pillars, black lacquered altars. It is strange, weird, unearthly. I am deeply awed. I dream long before the *Nehan-do*, and I have the impression of being an initiate who, proceeding from stage to stage, has at last reached his goal.

[1] The largest edifice in a Buddhist temple.

The Nanzenshi.

Of the Nanzenshi, inhabited in the thirteenth century by the Emperor Kameyana, and reconstructed by Ieyasu in the seventeenth, I remember in particular, besides its pretty façade, its double roofs and its artistic treasures, its garden which is designed in the sober, classical style called *Cha-no-yu*—so sober, in fact, that it generally bewilders the stranger. The garden of the Nanzenshi is, indeed, merely a small courtyard containing a few stones and bushes. Is that all? Yes, that is all. A certain tourist, who caught sight of the garden at an hour when it was forbidden to visit it, is said to have exclaimed: "There is nothing to see and yet it is forbidden to see it." A garden like this one only confides its whole secret to a Japanese soul—to a purified Zenist. Centuries of spiritual and aesthetic education, the whole thought of the Chinese sages, all the Japanese genius of delicate assimilation, have contributed to place these stones *here* instead of *there*—have conceived the unconstrained, intuitive order of this small space. A child and a wise man, simple and pure souls, alone can understand these things. And that is why the Zenist discovers therein a treasure, and the foreign tourist nothing.

The Tofukuji.

Who will ever describe the charm of long meditations in these wooden galleries in the company of a Zenist bonze—discreet artist and delicate dreamer?

In autumn the pilgrim's attention is first caught by two red masses of maples bordering a ravine spanned by a bridge, the *Tsu-ten-kyo*—"the bridge of the sky." Will I meditate standing upon this bridge, hanging between sky and earth, amidst the flame-coloured trees, waving in the wind, like symbols of the ardent passions of men? No, I prefer to return some other day when the bonzes exhibit for the veneration of the faithful, an admirable kakemono, a spiritual masterpiece, representing Buddha's entrance into Nirvâna, and due to the brush of Cho-Densu, who was a monk in this temple where he spent his life. The pilgrims often kneel before this magnificent picture. Or else, in order to meditate upon Zen thought, I will simply go and dream at night near the temple under the starry sky. The landscape is singularly varied, with many precipices and covered passage-ways spanning tumultuous torrents. *Satoris*, or sudden revelations and enlightenments, await one at each step. . . . Here the spirit may founder, or soar to luminous heights.

The Temples of Kenshoji, Enkakuji and some other sanctuaries.

At Kamakura one's imagination is exalted by the remembrance of the old Zenist Samurais. Here the visitor can lead the religious life and meditate upon the question asked by the Superior of the Temples of Kenshoji and Enkakuji, which seem to proclaim the Zen ideal with their sober lines and their scenery of beautiful green foliage. The first is hidden amidst trees. A gallery runs along its front. Its paved alley, flanked by two stone lanterns, presents that awe-inspiring mixture of poetry and severity so expressive of the effort of a soul striving to be complete. Inside the temple, an image of Jizô welcomes one. Jizô, the smiling God of the children. Does not Zen exact of its adepts, as several texts express it, "the soul of a little child"?

The temples and the charming shady nooks of the sanctuary of Okuyama, in the province of Totomi, also invite one to clear meditation, free of all pessimism.

A pilgrimage to the grave of the poet Bashô (1644-1694), a Zen Buddhist.

Lake Biwa is calm, blue and transparent. Its purity is strangely moving. It has a Zenist soul. As we follow its banks, bordered with glistening reeds, my companions remind me of the eight traditional beauties of Lake Biwa: The autumn moon seen from Hishiyama, the setting sun on the bridge of Seta, a snowy night at Hirayama, the evening bell at the temple of Miidera, the boats returning from Yabassé, the clear sky and the breezes of Awadzu, evening rain on the old pine tree at Karasaki, the flight of wild geese at Katata.

All the Zen School of Thought is expressed here far better than in books. Yet this evening I pass by without answering the silent appeal of all these marvels, for, accompanied by a few Japanese friends, I have decided to go and salute the grave of Bashô, the greatest of Japanese poets—a Zen Buddhist.

"He was, before all, a fervent Buddhist," one of my companions informs me. "If you do not sympathise with the Buddhist state of soul, you will be unable to understand him. His kindness extended to every living creature—to the butterfly. . . ."

Another interrupted smilingly :

"To the sparrows. . . ."

A third added, also smiling :

"To the dragon flies. . . ."

I knew to which of the poet's celebrated *haikaï* these remarks alluded to, *haikaï* so popular that my friends would have deemed it presumptuous to remind me of them more clearly.

> Awake! Awake!
> I will make thee my friend
> O sleeping butterfly!
>
> Sparrow, my friend
> Do not eat the bee
> Disporting itself amidst the flowers.

The third *haikaï* alluded to by my companions is the one which provoked a well-known incident. One day, inspired by Buddhist kindness, Bashô cleverly modified a cruel *haikaï* composed by his humorist disciple Kikaku. The latter had written :

> A red dragon fly,
> Tear off its wings,
> A pimento!

Bashô modified this to:

> A pimento,
> Add wings to it,
> Lo! a red dragon fly!

One of us sang the *haikaï* twice over, according to custom. The light caressed the blue lake, and from the oars of a distant fisherman the water dripped in cascades of diamonds. I thought of Bashô, who was indeed a Japanese Saint Francis of Assisi, as well as an ever-wandering poet-pilgrim, and I inquired:

"Which is, in your opinion, of all the different aspects of Bashô's sensibility, the one most characteristic of the Zen spirit?"

One of my companions replied:

"It is the ardent desire of liberating his soul. For do not deceive yourself. Gentle and kind as he was, Bashô wished to live his life. He wished to consecrate himself wholly to his need of loving Nature freely, without any ties, like a tramp—sleeping under the stars like a beggar, having for sole possessions his staff, his wallet and his bowl.

"He was born in 1644 in a family of Samurais in the service of a Daimyô, whose son became his most intimate friend. He might easily have exploited this friendship to obtain material advantages, but it never even occurred to him to do so. He wrote verses with his friend, and after the latter's sudden death he retired to a Buddhist monastery, where he discovered his 'Buddha nature'—his real self.

"On leaving the monastery, his reputation as poet was prodigious, and many admirers pressed around him in his little house at Edo surrounded by a garden full of banana trees.[1] Here, again, what prevented him from taking advantage of his popularity? When his house was burned down in 1683, in the great fire which destroyed nearly the whole of the

---

[1] He planted a banana tree near the window, and from it he took the name of Bashô (banana) by which he is known.

capital, it was in truth a deliverance for him. Since long his soul had perceived the impermanency of things, of which events reminded him. He therefore resumed his staff, his wallet and his bowl, as a mendicant monk. Poet, wanderer and free, such was Bashô. It was under this aspect that he found his true nature, his 'Buddha nature.'"

We continued our way slowly, admiring the transparent water—a white sail—the pink mountains.

Another of my Japanese friends remarked:

"You are giving too much importance to Bashô, the traveller. It was not wandering that tempted him, but direct contact with Nature. Now this commands that. One cannot love Nature without wandering in the woods, the fields, along the sandy shores, sleeping anywhere so long as he could see the moon, or admire the first ray of the dawn. . . . Remember his *haikaïs*:

> My lantern is out,
> I lie down nevertheless,
> Oh! the moon in my window.
>
> Spring evening,
> The cherry trees—the cherry trees,
> Ah! spring has come.

"To love Nature means wandering ceaselessly in all seasons to admire it. As Bashô himself declared: 'To admire the snow, let us walk, walk, until we are exhausted.' Bashô was especially a Zenist by his love of Nature. His true friends were the moon and the snow, the butterfly, the spring cherry trees, the red maples of autumn, this blue lake."

"I approve of your remark," interrupted my third companion, "but I wish to insist upon one of the characteristics of Bashô and of Zen: *Poverty*. Simplicity, purity and poverty are the three aspects of the fundamental virtue of a Zenist, which consists in possessing a completely purified soul. Some of Bashô's *haikaï* reveal not only that he was poor, but that he loved poverty and enjoyed its adorable charm. Thus when he speaks with love of a tiny hut, lost in the woods: 'Oh, little hut, so small that when I lay down my feet touched its walls.'

"When he died, in 1694, one found on him a standish, a bowl, a few books and an image of Buddha. That was all the fortune of our great poet. Yes, Bashô was indeed Zenist by his poverty."

We were approaching the temple containing the grave of the poet. Before entering the sacred enclosure, we asked the bonze Guessan Kanaï to express his opinion.

"I quite agree to all that has been said," he answered. "Mystic, poet, wanderer, lover of nature, a poor man, Bashô was indeed all of these. But did you not ask us to describe the Zen quality most characteristic of his soul? Well, in my opinion, that quality lies in his intuitive genius. Zen is an intuitive method. Now in Bashô, an extraordinary depth of feeling, coupled with a marvellous intuition, enables him to be directly in contact with the heart of things and of beings. Then the emotion becomes intense, of an unparalleled purity and quality. The soul of things, perceived by him, passes into him and is conveyed to us by his poems. On the seashore, in front of a fisherman who, according to Japanese custom, is catching poulps with the aid of an earthen pot tied to a string, Bashô, ever conscious of the common origin of all things, expresses in a few words the whole Buddhist philosophy of life. *Like a poulp, caught in the pot, we make a short dream looking at the summer moon.*

"How deep, how moving is this! Zen often uses very concentrated forms of expression, resuming a world of ideas and of sentiments. Bashô did so also. The great Chinese Zenists often speak a very concise esoteric language, which is also far from clear, and rather jerky. Thanks to Bashô, the *haikaï*, an ultra-concise poetic form, became a Zen means of expression, full, however, of charm and of grace.

"Let us enter into the grounds of this temple. We will remember the celebrated poem in which the poet succeeded one night in concentrating all human emotion, in the silence broken only by the noise of a frog plunging into an old pond.[1] It is here that you will best understand the exhortation of M. K. Nukariya, professor at the Buddhist College of the Zen sect: '*Go directly to the soul of things.*'"

But where is the grave of the divine Bashô? Ah, here it is! A simple stela, not even a stone—a stela caressed by the light dancing shadows of banana leaves. . . .

[1]   Ah! the old pond—
         And the sound of the water
         As the frog plunges in!

This celebrated poem evokes beautifully the park of a Japanese monastery with its calm old pond, the silence of which is only broken, from time to time, by the plunging of a frog.

CHAPTER IX

THE JÔDO SECT

(1) The Jôdo Sect. (2) Mr Kanei Okamoto, bonze of the Temple of Chion-in, tells me of the gentle life of Hônen, a Buddhist saint, and expounds the Jôdo doctrine: *" Whoever will invoke Amida-Buddha will, by pronouncing this name, enter at the end of his life the Pure Land of Paradise."* (3) Mr Mochizuki, bonze and professor, lecturer on Jôdo at the Faculty of Letters of Taishô, explains the principles of the sect. (4) The Monastery of Chion-in, or the Bell of Amida. (5) The Temple of Kurodani, or the Hermitage of Saint Hônen.

1. *The Jôdo Sect*

The Jôdo sect, whose name means Pure Land, was founded in Japan in 1175 by Genku, better known under the name of Hônen, who was a great saint. The doctrine is based on the sutras of Amithaba (literally, *Infinite Light*), and in particular upon the *Sukhâvativyuha* (description of the Sukhâvati Paradise), which are canonical texts. Before Hônen those texts had been commented in China by the sage Zendo in the seventh century, and in Japan itself by the celebrated priests Ekwan and Eshin. Hônen had more than a hundred disciples. Actually, the sect possesses 7118 temples or monasteries, of which the Chionin (Kyôto) is the most important and the most popular. The sect also counts more than 5500 abbots and priests, 2,200,000 perpetual subscribers, and 300,000 occasional and Shinto subscribers. Its annual budget amounts to more than one million yen. It has created 120 social assistance organisations. One of Hônen's disciples, named Shoku, founded the Seizan branch, the perpetual members of which exceed 700,000.

2. *Mr Kanei Okamoto, bonze of the sect, tells me of the gentle life of Hônen,[1] a Buddhist saint, and expounds the Jôdo doctrine*

Mr K. Okamoto is a young and very scholarly bonze of the Chion-in monastery. He knows the West well, having studied in Paris, and he expresses himself in very pure French.

"Genku, better known as Hônen, was born in 1133 in the family of an official of the province of Mimasaka. A very sad event made a deep impression upon his childhood. His father, who was murdered by bandits, adjured him before dying to forgive his slayers. '*Thou wilt not avenge my death,*' he said to his son. '*Shouldst thou do so other vengeances are bound to follow, and the cycle of evil would never end. Forgive them, pray for them, and for all. Strive to lead men into the way of eternal salvation.*'

"The child grew up and fully realised his father's wish. He forgave his father's murderers, converted them to the good doctrine and became one of the greatest saints of Japan.

"Hônen was first brought up in a seminary in his native province. Whilst there he revealed such aptitudes for a religious life that his master sent him to the monastery on Mount Hiéi. It is said that the letter of recommendation he bore contained these words: '*I am sending you the portrait of Monju.*' The monks asked where was the portrait of the sage Monju thus announced to them; then, discovering their error, they understood that the phrase alluded to the youth standing before them.

"Hônen remained thirty years in meditation upon Mount Hiéi. His saintly reputation continued to increase. His humility, gentleness and kindness attracted to him the sympathy of all men. Kakemonos represent him in meditation before flowers, or in the moonlight. His face is illuminated by the irradiation of his heart. All those who approached him went away convinced that they had seen a great saint.

[1] Curious details concerning Hônen will be found in Mr Ishizuka's work, *Hônen*, and in some lectures given by Mr Anezaki. See the Bibliography, page 297.

"The object of Hônen's meditations was to make of Buddhism a religion, the moral benefits of which would be accessible to all—to the poor and to the ignorant as well as to the rich and to the learned. Buddha had certainly not wished that the treasures of his wisdom should be the exclusive possession of the privileged members of the aristocracy, and of learning. Hônen's renown had attracted around him on Mount Hiéi a court of admirers and devotees who troubled his researches. He therefore retired as a hermit to Kurodani, where he re-read the five thousand books of the Chinese *Tripatika*, and the commentaries of the Chinese sage Zendo on the sutras of *Amithâba*. In 1175, at forty-two years of age, Hônen at last reached the end of his spiritual efforts and expressed his views in a book called *The Choice*. He then founded the Jôdo sect.

"These views are very simple. Faith in the kindness and merciful will of Buddha to save all men, replaces the necessity for prolonged meditations by which the other sects pretend to lead the faithful to final illumination, to Nirvâna. According to the Jôdo sect, whoever invokes '*with a sincere heart*' the sacred name of Amida-Buddha obtains at the end of his days access to the *Pure Land*, or Paradise (Japanese: *Gokuraku*; Sanskrit: *Sukhâvati*). The form of invocation generally used, and which you will hear chanted in our temples, is: '*Namu-Amida-Butsu*' (Adoration to Amida-Buddha), or, analysing the idea contained in the word Amida, 'I adore thee, O Buddha of eternal life and light.'

"Long stages towards perfection during successive lives and innumerable cosmic periods are not exacted by Jôdo. The hope, or rather the certitude of reaching the *Gokuraku*, the Pure Land, the land of Eternal Light, is opened to all, even to the ignorant, even to the sinner. To realise one's salvation it is only necessary to pronounce the name of Amida-Buddha with a sincere faith in his redemptive power. Until then, there had been but one way of reaching the supreme goal, that of progressing in the way of perfection which we call the 'holy way.' Very few people are capable of this. Hônen brought a gospel, a good news. He revealed to men that deliverance may be obtained much more easily by the enunciation or repetition of the sacred name. The first way—that of the 'holy way,' exacts a constant personal effort (*Jiriki*). The second contents itself with waiting confidently for the effect of grace, for the help which Amida-Buddha grants us through his compassion for us, irrespectively of all merit on our part (*Tariki*), and which we accept with humility.

"For what reason is this facility offered to us ? Because the men of the Latter Times, that is to say the men we are, living in a corrupt epoch far removed from that in which the Buddha taught, are no longer capable of deeply understanding Buddhist wisdom. You know that Buddhists admit of three decreasing periods from the point of view of our capacity to understand Buddhism. These are counted from the death of Buddha. The first period, which extends over a thousand years, is called 'period of True Buddhism.' The second, also of a thousand years, is called 'the period of the copied Buddhism.' The third, in which we are living, we men of the Latter Times, is that of degeneracy. The world is nowadays too degenerate to understand great things. We merely demand of men an act of faith in Buddha—and Buddha will save them. Our doctrine is based on the sutras of Amithâba (Japanese : *Muryô-jukyô-kammuryôjukyô-Amidakyô*), in which Buddha promises the access of the Pure Land to those who invoke him. On Buddha's part it is Charity. On our part it is an act of Faith."

"What difference should one see between Amida and Buddha ?" I asked.

"Amida is the Japanese term by which we express the Sanskrit term *Amithâba* (Infinite Light). Buddha came on earth to save us. Under that form he is the historical Buddha, that is, Sakyamuni, or Shaka. To speak only of Amida, he can be defined in two ways : a philosophical way, on which I will insist, and a vulgar way. From the highest philosophical point of view, Amida is both *Symbol* and *Container*. He is the essence of things and unobstructed Light, Time, Space, Life. One can in this measure conceive him as eternal. But he is not a transcendent, creative God—such as God is in the Christian conception. His natural activity—he who is universal essence—consists in working for the salvation of men. The vulgar explanation is less important than the one I have just given you, but it is useful to recall it, if only to avoid misunderstandings. In the great sutra (Japanese: *Muryôjukyô*; Sanskrit: *Sukhâvativyûha*) Buddha speaks of a Bodhisattva who became Amida. This extraordinary being is called in Sanskrit Dharma Kara, and in Japanese, Hozo. This fact explains how Amida, who is, as I have just said, Space, Light, Essence, has sometimes retained the aspect of a person in the eyes of the ordinary man. But I repeat that there is no question of a creative, omnipotent God, but of a qualitative identification of the eternal notions of Space and Time with that Force which is eternally working at our salvation."

"But Space and Time may only be the creations of human thought?" I suggested.

"That would in no way affect my explanation," returned the bonze. "To make myself understood I imagine for an instant that the Moon is the symbol of Amida, and I say: 'The Moon sheds its rays everywhere, *yet its light exists only for those who look at it.*'"

"Does not the repetition of the holy name, 'Namu-Amida-Butsu,' tend to become a purely mechanical formula, void of all thought?"

"The invocation of the sacred name is not a mechanical, empty formula. It must be accompanied by an absolute sincerity of heart, and by the most complete faith in the Goodness of Amida, who has willed that all creatures shall be saved. Taking the men of the Latter Times in pity, and in order to deliver them from the suffering of the world, Amida has wished to substitute to virtue and understanding that quality of the heart which can be found amongst the most simple folk—faith in the redemptive value of his grace. For it is clear that the understanding of so profound and arduous a doctrine as Buddhism could be in this world only the privilege of a few, whereas faith and sincerity of soul are immediately accessible to all. Do not let us discredit humility, which is especially suited to the men of our time, or faith and confidence, to the benefit of intelligence, meditation and acquired merits. The little child who addresses a prayer to Buddha with all his soul has not meditated upon the sutras, nor has he reflected much upon the doctrine. Yet would you say that his words proceeded from a mechanical or stupid act? Surely not! He gives all he can with all his heart, and that also is very beautiful. Well, the men of the Latter Times resemble this child. They are weak-minded, incapable of ensuring their salvation by their own thought and their own merit. That is why we merely ask them for their heart, for their absolute confidence in the promise and mercy of Buddha —for their Faith."

"So in your sect, faith suffices, by the grace and love of Amida-Buddha, the saviour of men, to assure the latter of Paradise? Under these conditions, what essential difference do you see between your doctrine and Christianity, which also comprises a Saviour, a Paradise and only requires of men— Faith?" I asked curiously.

"In Christianity, God is all, man is nothing. According to the Jôdo and Shinshu sects, man escapes from suffering and reaches the supreme goal, not, it is true, by his own merit, which is too weak, but thanks to the compassionate intervention of Buddha. But Buddha is a man. As I was saying to you a moment ago, Amida-Buddha can be compared to lunar light. This light is everywhere present, *but it only exists for those who look at it. If humanity did not exist, Amida-Buddha would not exist either*. Amida-Buddha exists in function to human life, and his beneficent activity is in function of men's desire to reach a refuge—salvation. In Christianity everything goes from God to man; the two terms apply to two entirely different personalities, the one being the creature of the other.

The one is All—the other nothing. In the Jôdo and Shin doctrines *a human ascent towards the Pure Land takes place.* We all become Buddha, and we are so already in a certain degree, since Amida-Buddha is space, Time, Eternal Life. But this human evasion from the sufferings of this world can, in our days and for the reasons which I have indicated to you, only take place with the actual help of Amida and not by the exclusive and proud effort of our intelligence, henceforth too weak—nor by the qualities of our heart, henceforth too corrupt.

"Let us resume the story of Saint Hônen.

"Later Hônen retired to another hermitage, at Yoshimizu —the Fountain of Joy. He hoped to live there in peace and simplicity—his thought solely occupied with the adoration of Amida-Buddha, whose ineffable grace was to fall on mankind like a soft and beneficent dew. But his reputation had spread throughout all Japan, and numerous persons belonging to all classes of society came to him in the hope of ensuring their salvation. It must be said that the souls of the people were very troubled by historical events. Civil war had broken out, in which not only the Samurais but also the monks of many monasteries took part. In the moral confusion which ensued, men were desperately seeking a faith. The success of Hônen was considerable. Aristocrats and plebeians, high dignitaries, merchants, soldiers, peasants, scholars and ignorant folk, all pressed around him, eager to hear his doctrine. All tormented souls were awed, and his words were balm to their hearts, because he preached a simple, trustful moral, announcing salvation for all. Nothing moves men as much as goodness. Hônen appeared as the mouthpiece of the infinite goodness of Buddha. It is said that criminals and prostitutes were amongst those he converted. Everybody wished to hear the good saint of the Fountain of Joy. These successes excited against him many jealous people who denounced him as being an enemy of public order, and obtained that he should be banished to a distant island.

191

"In 1207 the gentle Hônen started for his exile, at seventy-four years of age. His heart was full of serenity and he forgave his persecutors, for he thought that his exile would allow him to preach the Gospel of Amida in a region where in all probability none of the inhabitants had heard of it as yet. He would thus save more souls. On leaving he addressed the following words of farewell to his disciples and friends: *What matters separation? Nothing can stop the triumph of the reign of Buddha's grace. Keep your faith. Be confident. We will meet again in the light of the Pure Land.*'

"Four years later Hônen was forgiven. The gentle saint returned still smiling amongst his disciples, who welcomed him with the joy of men who perceived light once more after waiting long in the darkness. All communed in faith and in the hope of eternal beatitude. But this joy was of short duration, for in 1212, at the age of seventy-nine, Hônen fell ill and had to lie down. His disciples surrounded him, giving him all possible care, but each day the saint lost strength. He asked for his brush and writing-desk, and proceeded to write what is called *The Testament of Faith on a Single Sheet*. Here is this text:

"'Meditation, the spiritual method of wise men of ancient times, is not our spiritual method.

"'Science and wisdom, which formed the thought of the wise men of yore, do not form our thought.

"'The faith that Buddha, invoked by us, will welcome us in his Paradise, forms our certitude of our coming salvation. Our only practice consists in repeating the holy name *with confidence*.

"'All that we can teach proceeds from our absolute faith in the will of Buddha to make us be reborn in Paradise. Those of you who are scholars, and who have studied the words of Shaka, must consider themselves as ignorant. We are all equal by the effect of our common faith, and of our confidence in the grace of Amida-Buddha. In common with those who know nothing of doctrines, and taking no account of the methods of wise men, let us put all our heart into the practice which consists in uttering the name of Amida-Buddha.'

"On the day of his death the gentle saint, who was surrounded by his disciples, kept repeating the sacred name, 'Namu-Amida-Butsu, Namu-Amida-Butsu,' till his strength failed him. He said, thinking of Amida: 'His light bathes the world.' The voice repeating the name of Amida-Buddha became more and more weak, then hushed altogether. His disciples continued repeating for a long time: 'Namu-Amida-Butsu.' But the lips of the saint were silent for ever. His gentle face was smiling at the Pure Land."

3. *Mr Mochizuki, bonze and professor at the Faculty of Letters of Taishô, lecturer on the Jôdo doctrine, expounds the Jôdo ideal*

"The supreme ideal of Buddhism lies in access to Nirvâna. The Jôdo ideal is to go to the Paradise of the Pure Land after death. The doctrine is characterised by the following points. We are all men of our time, mediocre and stupid, and incapable of understanding the far too wise and too superior thought contained in the Buddhist texts. The virtues and practices which Buddhist wisdom exacts of us are also too difficult and far above our capacities or our feeble means and merits. The Jôdo doctrine and its practices are within the reach of all. The most ignorant can come to us. Truth and the profound ideal of Buddha are concentrated within the Pure Land which is the issue of the great vehicle.

"What should one do in order to be reborn in the Pure Land after death? Nothing is simpler. It is merely necessary to have pronounced *ten times* during one's life, heartily and in all faith and sincerity, the formula of invocation: 'Namu-Amida-Butsu.' If you have done this the access to Paradise is yours by right—that is to say, you accede to the state of Buddha. He who for some reason or other has not invoked the holy name cannot become a Buddha.

"But how can one define the Pure Land? When we say Land this naturally does not mean an ordinary land, a geographical country. By the term Pure Land, or Paradise of

Amida, we express the idea of an unlimited, abstract land. It is Nirvâna, the supreme state of Buddhist perfection, or Buddhahood. Ordinary words fail to express the absolute. A land, a branch of a tree or a leaf, seen in the light of profound truth, are not ordinary land, branch or leaf. The Paradise of the Pure Land is Amida himself, who is essence, time, space and absolute wisdom. If I may resume myself thus, I would say that Amida-Buddha is the absolute, and that his Paradise is also an absolute notion. To reach it we must rely upon the help of the absolute, *upon grace*. The absolute, which resides in the name of Amida-Buddha which we recite, is willed by Amida-Buddha, who *is* absolute.

"In practice the Jôdo method consists in this: Let us be humble, full of modesty and humility, for we are merely poor, incapable creatures, who are born and who die, burdened by faults and by crimes. Let us believe in the redemptive virtue of Amida-Buddha, and let us live in that idea. *The only means of salvation which is opened to us is an act of Faith—an act of the heart, and not of the intelligence.*"

4. *The Monastery of Chion-in, or the Bell of Amida*

The Chion-in, great monastery of the Jôdo sect, founded by Hônen in the thirteenth century, rises on the flank of a hill, in a marvellous site. In order to reach it I climbed numerous steps and did not regret doing so. Along the road I spoke to some pilgrims who were also on their way there. Children, accompanied by their mothers, smiled at me in passing. The soul of Saint Hônen seems to hover over this blessed land. Am I being prejudiced? But it seems to me that the worship of Amida has communicated an unaccustomed joyfulness to all minds. Here those who would pretend that Buddhism is pessimistic would find themselves in the wrong. It is true that, for the followers of the Jôdo sect, as for all Buddhists, life remains an ocean of suffering. . . . Nevertheless, the haven is in sight. . . .

Chion-in Temple

Magnificent alleys, bordered with old trees and cherry trees, lead us to the temples. I cross monumental gateways. All the buildings are not of the thirteenth century; several were reconstructed in the eighteenth century, and there are many modern additions. Shall I confess it? The sight of these successive reconstructions in Japanese temples does not displease me. Nothing proves better the living value of Buddhism. Nothing demonstrates better that Japanese temples are not architectural constructions like others, but the expression of a progressing thought, and themes offered to our spiritual needs. Their aesthetic value is in function of spirit. Here the primacy of the spiritual is not a theory but a fact, which is instinctively realised. That which constitutes the permanent value of this old monastery is the thought of Hônen, everywhere present, and also those adorable statues of Amida, the golden treasures of the sanctuary whose sight alone suffices to remind one of the reign of Buddhist love and of the Pure Land. There are also in the *Shuei-do* two charming golden altars, one of which supports an image of Amida by Eshin-Sozu, and the other a large golden statue of Amida by the brothers Kebunshi and Kebundo. To the right stands Monju [1] the sage, dressed as a bonze, who reminds me of the letter of introduction borne by the youth Hônen when he presented himself at the monastery of Mount Hiei: "*I send you the image of Monju.*" In another more recently built temple I noted an altar all agleam with gold, and on which was placed an enormous statue of Buddha.

On the 24th of each month the monumental and celebrated Bell of Chion-in peals for an exceptional service. At that moment it seems as if the golden Amidas express themselves by this voice, and send forth, on infinite vibrations, the good news of a promised deliverance calling the universe to prayer. "*Namu-Amida-Butsu!*" At the sound of this bell, how many Japanese, and, amongst them, how many poor, unhappy people, collect their thoughts and murmur, "*Namu-Amida-*

---

[1] A disciple of Sakyamuni, renowned for his wisdom.

Butsu!" It is thus that all the poetry of the Angelus appears to me in this land of Nippon. And I say to myself that if the religious evolution of Japan results in aspects so analogous to our own, it may be because the Japanese and the European races possess in common many psychological elements which command, and, so to speak, pre-ordain their *entente* and their destiny.

5. *The Temple of Kurodani, or the Hermitage of Saint Hônen*

The temple of Kurodani, founded at the end of the thirteenth century and rebuilt in the seventeenth, rises on the side of a wooded hill amidst a charming landscape. My first thought is that it was on this very spot that the humble hut of the hermit Hônen stood in the past. I imagine the hermit in his retreat as one can see him on the kakemono preserved in the temple, murmuring with bent head and dreamy gaze, *"Namu-Amida-Butsu."* It is said that he repeated the holy name sixty thousand times a day as a sort of breviary concentrated into a few syllables.

But the Kurodani temple does not merely perpetuate the touching remembrance of Hônen-Shonin; it also proclaims the glory and benefactions of Amida-Butsu. These three successive visions pass before my eyes during the visit to the sanctuary—the saintly hermit, Hônen; Amida, the radiant; and Kumagaï Naozane, the repentant sinner, of whom I will speak later. These form the spiritual Trinity of the Kurodani: Hônen, Amida, Kumagaï—the Doctrine, Buddha and Sinning Man.

Pilgrims can admire at the Kurodani several wonderful kakemonos in which the whole history of Saint Hônen is retraced in high colours, with the same minute details which characterise the paintings of our old masters, and which are infinitely touching because sincere. The artist who created these masterpieces is unknown. Looking at them I saw depicted all that had been told me: Hônen on Mount Hiei, in the Kurodani, in exile, etc. Here the amateur of art would fatally become Buddhist. The pilgrims also halt before the golden reliquary containing the statue of the saint, carved by himself in 1207, the year of his exile, and before the kakemonos of the fifty Buddhas whose bodies and aureoles consist of the inscription "Namu-Amida-Butsu," repeated a thousand times. Then the pilgrim bows before the radiant glory of Amida.

In the chief temple of the sanctuary the altar, which is a mass of gold surrounded by magnificent silken banners, gives the impression of a radiant apparition illuminating the world. I feel bathed in a celestial atmosphere. Reason abdicates. Faith, confidence in a wisdom higher than our own, take peaceful possession of the hearts of all present. Lastly, the pilgrims find at the Kurodani a celebrated example of the grace Amida reserves for sinners. It is in this temple that the warrior Kumagaï retired in despair of having, during battle, severed the head of Atsumori, a young noble of sixteen, belonging to the Taira clan.

Legend and literature have popularised this story. In the delightful garden of the sanctuary one can still see the pool into which Kumagaï threw his armour before taking the habit of a monk. We have all, each of us, destroyed and sinned. Each of us is responsible in his conscience for the innocent head of an Atsumori. But the mercy of Amida extends to us all.

CHAPTER X

THE SHINSHU SECT

(1) The Shinshu Sect. (2) A conversation with Messrs Kenryo Kawasaki and Fujioka, bonzes of the sect. A simplified indulgent religion, adapted to modern life. (3) The Shinshu doctrine according to the popular text-book of the sect: (a) The Life and Work of its founder, the Shonin Shinran, called "the bald man with the simple heart"; (b) The doctrine of absolute faith in the saviour, Amida-Buddha, who promises us the Paradise of the Pure Land, where we become Buddhas, on the sole condition that we invoke him sincerely by pronouncing his name; (c) The two ways; (d) Amida wishes to save men for the love he bears them; (e) The Pure Land; (f) What is required of the faithful. (4) A visit to the *Hongwanjis* of Kyôto, celebrated sanctuaries of the sect. (5) Mr K. Kawasaki, bonze, demonstrates to me that if all men believed in *Karma*, universal peace would be established. (6) Mr Tsumaki, bonze and professor at the Faculty of Letters of the Nishi-Hongwanji, expounds the practical character of Shinshu and situates it amongst the different sects. (7) Mr Shugaku Yamabe, bonze, insists upon the analogies and differences existing between Buddhism and Christianity: Amida is only Love, not Judge. (8) Mr Gessho-Sasaki, bonze, President of the Otani University, Kyôto, explains religious life and the conception of the 'ego' according to the Shinshu doctrine. (9) Mr Otani, bonze of the Shinshu Sect, gives us his opinion about the moral value of Shinshu and the place it occupies in relation to Christianity. (10) A Psalm beneath the Dew.

1. *The Shinshu Sect*

This sect, whose complete name is Jôdo-Shinshu (True Sect of the Pure Land), professes the same principle as the Jôdo sect. Like the latter it is a Japanese creation. Its founder was the Shonin [1] Shinran, who lived from 1173 to 1262. Its two principal texts are the *Daï Muryojukyō* and the *Amidakyō* (Sanskrit: *Sukhâvativyûha*). These are also the canonical texts

---

[1] Title given to virtuous bonzes.

of the Jôdo sect, and in them Amida promises Paradise to whomsoever will have invoked him *sincerely* by pronouncing his name.

The Shinshu sect is the most important sect of Japan. It counts ten branches which all practise the same doctrine. Those of the Hongwanji (the original vow), which possess the celebrated and magnificent temples of the same name, and in particular those of Kyôto, are the best known and the wealthiest of these branches.

The Hompa Hongwanji branch alone possesses 10,800 temples, monasteries or chapels, and counts something like 19,400 priests, either ordained or probationers, more than 7,200,000 perpetual subscribers and 140,000 occasional or Shintô members. Its budget exceeds 1,300,000 yen, and the annual revenues of its incorporated temples, monasteries and religious associations exceed 5,400,000 yen. Besides founding the Faculty of Ryûkoku, the Hompa Hongwanji branch of Shinshu has created numerous schools, colleges and organisations of social welfare (relief for the poor, old and sick people, and the victims of war, legal help, feminine organisations), with a membership exceeding 400,000.

The Otani Hongwanji branch possesses more than 8400 temples and monasteries, counts more than 30,000 priests, 790,000 perpetual members and 570,000 occasional members. It has created a Faculty, numerous establishments of primary and secondary education, social works (protection of childhood and motherhood, workhouses, co-operative societies, medical assistance and back-to-the-land schemes, etc.).

The other branches still possess between them more than 1800 temples, and group about 3,000,000 perpetual subscribers. Most of the branches have many possessions such as fields, rivers, forests and real estate.

2. *A conversation with the bonzes Kenryo Kawasaki and Fujioka*

I had several interviews with Mr Kenryo Kawasaki, bonze of the Hongwanji Sanctuary of Kyôto. He is a very popular priest in Japan, and his competence, modesty and charming discretion of manners impressed me deeply. The venerable priest lent himself very kindly, and with much good will, to my philosophical inquest, and even encouraged me to question him, whilst he in turn plied me with questions concerning the moral and religious dispositions of my compatriots towards Buddhism. He was generally accompanied by Mr Fujioka, bonze of the same sect, with whom I later became very friendly, and whose obligingness and gentleness of character were untiring.

The bonzes of this sect all profess that one must live practically, according "to the honourable customs of one's time." They admit the marriage of priests; they eat both fish and meat, and the relations one may have with them in daily life are hereby considerably simplified. I remember a delicious luncheon during which we partook together not only of "autumn dew soup," but also of "*shajimi*" (raw coryphene), whilst conversing of Amida and the Pure Land.

The doctrine of the sect rests on the same principles and on the same texts as the Jôdo doctrine. The men of our times being too corrupt to reach Nirvâna by their own merits, are merely asked to possess a sincere faith in the merciful will of Amida-Buddha, who has promised the faithful that they shall be born again after their death in the Paradise of the Pure Land, that is to say, to make Buddhas of them.

This promise, which is called the "original vow" of Amida, can be found in the following form in the canonical text:

"I will not obtain perfect understanding if one of the living beings of the Ten Points, who believe in me with the true thought and desire of being born in my country, and who repeat my name ten times in thought, was not born again in my Pure Land (Sanskrit: *Sukhâvati*)."

One knows that the formula "*Namu-Amida-Butsu*" or, more simply, "*Namu-Amida-Bu*," is used for the repetition of the saint's name.

Mr Kenryo Kawasaki was kind enough to offer me a copy

of *The Fundamental Teachings of the True Sect of the Pure Land*. In this popular text-book adopted by the sect, different points of the doctrine are explained. So many errors have been voiced concerning the worship of Amida, and the beliefs and practices of Shinshu, that the Buddhists of this sect decreed it useful and prudent to make a résumé of the essential teachings, at least for the use of beginners. I quote, further, one of the most characteristic passages of this text. Of our conversation on Buddhism and on the sect of the Pure Land I will merely note here the following declarations, which preface and complete the explanations contained in the pre-mentioned document.

"It is in nowise necessary," said Mr Kenryo Kawasaki, "to retire from the world, or to practise special austerities to become a perfect Buddhist. Our founder, the Shonin Shinran, was married and lived in the world. Our duty is to live according to the family, professional and national morals of our social station, and not to distinguish ourselves from other men by exterior acts or manifestations. The believer of the Shinshu sect can lead the life of his own choice provided it is an honest life. He can be a merchant, an industrialist, an official, soldier, peasant, workman or fisherman. He *must* be a good citizen, a good husband, a good father and a good son. Buddhism is not in antagonism with the exactions of modern life and civilisation. On the contrary, modern civilisation would be incomplete if it was obliged to reject all doctrine and all hope of a spiritual order."

"What hope can Buddhism offer to men ?" I asked. "When an unfortunate man addresses a prayer to Buddha, imploring his aid, Buddha can surely not wish to satisfy him, since Buddha is in Nirvâna, and, in consequence, ignores desire."

"Your question denotes that you place yourself from a Christian point of view," answered the bonze. "Buddhist prayer and Christian prayer are acts which cannot be compared the one with the other. The Christian wishes to *obtain some advantage from God*, and if he fails to obtain it, I fear the consequences his deception might have for him. The Buddhist *asks nothing of Buddha*. His prayer is an act of faith, a homage, an *affirmation*, an effort towards the purification of his consciousness. There is nothing to be done against unhappiness, the tribulations of life, sickness or death. One must accept the inevitable. But, according to our sect, sincere faith and an absolute confidence in Amida-Buddha always find their recompense after death by the access of the faithful to the Paradise of the Pure Land. The hope offered to men is not that of a mediocre advantage in the course of this life, but the certitude of a complete and early deliverance. One only demands of the believer his faith, his confidence in Buddha's mercy. Our doctrine is so simple, and our practices are so simplified, that the man most absorbed by modern life can come to us."

I next asked the two bonzes the question I had previously asked the bonze Kanei Okamoto, of the Jôdo sect.

"Since, according to your sect, Buddhism exacts from the believer faith in an adored Saviour, what essential difference do you establish between Christianity and your doctrine?"

I received the same answer—*i.e.* that Buddhism does not recognise any omnipotent God exterior to the creature, to whom He dictates his duties. *Buddhism is exclusively a human, moral and philosophical system.* Amida-Buddha, the Saviour, is in function with humanity which needs to be saved. And Mr Fujioka resumed this in the following impressive formula:

"*It is not because there is a Buddha that Humanity exists. It is because Humanity exists that there is a Buddha.*"

3. *The Doctrine of the Shinshu sect according to the popular text-book*

The life and work of its founder, the Shonin Shinran, "the bald man with the simple heart."

The doctrine of the True Sect of the Pure Land was preached by the venerable Sakyamuni himself. Nevertheless it is only a little more than seven hundred and fifty years ago, that is to say, only at the epoch when the Shonin Shinran, founder of the True Sect, sojourned in the province of Hidachi, to spread there the new Buddhist teaching, that this sect was recognised as such and formed a distinct Buddhistic organisation.

The Shonin Shinran was born in 1173 in the village of Hino, near Kyôto. His family belonged to the all-powerful Fugiwara clan. As the eldest son of a noble family, he could have aspired to some high office, or he could have abandoned himself to the delights of a purely worldly existence. The death of his parents when he was still a mere child made a deep impression upon his young soul, which, being naturally sensitive, meditated from then onwards on the uncertainty of human life. At nine years of age he left his home to enter the Buddhist monastery of Shorene-in, at Awada-Guchi. Then the Shonin went to Mount Hiei, and there he pursued his studies under the direction of professors of the Tendai sect. He also strove to penetrate the doctrines of the other sects, but was unable to discover the true way leading to deliverance from this world of affliction. At the age of twenty-five he was named *Monezeki*, or first priest of the *Shôkôin*. But we find him at the age of twenty-nine years still in the same state of uncertainty. At that epoch he used to address prayers daily to Kwannon Bosatsu in order that light might be given him. At last he had a vision of the Bosatsu, and obeying the instructions he received from her, he went to Yoshimidzu to be taught by the Shonin Hônen. Now, according to the Hônen doctrine, any creature, however sinful it may be, is certain to be saved and to bathe in the light of Amida and obtain a place in the eternal and imperishable Land of Happiness. It need only believe in Amida-Buddha, and, renouncing all the small present and past cares of this world, take shelter between Amida's liberating hands, so mercifully extended towards all creatures, and utter His name with a complete sincerity of heart.

On hearing this doctrine every shadow of spiritual doubt

disappeared from the soul of the Shonin Shinran. At that moment, and for ever after, he understood that Amida was the name of his true father, and he could not help remarking that during the twenty-nine years of his existence his life had been directed by the desire of salvation of this true father who, since the beginning of the world, had ceaselessly striven to save his sinful child, thanks to his eternal grace. The Shonin was filled with a joy and gratitude impossible to describe. Renouncing his preceding attachment to the beliefs of the Tendai sect, he embraced the faith of the sect of the Pure Land, or, in other words, abandoning the uncertainty of salvation by "one's own self" (*Jiriki*, *i.e.* personal power), he became an adept of "salvation by a power other than one's own" (*Tariki*, *i.e.* "power of another").

Then he resigned his post of *Monezeki*, and, becoming a black-robed Buddhist monk, he built himself a humble hut at Okazaki and continued to learn of the Shonin Hônen.

In October 1203 our Shonin resolved to follow the advice of Hônen, and he married so as to prove to all that a family man could be saved just like a bachelor monk. He therefore married Princess Tamahi, the daughter of Prince Kanezane Kujô, former Prime Minister of the Emperor. Shinran was then thirty-one years of age, and the Princess was only eighteen. His marriage was in reality celebrated to dissipate the then predominant religious doubts concerning the final redemption of those secular married men who, living in the midst of their families, had not succeeded in destroying their passions to their very root. Prince Kujô was one of those who shared this uncertainty, and our Shonin gave the practical demonstration of his conviction by marrying one of the Prince's daughters, and leading the life of a man of the world. The following year there was born to him a son whom he called Hâne-i.

When Hônen was exiled, Shinran, who was his first disciple, was unable to escape the same lot, and he was exiled in his turn to Kokubo, in the province of Echigo. There he displayed an indefatigable zeal as missionary.

Five years passed, then, in November 1211, the Court published an edict putting an end to Shinran's banishment. It was then that he adopted the name of *Gutoku* (literally "the bald man with the simple heart"). By this appellation he intended to fix, on the one hand, his situation amongst the disciples of Buddha, which was neither that of a priest nor of a layman—and, on the other hand, affirm that he was merely a simple-hearted Buddhist, deprived of wisdom, intelligence or learning. The name Gotoku signified that he sincerely considered himself an ignorant and sinning man.

In January 1217 he settled at Inada, in the province of Idachi, and began to write his *Kyo-Gyo-Shine-Sho* (the teaching, the practice, the faith and the goal), in which he expounds the fundamental principles of the True Sect of the Pure Land. This was his first as well as his most important work. Its object was to safeguard from all possible misunderstanding the true signification of the principles of the sect, which had been often grossly misconstrued after Hônen's death. Shinran finished his book in 1224, at the age of fifty-two. The following year he erected a temple at Takada. There, as at Inada, he devoted himself untiringly to the cause of the True Sect of the Pure Land. He next returned to the capital. He was then sixty years old. He was never tired of preaching the Good Law of the Merciful Buddha to all who sought him either as a spiritual guide, or to solicit the help of his teachings. To those unable to visit him in person he sent letters describing the joyous life of a fervent Buddhist. Towards the end of his existence, the Shonin Shinran wrote divers messages for those adepts of his faith who were deprived of instruction—messages in which he expounded in very simple terms the principles of the True Sect.

In 1262 he reached the great age of ninety, and on the 23rd of November of the same year he began to feel the first symptoms of illness. But he did not complain, speaking only of the deep love of Amida, whose name he uttered with the greatest devotion. On the 27th he made his farewell to his disciples, telling them that he would await them in the Pure Land when it was time for them to join him. He then continued to murmur the name of Amida. The next day, following the example of the great Muni of Sakya, at the instant of his Nirvâna he asked to be placed in a chamber of the Zenho-in, with his head turned towards the north, facing the west, and resting on his right side. At midday his murmuring ceased gently. He had definitely departed for the Land of Light, and it is said that a suave perfume of an indescribable sweetness permeated the chamber, whilst in the western sky appeared a white light which resembled the unfolding of a large piece of immaculate silk.

A brief outline of the doctrine and practice according to the Kyo-Gyo-Shine-Sho (teaching, practice, faith, goal) by the Shonin Shinran.

(i) *The Teaching.*—Amida assumed one day a human form and came on earth to save us from sin and ignorance. He incarnated himself under the name of Sakyamuni.

The true reason of his coming on earth was to establish the basis of the True Sect of the Pure Land. In other words, we may say that the True Sect is the direct revelation of the Buddha Amida.

(ii) *The Practice.*—We know the name of Amida by the preaching of Sakyamuni, and we know *that in this name is enclosed Amida's strength of desire to save all creatures.* To hear this name is to hear the voice of salvation saying, "Have confidence in me and I will save you surely," words which Amida addresses directly to us. This signification is contained in the name of Amida. We must therefore express to him our deepest gratitude by reciting his name according to his will, having listened to the call of our Father so full of love and compassion. The formula of recitation is: "*Namu-Amida-Butsu* or *Bu.*"

Whereas all our other acts are more or less tainted with

impurity, the repetition of *"Namu-Amida-Butsu"* is truly an act exempt from all impurity, *for it is not we ourselves who recite it, but Amida himself who, giving us his own name, obliges us to repeat it.*

(iii) *Faith.*—When we hear the name of Amida we acquire belief in a certain salvation, belief which also comes to us by the grace of Amida.

When we think of Amida's desire to save us, we become incapable of dissimulating to ourselves the insufficiencies and lies of our inner life, and we understand from henceforth that it is impossible for us to act as if we were wise. This is the proof that the pure desire of Buddha, exempt from all lies, has descended upon us.

From the moment we hear the name of Amida and abandon ourselves to his will, only hoping to obtain our salvation through his grace, we gain spiritual peace. This sentiment would not exist if the desire of Amida to save all people had not affirmed itself in us.

From the moment we believe in our salvation, through the grace of Amida, we awaken in us the desire of being reborn in his Pure Land, and we are happy because we are convinced that this wish will be realised. This is an effect of the overwhelming love of Amida, who invites us to rejoin him in the Pure Land.

This is why one must conclude that if we entrust ourselves to Amida for our salvation, that act is entirely due to his grace and in nowise to our own personal efforts. Indeed this faith in Amida, this sentiment which subordinates us to his action, is nothing else than a consequence of his own will.

(iv) *The Goal.*—As soon as our belief in our salvation by Amida has been awakened and consolidated, our destiny is fixed. *We will be reborn in the Pure Land, and will become Buddhas.* It is said that we shall then be wholly bathed in the light of Amida, and that under his loving direction our life will overflow with an indescribable joy—gift of the Buddha.

We have therefore no need to implore the gods or the Buddhas to grant us more happiness in this world, for do we not already enjoy all the happiness we can reach here ? If we still have to endure unhappiness, this results from faults we have committed in the past, and no prayer can save us from it. It is only after our rebirth in the Pure Land that we will be allowed to live a life absolutely devoid of suffering.

At the end of our earthly life we throw off the last trace of this corrupt existence and, being reborn in the Land of Purity and Happiness, we obtain the Illumination of Buddha. The Land of Happiness is the Garden of Nirvâna. Those who are born therein obtain the Great Illumination of Nirvâna, enjoy eternal life, and are for ever delivered from the fetters of Birth and Death. *They can then incarnate themselves indefinitely, and return to this world of suffering to deliver other creatures from sin and ignorance.* All these innumerable happinesses which we then enjoy come solely from a unique source : *the grace of the Buddha Amida.*

The Two Ways: the Holy Way and the Pure Land.

Buddhism is one of the most complex of religions. Its founder, Sakyamuni, taught his followers by different means according to their aptitudes and characters. Buddha opened to his disciples different means of approach amongst which we generally distinguish two principal ways of salvation. The one leads directly to the goal, which is to escape from this world of suffering. The other is only a provisory way which prepares one to enter finally into the way of truth. It is indispensable that students of Buddhism should remember this distinction.

Buddhism is divided into two principal schools. That of the Lesser Vehicle (*Hinayana*) and that of the Greater Vehicle (*Mahayana*). The first addresses itself to those disciples and Pratyeka-Buddhas (individual Buddhas), who are content with attaining a comparatively mediocre result. The second school, that of the Greater Vehicle, teaches the way of Great Illumination, permitting us to reach Buddhahood. The latter must therefore be considered superior to the former. According to the School of the Greater Vehicle we can also distinguish the doctrine called the Way of the Wise (*Shôdomone*) and the Pure Way (*Jôdomone*). The Way of the Wise is the teaching which leads a Buddhist to wisdom here below. It exacts that he should practise all virtues, and extirpate his passions. The Way of the Pure Land teaches us that we become Buddhas simply by being born again in the Pure Land of Amida. According to the Way of the Wise, you must attain Illumination by your own strength, which is very difficult to do. This is why this method is called *Jiriki-Kyō* (doctrine of personal salvation) or *Manegyô-do* (the way which is practised with difficulty). By following the Way of the Pure Land we must reach the means of attaining Illumination by a power other than our own, *i.e.* by the grace of Amida. This latter doctrine is called *Tariki-Kyō* (strength of another), or doctrine which teaches the means of salvation without appealing to personal merit, or *Igyo-do*, the way which is easily practicable.

It is almost impossible for any man not endowed with extraordinary intelligence and wisdom to follow the Way of the Wise. For creatures such as ourselves, born in this century far removed from Buddha's time, the best method is to follow the Way of the Pure Land, by having faith in salvation through the grace of Amida.

Amida wishes to save men out of love for them.

In the True Sect of the Pure Land, we discover the true and universal love of Amida, who wished to save all creatures from suffering and ignorance. His love is the net of infinite mercy cast into the sea of miseries in order to catch there the ignorant rather than the wise, and the sinner rather than the just man. This infinite love and mercy reside eternally in Amida–Buddha, whose will to save all creatures knows no limit, and who, for this very reason, has been called *Amitayûs* (life eternal). His power of salvation is borne in his light. Although invisible to our limited sight, his light is continually shedding its rays upon all creatures endowed with sensibility, and leads them untiringly towards faith. Those whose faith in the saving power of Amida has been awakened, are immediately bathed in his light, and destined to be borne again in the Pure Land after their death. The Light of Amida, whose merciful solicitude watches over all creatures, reaches into all regions of the universe and knows no limit in space. It is for this reason that Amida has also been called *Amithâba* (infinite light). His desire to ensure the salvation of all living men is infinite, not only as to time, but also as to space. From thence his two aspects: *Amitayûs* (eternal life), and *Amithâba* (infinite light).

Amida is the Father of all creatures. He is the One Being, and since the beginning of all things he has been working at the task of saving the world.

The Pure Land to which we are carried by the "Barque of Love," manned by Amida.

This earthly life is filled with sin and suffering. Neither the wise nor the ignorant are out of reach of sin. Noble and poor alike are subjected to suffering. He who believes himself stainless is either mad or an idiot. Even when, according to the judgment of our ignorance, we believe ourselves happy, it is quite possible that we are mistaken, for in the eyes of Buddha our apparent happiness may be only real suffering. In a world of impurities such as our own, it is impossible to find a true state of peace or happiness. Where can we therefore discover a region containing no pain? Let us turn our gaze towards Amida who shows us his Land of Purity and Happiness, in which the sufferings and tribulations of this world no longer exist. It is a place of perpetual smiles flowing from the source of all happiness. There one meets neither suffering nor sin, only beauty, goodness and joy. Those who are reborn there enjoy unending bliss. They are endowed not only with infinite freedom and wisdom, but also with that pure love and compassion which gives them the power to save all the creatures of the world from pain. This immense happiness, devolved to those of the Pure Land, is the result of Amida's love and of his desire to save human beings.

The True Sect of the Pure Land teaches the doctrine of the Pure Land, or the Way of Truth which ensures the believer of being born again after death in the Pure Land of Amida.

One can conceive several ways leading to the Pure Land of Buddha. Some are narrow and arid. The wide and sure way is that which leads us to the certitude of being reborn in the Pure Land.

The Pure Land of Amida is a land of perfect beauty founded on truth and goodness. Not a single particle of impurity can penetrate it. Now, whatever may be the merits of a moral human conscience dwelling in a corrupt human heart, one can never affirm that it is absolutely free from all trace of impurity. It is therefore impossible for us to be born again in the Pure Land on the strength of our own personal merits and will. Whoever aspires to be born there must absolutely abdicate all personal pretension. The will of Amida leaves no doubt as to this point. This pure and magnificent Land of Happiness is reserved for us. Amida, desirous of seeing us join him in the Pure Land, ceaselessly pours his light upon us so that we grow in wisdom, become conscious of our sins and lies, and cherish the desire of being reborn in the Land of Goodness and of Truth.

Thus, it is solely thanks to the supreme light of Amithâba, "infinite light," that we become conscious of the blackness of our own hearts, and that an aspiration towards the Land of Eternal Light awakens in us. After having brought our intelligences to this point, and while we completely ignore his existence, Amida is already calling us to him, saying: "Listen to my name of Goodness and Truth. Free your consciousness from the impurities and the lies which darken your hearts, and entrust your destiny wholly into my care. I will save you from sin and ignorance!" Those who, realising their sinful state, listen to Amida's appeal, comply to his wish, and seize with perfect trust his outstretched hands, are embraced by the Good and the Truth of his saving grace, and are delivered after their death from the corrupt body and spirit they now possess. They will be born again in the Land of Happiness and Purity where they will receive infinite wisdom and love.

Without the love and grace of Amida, who wishes to save all creatures, we would have no possibility of being born again into the Pure Land. That is why the true way one should follow to obtain this rebirth in Buddha's country, consists in crossing the Sea of Suffering in the barque of Love manned by Amida.

What is asked of the faithful?—Faith and nothing more.

What faith does the True Sect exact of its adepts? Very little. Compliance with the desire of Amida which can be expressed thus : "*Trust yourselves to me in all sincerity of heart, and you will be saved.*" So let us trust in his grace. Let us take shelter in his merciful arms in the hope of being saved in the future life. Amida is the guide of all the Buddhas. It is he who holds the key to all the mysteries of existence. If we prostrate ourselves before him in all humility, all the gods and Buddhas will protect us from all evil. *The believers of the True Sect who address their prayers to a Bodhisattva or to a Buddha other than Amida, are in the wrong, or lack faith in the redemptive virtue of Amida. The faith one has in a perfect being should be perfect and absolute.* That is why we must only trust ourselves to the mystery of Amida alone, since he is the mystery of mysteries, and he alone can absolutely save us.

The name of Amida is the most honourable name in the whole Universe. All the roots of goodness and all merits are contained in it, and the recitation of this name *is the most noble act one can perform in this world—and the best of acts which can be accomplished here below.* Whilst repeating the name of Amida, one understands how inferior all other acts are to this recitation. Noble, honourable and beautiful as a meritorious, moral or religious act may be to our profane eyes, it has not the power of leading us to the Pure Land, where resides Amida, who alone can deliver us.

4. A visit to the Shinshu sanctuaries of Kyôto, the Nishi-Hongwanji and the Higashi-Hongwanji

The temples of the Shinshu sect present a very grand appearance which at first rather frightens me. I fear I shall not find in them the special charm, the Buddhist charm, the perfume permeating those small sanctuaries and temples in which I have left a part of my heart. But I soon repent of this hasty impression. At the Nishi-Hongwanji, the doors, ceilings and columns are all of a perfect taste, and reveal a sense of proportion which is like a homage rendered to the poise of a peaceful soul. I have wandered in the wooden nave of the *Keyaki* where flicker dark shadows and soft lights, in the halls of golden columns decorated with lotuses, and I have meditated before the invocation to Amida traced in large golden letters on a kakemono. In this environment I understand better all that these few words, "*Namu-Amida-Butsu*," may contain of moral power. This one formula contains, in fact, as I was told, the whole of Buddhism. In the more intimate *Amida-do*, of rather smaller proportions, before the portraits of Shotoku-Taishi and of Hônen, a thousand remembrances culled from my lessons, lectures and pilgrimages come back to my mind. Let us give up judging these things as a tourist and even as an artist. It is first of all necessary to learn to understand and to love.

But it must be said that in the Nishi-Hongwanji the visitor is less impressed by the temple than by the sumptuous gateway leading to the apartments, decorated with sculptures which, according to the Japanese, would require a whole day to be examined in detail. He is also deeply impressed by the halls —those immense and splendidly decorated halls. Here great art and exquisite taste have joined forces. These halls follow each other without an overcrowding of objects, like a series of fairy-like yet sober visions, where each marvel of art, painting, sculpture, ironwork, lacquered colonnade, detaches itself without being overladen. We are indeed in presence of a *Force*, of a *Thought* which is sure of itself. It is the Vatican of Buddhism. Here splendour is not pride but in function of the immense universal rôle of the idea—of Faith.

The decoration of the first hall, which represents bamboos and birds, against a golden background, is extraordinarily masterly. Great painters, such as Kano Kyokei and Yusetsu, decorated other halls, the former with wild geese, the latter with chrysanthemums. Cedar doors marvellously carved are decorated with great violet cords. But the larger room "of two hundred and fifty mats" especially provokes my admiration by its harmonious dimensions, its sober structure, its decorated panels, its lacquered columns, and by the majesty and amplitude of its architectural conception. It is a Council Chamber. Indeed, important assemblies have been held there. Predications are given there. It is also in this magnificent hall that one assisted in former days at the representations of Nô, those lyrical and Buddhist mysteries which were played in the neighbouring courtyard. My imagination resuscitated for a moment those celebrated masked actors of yore describing heraldic gestures before a pine tree, the obligatory setting, amidst symbolic accessories, and the blue smoke of incense. I see them measuring their slow dances according to the traditional rhythm—a whole art in itself—in such plays as *The Meeting at Chara*, a scene of the transitory glory of the great ones of the earth, and which ends in Buddhist wisdom—or *The Dwarf Trees*, in which an Emperor, disguised as a monk, wanders in the snow and is helped by some poor folk in the name of Buddhist charity.

When I come back to reality, still in that splendid hall, I see the immense picture of Tanyu which represents a reception of Chinese Ambassadors on a golden background. This composition, majestic but easy in style, makes one think of the Veronese, and lends to the hall a sort of official character. I have distinctly the impression of being in the presence of a religion freed from popular puerilities—whose chiefs are also politicians—and which aims at universality, like Catholicism.

We continue our pilgrimage by a visit to the Higashi Hongwanji, a vast modern edifice built in 1895. It is the largest temple in Japan. It alone would suffice to attest the sincerity of the Shinshu sect. It was built, we are told, with the subscriptions of the faithful, which amounted to several million of *yen*. The pieces of wood forming its framework were erected with the help of twenty-nine stout ropes made of the plaited hair of women worshippers who had sacrificed their locks as a pledge of faith, for the building of this new temple dedicated to Amida-Buddha, Saviour of the World.

The pious visitors then go and pray in the temples of Nishi-Otani and Higashi-Otani, where rest the earthly remains of the Shonin Shinran.

5. *Mr Kenryo Kawasaki, bonze of the Hongwanji, demonstrates to me that if all men believed in Karma the foundations of Universal Peace would be laid*

I took advantage of Mr Kenryo Kawasaki's kindness to pursue my investigations.

"Tell me how Shinshu, which aims at playing an important moral part in modern life, and whose optimistic conceptions have sometimes been compared with those of Christianity, has succeeded in adapting the classic notions of Buddhism, which it does not deny, to its practical ends?"

Then Mr Kenryo Kawasaki proceeded to expound his ideas on the *Karma* and the *ego* in function to human fraternity, universal peace, and to the dominating preoccupations of our times. His thought, in spite of the technical expressions and classifications it makes use of, never loses sight of the goal, which is the good of humanity. It is characteristic of the Shinshu attitude to strive to avoid the shoal of exclusively specu-lative philosophies to return directly and practically to actual human needs—such as the solidarity of mankind, charitable duties, racial equality and the disparition of the causes of conflict.

"The fact of being born a man," remarked Mr Kenryo Kawasaki, "involves particular characteristics. There exists in us three fundamental desires : the desire of comfort, the desire of various satisfactions and the desire of liberty. These desires find their expressions in all forms of our activity. We have sought through successive lives to realise them without ever succeeding completely in doing so. And we reach this present life still aspiring towards the realisation of these desires. The nature of the 'self' through all these successive lives may be compared to the waters of the ocean which rise and fall in waves of different aspects. The waves change form continually, but the nature of the water does not change. Like the water of the ocean our true self continues to exist eternally, although its physical and spiritual expression may ceaselessly assume new aspects. In the teaching of Buddha, the force which directs these changes is called *Karma*. Karma appears in the human self under three forms : thought, word and action. These are called the Three Karmas which react upon our true selves, and are responsible for the transformations of existence of a being. This Karma force does not merely direct our present life : the Karma of today prepares our future. Karma has existed since the beginning of life until our actual life, and will act until the eternal future. For eternal life should be understood under its true aspect of continual change. The reason why we were born human beings and not in some other animal form resides in the fact that amongst the multiple currents composing the Karma, that resulting in the human form was stronger than those currents resulting in the animal form.

"We call '*Ingo*' (a commenced Karma) that form of Karma which creates a new general form of life. We also call it '*Soho*' (general fruit) because from the point of view which interests us, all beings find themselves in the same situation. Or, again, we call it for the same reason *Kyogo* (universal Karma). That which appears in *Ingo* is our human quality—

our common quality. But another Karmic current called *Mango* (accomplished Karma) will perfect our *self* and stamp it with its personal mark. The *Mango* is essentially different in the case of each individual, that is why it is so often opposed to the *Soho* under the name of *Beppo* (special fruit), or of *Fukyoko* (individual Karma). This individual Karma remains in constant and intimate relation with the universal Karma.

"It is the *Mango* which creates the individual differences between men, who all, nevertheless, possess in common the same universal human nature. The *Ingo* creates humanity. The *Mango* creates the individual. On learning these facts, we reach the necessity of respecting humanity and each being taken individually, and of admitting that all men and all nations are equal and have the same rights.

"A familiar example will help you to understand better what I mean. Life resembles a journey in a train. Those who go from San Francisco to New York, whatever may be their rank or condition, all travel in the same direction. Thus the *Ingo* or *Soho* gives to all beings a same human direction. But in the train each traveller acts differently; none accomplishes exactly the same gestures as his neighbours although respecting their peculiarities. This is the realm of *Mango*; the principle of differentiation. We Buddhists practise this tolerance in regard to all. Unfortunately we often see in life men who pretend to destroy or level individual differences, or to crush others by their own individuality, or to oblige others to think as they do. This is infinitely regrettable. The life of all men should be as tolerant and happy as that of the passengers in the train.

"The deep cause of the present conflict one sees amongst nations and men is, in reality, the misunderstanding of the teachings of Buddha, that is to say, of our general universal nature, and of our special Karma. If men understood the nature of Karma, and admitted that each individual man has his *accomplished Karma*, which distinguishes him, and if they considered human equality as a logical and reasoned consequence of universal Karma, Peace would be established in the world for all eternity. A civilisation which would only comprise material, technical progress, would not be complete. *There are two means of eliminating causes of conflict in humanity: the one consists in maintaining social equilibrium by reforms, by the excellence of institutions and of the political and economic system. This is an exterior means. The other method consists in purifying, perfecting the inner life of men who should be directed towards peace by that effort of moral purification. We Buddhists practise this second way. We believe in the primacy of the spiritual, principle of all action.*

"We make an effort to purify and to enlighten our mind, and we do not disdain our neighbour's different mind. But we strive to help others in their moral perfecting, because the life of humanity is not made only of those special and individual fruits, but forms a whole. All beings are jointly responsible the one for the other. As it is impossible to have a perfect part of anything so long as the totality is imperfect, we Buddhists wish to create a superior life in which men co-exist in mutual brotherhood and happiness. The welfare of all commands our particular satisfactions. To purify one's mind, to do good, to create Peace, such is in short the teachings of Buddha."

6. *Mr Tsumaki, bonze, professor at the Faculty of Letters of the Nishi-Hongwanji, expounds the practical character of Shinshu and situates it amongst the sects*

"In Japan, long before Eisai, Shotoku-Taishi amalgamated the traditional principles of Japanese psychology with Zen. These are characterised by intelligence, large-heartedness (*i.e.* charity) and active courage. Our Zen is born of a combination of Chinese Zen and of our racial qualities. That is why one finds therein, in the first place, *action, courageous activity*, which unceasingly seeks to realise Buddha on this earth. Buddhism, which in India was pessimistic and 'mountainous' (that is to say, retired from the world like a hermit upon his mountain), has become with us a doctrine of life and action, which can be practised by all men and women, and is capable of educating a child. It is the glory of Shotoku-Taishi to have known how to combine our racial qualities with the pure Zen philosophy he brought us. He used to say : 'It is not necessary to put on Buddhist clothes in order to be a good Buddhist. One can preserve the pure, detached, active soul of a Zenist just as well under the garb of a layman.' Therefore, thanks to Shotoku-Taishi, Zen became in Japan a philosophy made in our image, *living, active and practical*.

"After the death of Shotoku-Taishi the fine qualities of Japanese Buddhism slumbered for a while. The Buddhism of Nara was not very interesting in character, being tributary to India and to China. But after the era of Nara, during the era of Herian (Kyôto), Dengyô-Daishi, founder of the Tendai, and Kôbô-Daishi, founder of Shingon, restored its true aspect to Japanese religious philosophy. It appeared once again, such as it must always be, active and practical, immediately available and applicable in daily life. Dengyô and Kôbô borrowed their ideas from China, but they adapted them for Japanese use, and gave them a human and salvationist character. One knows the success of the Tendai and the Shingon sects, the importance enjoyed by the priests of Mount Hiei, whose bonzes, reaching the summit of powers and honours, were garbed in robes of gold.

The Tendai philosophy, *Ritsu* (disciplinary practices), *Shimizu* (or secret doctrine) and Zen were the four spiritual values which penetrated Japanese civilisation. The irradiation of Mount Hiei is a great historical fact. Thanks to it, the ideas of national unity, national teaching and national religion were for the first time born in our land.

"Kôbô-Daishi knew how to give a popular value to his secret doctrine. Before him only the nobles and a few privileged persons had enjoyed the practical possibility of studying Buddhism. Kôbô-Daishi strove to induce the people to frequent his temples. He created several centres of teaching, and addressed himself to all—peasants, warriors, merchants and artisans. Different religious philosophies sprang out of Tendai. After the Heian period came the Kamakura period. Zen Buddhism was brilliantly represented by Eisai and Dogen. From this period came modern Japanese Buddhism, *i.e.* the four great modern sects—the Zen sect, the Shinshu sect, whose founder was Shinran, the Jôdo sect, whose founder was Hônen, and lastly the Nichiren sect.[1] It is the study of these sects which gives us the true aspect of modern Buddhism.

"The Zen and Nichiren doctrines can form a group which I will oppose to the Jôdo and Shinshu doctrines. Zen is a philosophy—a method of appealing to inner power. The Zenist thinks and acts *in* his self and *by* his self. Zen is the characteristic doctrine of personal effort, of acquired merit, of an inner ideal. In what concerns the Nichiren doctrine the question is more delicate. Indeed, the latter derives its power from the *exterior*, appeals to the *exterior*, expects salvation from the *Hokkekyô* (Lotus of the Good Law). But do not let us forget that the follower of the Nichiren sect acts thus *consciously*; it is a doctrine of *conscious, exterior power,* and is not merely passive. The words '*Namu mihoho renge kyo*' must be weighed and pronounced fervently. In short, the individual is conscious of his community with Buddhist power, that exterior virtue upon which he calls. Nichiren created a complex doctrine. He borrowed from the Jôdo doctrine the principle of an easy prayer, but he also practises a *mandara* of a deep scope, and strongly recommends a centre of adoration and activity. Like Zen, the Nichiren sect believes that Paradise is here on earth, and that its doctrine possesses an immediate, a present value.

"On the contrary, the Jôdo and Shinshu doctrines consist exclusively in faith in a principle of *exterior power*. These two doctrines have not the *present* character of the two preceding ones. The Pure Land sects attribute necessarily more importance to *tomorrow* than to *today*. Yet Shinran, the founder of Shinshu, who venerated Shotoku-Taishi, rejoins the funda-

[1] See next chapter.

mental ideal of the latter. Shinran sought to vulgarise, to facilitate goodness and the duties of daily life. He believes that one should go directly to Buddha *'with a virgin heart,'* and he never loses sight of the practical activity of men. If, for example, he admits that one can eat meat in spite of the traditional Buddhist precepts, it is because he knows that it is practically impossible for working people to do otherwise. But even that action, if accomplished with a pure heart, and according to Buddhist charity, becomes incorporated to Buddhist life itself. The principle of Shinran's teaching is, like that of Shotoku, to allow the heart to lead one directly to Buddha, and to act in a practical way. The idea of activity, and not of sterile isolation, which is characteristic of Japanese psychology, and which Shotoku-Taishi had made his own, is also in the foreground of the Shinshu doctrine. Like Shotoku-Taishi, Shinran teaches the vanity of this world and shows the way to true life into which one must enter actively and practically. For him the truth consists in detaching oneself from this ephemeral life, and directing oneself by faith, which proceeds from truth, to that genuine Buddhist life, to the life that is truly active and charitable."

7. *Mr Yamabe, bonze and professor at the Faculty of the Nigashi-Hongwanji of Kyôto, insists on the analogies existing between Buddhism and Christianity and foresees the one future of the two religions*

"Like Christianity, Buddhism, in the countries where it has developed itself, has compromised with the spiritual nature of the different peoples. And yet both religions always preserve their essential principles.

Buddhism is not a dead abstraction, and it has for this very reason modified itself as the spirit of men developed—enlarging its conception of truth. Like in the other religions, when man's insight develops, he discovers as from the summit of a mountain unsuspected regions, and proclaims that which appears to him as being new truths, and which are, in fact, only new aspects of the eternal. Japanese Buddhists always found themselves on the teachings of Buddha, certainly, but they have enlarged their vision of Truth. They pretend that new flowers and fruits have grown from the old roots which existed in India in the times of Gautama Buddha, and that a hundred different flowering branches now rise towards the sun.

"Buddhism has followed the general trend of the religious history of humanity. The development of Mahayana Buddhism, notably, issued from the teachings of Gautama Buddha, has been compared to that of the Christian faith issued out of Judaism. Better still, one could compare it to the development of a whole sacerdotal system born of the simple Gospel of Saint Mark. A parallel can be established between the evolution of the thought and doctrines of the two religions, which doctrines appear only to have been marked, modified with us Japanese, by our Oriental mentality and by circumstances of *milieu*. This fact, if it is not a miraculous coincidence, can only be explained by admitting points of contact in the past between Christianity, which filtered through the Orient by means of the great commercial roads of antiquity and Buddhism. It is every day more certain that this must have been the case, and that the points of fusion were far more numerous than supposed. If this is exact, if it is true that in spite of differences of race, mentality and circumstance, the religious thought of the East and of the West have so many points in common, one can foresee a unique future for spiritual needs and entertain the hope of a future union between the two systems of thought. But, of course, this is only a dim vision—a mere hope."

Mr Yamabe then proceeded to underline one difference between Buddhism and Christianity: Amida is Love and not a Judge.

"The orthodox Shinshu sect, which teaches the doctrine of Redemption, finds its justification in the conception of Amida, the Buddha of Infinite Light and Eternal Life. The name of

Amida is mentioned for the first time in the 'Sukhâvati-Vyûha-Sutra' (The Land of Felicity).

"This is what we find in that text:

When the Buddha Sakyamuni lived at Râjagriba, on Mount Gridhrakuta (the Vulture's Peak), and took part in an assembly of Bhikshus, the venerable Ananda having risen to his feet, addressed the Blessed One in the following terms:

'The organs of thy senses, O Blessed One, are serene; the colour of thy skin is clear; the tint of thy face is bright and golden. Just as an autumn cloud is pale, clear, brilliant and golden, so the organs of the Blessed One are serene. Besides, I do not believe, O Blessed One, I have ever seen the organs of the senses of the Tathâgata as serene, or the colour of his face as clear, or the tint of his skin as brilliant and golden as to-day. . . . Therefore this thought comes to my mind, O Blessed One: without doubt the Tathâgata dwells today in the state of Buddhahood, without doubt the Tathâgata dwells today in the state of a Mahânâga, and without doubt he beholds the fully illumined saints and Tathâgatas of the past, of the future and of the present.'

Ananda's question was most pleasing to Buddha.

'Well said, well said, Ananda! Your question is really excellent. Your philosophy is wise and your understanding is very beautiful. You, O Ananda, have come for the advantage and benefit of many people, apart from the compassion of the world, for the salvation of a great multitude of men and for the advantage and happiness of both gods and men, when you deem it wise to question the Tathâgata on this subject.'

"The fact is this: When Sakya, *filled with love for humanity*, was on the point of preaching the doctrine of great felicity and redemption for all, his face shone with a marvellous glow, and his whole being became as serene as an autumn cloud. That is what inspired Ananda to ask the Buddha the above-mentioned question. The words came to Ananda's lips, but the master's inspiration was clearly visible in them. The heart of Sakyamuni, who had reached the highest summit of purification, naturally moved Ananda, who was his beloved disciple, so that the latter's heart reflected like a mirror that which was taking place in Buddha himself. Ananda understood the supreme state of 'mutual contemplation' of the

Tathâgatas. To obtain a good harvest, it is first necessary to till one's field and to prepare it to receive the seed. Thus also the apparition of a great spiritual movement in the world is preceded by the advent of very spiritualised minds, ready to receive the doctrine of the saint, for then it will be easier for the latter to penetrate into the hearts of men. The moment was propitious, now, to propagate the religion of salvation by faith side by side with the monastic religion of personal initiation.

"It is thus that was opened the way to the doctrine of salvation by faith. Before pronouncing the more excellent vows (*Pranidhânas*), as they are called in the *Sukhâvati-Vyûha-Sutra*, in the presence of his master Lokesvarâraja, Dharmakara, who was still undergoing his disciplinary stage, declared his intentions in the following *Gâthas*:

'May my fatherland be exactly like the state of Nirvâna and unequalled. I will be full of pity and deliver all creatures.

May those who may be born here coming from the Ten Quarters, be pure and joyous, happy and fortunate when they reach my country. May Buddha prove that this is my true realisation. I address strong and vigorous prayers for the accomplishment of this wish. May the Bhagavats of the Ten Quarters whose wisdom is unimpeded, know my thought and my practices. Even when I suffer in the midst of affliction and of pains, I will always practise strength and endurance and will be free of all regret.'

Then, after having thus affirmed the forty-eight *Pranidhânas* (vows and prayers), Dharmakara recited the following verses by the grace of Buddha:

'If these prayers I have made, reaching farther than the world, and by which I will certainly obtain the highest peace, were not granted, may I not reach perfect understanding.

'If I do not become a great donator so as to save all the poor, thanks to incommensurable sums of money, may I not reach perfect understanding.

'If, when I reach Buddhahood, my name be not heard in the Ten Quarters, may I not reach perfect understanding.

'May I become the teacher of gods and men, having sought the highest peace by my generosity, my loyal and profound meditation, and by the practice of the purest virtues. ·

'The great light produced by the spiritual power of the Tathâgata shines on limitless countries, and destroys the darkness of three kinds of foulness, by saving beings from unhappiness.'

(Extract from the Chinese Version.)

Having recalled this, we can judge men according to their desires and class them into three groups. (i) Those who line their nests comfortably with the feathers of others. (ii) Those who, being satisfied with themselves, neither insult nor praise others. (iii) Those who sacrifice themselves for the good of humanity. Dharmakara was the greatest and the most remarkable amongst this last group. He considered himself absolutely *at one* with all the creatures of the Universe, and believed that no individual perfection can be reached if one does not strive at the same time to perfect others. This signifies in other words, that, in order to reach infinite mercy, supreme wisdom and power, these qualities must be incarnated in the person of a Redemptor.

"The number of what are called his *Pranidhânas* (vows or prayers) differs according to the texts. Five of them subsist in Chinese translations, and the sixth is known in Sanskrit under the name of *Sukhâvati-Vyûha-Sutra*. These prayers have sometimes been numbered at forty-eight, whilst at other times they are said to be only twenty-four. The most important are those which speak of his accession to understanding, to infinite life and wisdom, of the glorification of his name, of faith as to the reason of the teaching, and of his reincarnation for the salvation of the world. In consequence, if one obtains faith by listening to the doctrine of Amida such as it is expounded in the sutras and discourses, such a one will surely be born again in the Pure Land after his death, will possess infinite light and wisdom, and will wish to devote himself in his turn to the salvation of all creatures. He will accomplish his 'great vows' by practising the Six Virtues of Perfection during innumerable existences.

P 225

"We read in the Buddhist Psalms of Shinran Shonin :

Since He who is Infinite (*Amida*) has reached Supreme Wisdom, the long, long centuries of ten generations have passed by, and the light of his Dharmakaya is, in the world, like eyes for blind people.

The Buddha of Infinite Light having, together with the Bodhisattvas of Compassion and Wisdom, taken possession of the Ark of the Divine Promise floating on the Ocean of Birth and Death, has assembled and saved humanity with himself.

"One might ask, Does not Amida, the Shinshu saviour, resemble up to a certain point the God of Christians ?

"What differentiates Shinshu from Christianity is our conception of sin. The Christians' God is a God of Love and of Justice, whereas Buddha is Mercifulness itself, and nothing more. Buddha never judges. The God of Judaism, represented later by the Christ, became the God of Love, but nevertheless He remains the judge of men's sins and measures out punishment in proportion. The Amida of Shinshu, on the contrary, knows only infinite Love for all beings, and wishes to deliver them from the eternal circle of ignorance and suffering in which they are plunged. Therefore in Amida there is neither wrath nor anger. He is only Love."

8. *Mr Gessho Sasaki, bonze, explains as follows, religious life and the conception of the "self" according to Shinshu*

"What is the true life ? How do we reach the true life ?

"Such are the chief questions which must preoccupy those who study Shinshu.

"Is life really suffering or is it a very agreeable thing ? It is not so easy to answer this question as might be supposed. Daily experience teaches us that life contains both pain and pleasure. On the other hand, personal considerations must be taken into account, for what seems agreeable to the one may produce quite a different impression on another person. We all evaluate our personal experiences in our own way. From a general and reasonable point of view one can consider life as a whole as containing both pains and pleasures. The practical consequence of the truth is that we flee from what is disagreeable and pursue what is pleasing. Certain men seem exteriorily to avoid agreeable things, such as, for example, those who mortify themselves like the aesthetics of India. But indeed even these are seekers of joys; joys which cannot yet be realised, but which must become so, by the virtue of their penances. The aesthetic even often feels pleasure in acts which others would consider the most unbearable of tortures. From this point of view one can say that stoicism is, at its basis, a form of hedonism. We are all epicureans in some way. I do not know whether all men are Hamlets or Don Quixotes, but I do know that for each of us life is partially agreeable and partially painful, and that we strive to avoid the one to seek the other.

"This merely practical view on life is expressed in *The Four Times Noble Truth*, as enounced by Buddha. The first truth is that life is suffering. The second truth is that suffering comes from the accumulation of the causes of suffering. The third truth affirms that in suppressing these causes of suffering the state of absolute blessedness is reached. The fourth truth teaches us how to reach this state. I specify: the idea of pain or of pleasure must not be the final principle of our spiritual life. This has been expressly taught by Buddha, and in all the texts of the Hinayana we find the following advice:

Do not avoid pain when it presents itself to you.
Do not withdraw from pleasure when it presents itself to you.
But remain quiet and serene.

"Whereas pain and pleasure enter so largely into the composition of human life, we say *that life, devoted to truth, should not depend upon these contingencies, but seek beyond them its definite foundation.*

"As long as man is incapable of rising above the simple notion of pain and pleasure, he has hardly evolved from the animal age. To rise, as we have just said, exacts on his part the will of seeking some moral signification which distinguishes him from the rest of creation. He cannot deliver himself from his sensations, as he is a sentient being, but his sensations can be sanctified and ennobled so as to further his moral conduct. Thus a pain may be experienced when we have not acted according to morality, and an agreeable sensation may result in us when we have accomplished our duty. Cultivated minds can therefore create for themselves a moral world which uplifts them above the life of sensations, and they can thus discover, in this existence, the notion of an attitude protecting them against evil. *Moral life can only be born and progress in the man who knows how to control his sensations.*

> Do all that is good.
> Eschew all that is evil,
> And preserve a pure heart.
> Such is the teaching of all the Buddhas.

"Such is the well-known *gâtha* constituting the teaching common to the Buddhas, and which characterises the moral aspect of what is called primitive Buddhism. The *Vinaya* (Disciplines) is but the codification of moral rules applicable to the life of Buddhist monks.

"Now Shinran Shonin could not be content with this simple moral. *He felt the urge to go beyond good and evil, with the aim of reaching the other shore of religious life.* Thanks to him, the last Buddhists learnt the existence of another world which moral life alone could not reach, and which was unknown to the adepts of the Vinaya. In this world spirit enjoys perfect freedom, being henceforth liberated from the fetters of the double chain of good and evil.

"On hearing me speak thus, one might think that the teaching of Shinshu Buddhism is immoral, and could not, in consequence, interest our daily life. But, on the contrary, Shinshu possesses a very sure critical sense of our moral imperfection, and teaches us that precisely on account of our imperfections we must be humble, repentant and faithful.

Better still, Shinshu is conscious of what is unnatural in monastic life, and it therefore advises its adepts to live ordinary family lives, which in no way distinguishes them from other men. It thus consecrates family and social duties.

"Shinshu takes into consideration *the human side of humanity*, and Shinran audaciously turns away on this point from the way uniformly followed by other Buddhists. For this reason the Sutra of the Great Infinite (*Sukhâvativyûha*), the canonical basis of Shinshu, is also called the Sutra of Humanity. In no other Buddhist school is the link between religion and morals more complete than in Shinshu.

"Let us examine this next point: the problems of the relation between religion and morals are discussed by Buddhist Shinshu scholars under this special title—'Relative Truth and Absolute Truth.'

"During the Meiji era, that is to say during the latter part of the nineteenth century, Shinshu scholars divided themselves into two groups over this question. The one professed a unitarian point of view, the second a dualistic opinion. In this second group, moreover, some affirmed a sort of parallel between the moral idea and the religious life. These two systems of life were like the two wings of a bird, or the two wheels of a carriage: the one could not advance without the other, for they completed each other. One of these categories of thinkers gained an advance on the others. In general the conservatives inclined to support the dualistic theory, whereas the liberals strove to establish a unitarian relation between religion and morals.

"Those who make themselves the apostles of a theory of anteriority believe that a moral life was the necessary result of religious faith, or, in other words, that religious faith was pre-existent to moral law. The late Reverend Manshi Kiyozawa (1863-1903), who was president of the Shinshu College and leader of the liberal party of that epoch, himself energetically opposed the doctrine of the priority of the religious faith. He used to say : 'All moral acts are the products of our deliberation and must proceed from the will. Therefore those acts proceed from our inner needs. Nevertheless the salutary results they can bring into our intellectual and social life cannot be regarded as moral acts. In consequence, and especially in the teachings of Shin Buddhism, moral life must precede the accession to Faith.'

"Conformably to this doctrine, a religious life is only possible when one has acquired the consciousness of one's moral imperfections. The motto of the Reverend Kiyozawa was that morality is our guide towards religion, which reminds us of the saying of the Middle Ages : 'Philosophy is the servant of Theology.'

"When we consider the practice of Buddhist life we must not forget the Six or Ten Virtues of Perfection (*pâramitâs*) which are our lot as disciples of the Buddha. These six *pâramitâs* are : Charity, Morality, Patience, Energy, Meditation and Wisdom ; to which must be added, in order to reach the number of Ten, the Causes (*upâya*), the Vows (*pranidhâna*), Power (*bala*), and Science (*jnana*), or another group of moral qualities known as the Four Incommensurable Thoughts, *i.e.* Energy, Compassion, Goodwill and Impartiality. These virtues constitute what is called the Holy Life (*Brahmacharya*). The saints who practise such virtuous acts will all reach the state of Buddhahood. Ten degrees of spiritual development, corresponding to the Ten Virtues of Perfection, lead Mahayanists to the perfect Supreme Initiation of Buddha. These Ten Degrees are Joy, Purity, Light, Inner Fire, Superiority, Manifestation, Advancement, Immutability, Good Intelligence, and the Clouds of Dharma. When Charity, which is the first Virtue of Perfection, is practised in the most complete way possible, the Mahayanist reaches a spiritual state where he is liberated from all passion, and where his heart is filled with a sensation of Joy which lifts him above all limitations of Time —both present, past and future. This is the first degree, that of Joy. Pursuing his course of spiritual development he finally reaches the tenth degree and becomes the master of Love and Wisdom. Like the clouds enveloping the Universe, he has identified himself with the Dharma, and his heart embraces all things in Love and Wisdom. He is now an initiate, a saint, a Pure One. He has gained an infinite world built in, and upon, the world of relativity and of perfection.

"These Six or Ten Pâramitâs are the acts of purity and sanctity Buddha prescribed for his disciples of the Mahayana. Those who are capable of completely acquiring these virtues are saints and 'pure.' Those who are too weak-minded to follow the way of perfection and to uplift their spiritual level to that height, are the common herd of mortals who are technically called the 'ignorant' (bala).

"We see therefore that Buddhism has taken into account the opposition between the purity and pollution existing in the life we lead in this world. The principle which governs the life of a saint is purity. Now Shinran Shonin, founder of the Shinshu sect, makes a distinction in Buddhist religious life between this 'Way of Holiness,' as he calls it, and the 'Easy Practice,' which is quite different. The object of the 'Way of Holiness' is to follow the way of perfection, that is to say, to practise acts of purity and holiness until the whole world be entirely transformed into a kingdom of purity and holiness. We agree that the idea of universal sanctification is the highest goal of Buddha's disciples. But this is not an easy task in our present limited and worldly life. Perhaps it is impossible to practise completely even one of those Six Pâramitâs in our relations to other men. One must recognise that the distance separating the Mahayana ideal from our ordinary, practical, daily life is incommensurable. We must take into account our reality, and the way things take place in a life as limited as ours. The wall of holiness is too high for us to scale it with success, and if this scaling should be the absolute condition of our salvation, very few mortals would ever reach the light. That is why Shinran Shonin, wishing to establish the basis of religious life on something else than the 'Holy Way,' so difficult of access, composed the following psalm:

> From eternity to the present time,
> The proof exists that he loves me.
> For is it not thanks to him
> That I have penetrated the mystery of Buddha's wisdom?
> In which exist neither good nor evil,
> Neither purity nor impurity?

"We will understand these thoughts better after having studied the problem of 'self' according to the Shinshu doctrine.

"Whereas the philosophers prior to the Upanishad sought God in the exterior world, the writers of the Upanishad discovered Him in the Atman (soul). Buddhists, for their part, not only deny the existence of an exterior God, but also the reality of a soul, substantially conceived. It is for this reason that Buddhism has sometimes been accused of Atheism, of destroying the notion of soul, by those who have the habit of considering the world as the creation of an historical God, and the body as the residence of an immaterial soul. This explains why Buddhism has so often been confounded with Nihilism, with absolute nihility—because the sense of Buddhist negation, which implies not only an idea of thesis, but also the idea of anti-thesis, was not always understood. By this method Buddhism intends to rise above the dualism which intelligence has put into things. The Absolute is the point where one can no longer pretend to anything. It is the refusal of Buddha to admit an exterior God, and ends in the absolute notion of the Eternal Dharma. Buddha placed himself above dualism after having realised his perfect Illumination and when he declared: 'I alone am the Honoured One,' instead of saying, 'None others than myself are honoured.' For he made no distinction between *I* and *Thou*, between the I subject and the I object. For at the moment of his Illumination, what dominated in Buddha was the 'Great Self,' or Nirvâna. This is what should be understood when Buddhists oppose the *non-Atman* to the *Atman* of the Hindus.

"There was no personal substance, if I may express myself thus, in the 'self' of Buddha, at the moment of his Illumination. The purely relative human ideas of subject and object, of 'self' and non-self, are not found therein. We see here the 'pure' self, but with the possibility for this unique self to pass through different stages, to present itself under the relativities and the superficialness of the subject 'self,' the possessor 'self' and the object 'self.' If you consider these three stages independently the one of the other, you will see that the abyss deepens between each of these notions involving the rupture of Buddhist religious life and of human harmony.

"The multiple difficulties one observes in the social organism proceed from a belief in the independence of these three manifestations of the self. Each considers itself absolutely independent from the others, and the result of this error is that a human being brutally opposes his own interest to the interest of others. Absolute monarchy or statism dislocates and exalts one of these manifestations of the 'self' to the detriment of the others. The revolution which ensues signifies that the two other *selves* feel the need of rejecting the subject 'self.' When a privileged class monopolises the possession of 'self' by oppressing the working classes, we have capitalism. The present social instability does not only come from the question of salaries. Its more profound cause resides in the separation of the 'self' which possesses from the other *selves*, and in its autocratic affirmation. Feminism has also allowed itself to be influenced by the same error. Yet we believe that this social and moral instability can be remedied by transforming in the Buddhist sense, the consciousness of the 'ego' of the different classes of society and that of the individuals of both sexes. As long as the notion of personality continued to be misunderstood and divided, and as long as one of its aspects continues to be monopolised by one party to the detriment of the others, social unrest cannot cease. *The 'self or ego' must be restituted to its initial state, fluid, indivisible and non-crystallisable, in order that it may never be hampered nor con-*

strained in its movement of progressive evolution which defines its very essence.

"All the factors of the social organism should benefit by the possibility of undergoing these three stages of the 'ego' as they find it proper and advantageous to do so, without causing any harm to others. We thus affirm our personality, a privilege granted to the human spirit which is conscience and reason. We should be able to be, turn by turn, masters, landowners or servants receiving a salary, having the freedom to transform our being according to circumstances, and to those psychological, social or other needs amongst which we progress. Buddhism reminds and teaches us that there is no 'ego,' no *atman*, and lays down, in principle, the constant fluidity of what we call 'the self.' The rigidity of the notion of the 'ego' must disappear. In the Buddhist act of charity, one finds an example of the triplicity of the 'ego' which ought to be of help in the practice of our daily life: in the light of the charitable sentiment, the three aspects of the 'ego' blend together as one. The object of Buddhist religious life is to lead us to the perfect fusion of the three stages of 'the self.' When this mutual, absolute fusion is accomplished, *we find peace, and glory reigns in the world.*

"To resume, I group men into five categories:

"(i) Those whose lives are regulated by the sensations of pleasure and pain.

"(ii) Those whose lives are regulated by the notion of good and evil.

"(iii) Those whose lives are regulated by the notion of purity and pollution.

"(iv) Those whose lives are regulated by the idea of being and of non-being.

"(v) *Those whose lives are regulated by the truth of their ego.*

"And as we distinguish in humanity these five types of spiritual life, we must also consider the degree of spiritual development in each individual. *True life is nothing else than that which follows an experience of the vanity of the 'self'."*

9. *Mr Otani, bonze of the Shinshu sect, gives his opinion on the moral value of Shinshu, and situates it in relation to Christianity*

Mr Kaworu Otani, who was born in a temple of the sect, knows all its subterfuges. He is a scholar who expresses himself in perfect French and he replies amiably to my questions, which are, I believe, those which any stranger studying the doctrine of Amida would be led to ask.

"What are, according to you, the essential differences between the Shinshu doctrine, which is a doctrine of Faith and Redemption, and Christianity?"

"*The essential difference is that we have no God.* All the philosophy of Shinshu, like all the philosophy of Buddhism, remains purely *human.* Infinite Life and Eternal Light (Amida) come only to help our finite and incapable life, to aid our distress and moral insufficiency. We shall ourselves be able to participate in this task of salvation when we reach the Pure Land, or, if you prefer it, the light of Amida. The salvation of Humanity is thus the act of humanity itself, not that of a creative God, of a different essence than our own."

"Some Buddhist priests pretend that an entente is possible between Shinshu and Christianity," I observed. "Is this your opinion?"

"You can see the serious doctrinal differences which separate us from Christians," answered Mr Otani. "I believe these to be irreducible. But Buddhism is essentially tolerant. We admit that different means should be used to uplift souls which are different. We are agreed to recognise that equally moralising religions could develop along parallel lines in a reciprocal tolerance."

"In what concerns the moral value of Shinshu, is it exact to say that honest men and criminals will all be admitted *without distinction* to the Paradise of Amida ?"

"Yes, all, without distinction. We are all guilty—we can hardly not be so—and the doctrine of Amida is a doctrine of Grace, of universal redemption. What *would* be immoral, would be to distinguish between the different categories of sinners. Amida is Love."

"How can this affirmation be reconciled with the nineteenth vow contained in your canonical text, the *Sukhâvativyûha*, in which it is said that all men will go to the Paradise of Amida, with the exception of those who have infringed the Law of Buddha ?"

"We do not read the text in the same way as you do," replied Mr Otani. "It is vow number eighteen which signifies that all men will go to the Paradise of Amida, which dominates and illumines the whole subject. But there is a condition to this accessibility to Paradise, *i.e.* one must practise a sincere belief in the grace of Amida. The texts which appear to make an exception to the universally merciful thought of Amida, signify simply that he who does not believe in Amida-Buddha is excluded from the promised liberation. The sincere belief in Amida-Buddha is in itself a moral practice and perfumes our states of consciousness. In fact, statistics prove that criminality is inexistent amongst the adepts of Shinshu. Amida's unconditioned love for us, the gratitude it engenders in our hearts, are, for us who are both blind and guilty, the operating and fundamental elements of earthly morality."

10. *A Psalm beneath the Dew*

Early one morning I strolled in the company of one of my friends, a bonze, through the grounds of a temple in Kyôto, all bathed in dew. The dawn, the leaves, the golden sand, the blue sky delicately tinted each dew-drop. The doctrinal explanations on which I had concentrated my thought, to the exclusion of all other questions, during the last few days, had rather tired me. I was therefore grateful when my friend, smiling calmly, restored Buddhist peace and charm to my heart, by reading me some Psalms composed by the Shinran Shonin, founder of the Shinshu sect. He read them to me in an English version, and gazing at him whilst he read, in a grave voice, I had the impression of seeing before me a clergyman or an evangelist.

"*Seek refuge,*" he read in fervent tones, "*seek refuge in the heavenly harmony.*"

And this expression *Seek refuge* was repeated again and again like a rhythm or a litany. . . . The whole of Shinshu was thus contained in two words.

Seek refuge in the heavenly harmony.
The alleys of Paradise are full of trees
Laden with jewels and precious stones,
Which quivering all together and with a same rhythm,
Emit exquisite sounds and make delicious music.

Seek refuge in the Divine Promise,
In the Treasure of Merit !
From the seven gem-laden trees
Emanates a sweet-smelling perfume,
The flowers, fruits, branches and leaves of Paradise
Set aquivering their colours and lights.

Seek refuge in the Perfect Just One !
The breeze passes in the trees replendent with gems,
And plays a melody five times harmonious ;
In the whole world there is no place
Which is untouched by the glorious light
Irradiating from a hundred thousand rays,
Emanating from the hearts of the flowers of Paradise.

Seek refuge in Amida-Buddha !
Just as a golden mountain
Reflects the myriads of luminous rays
Which emanate from the hearts of flowers,
Such is the form of the Infinite.
From the sacred body of Amida-Buddha
Light flows as from a spring,
Upon the ten regions of the earth,
And His blessed teaching guides all that lives
In the way of His Light and of His Love !

CHAPTER XI

THE NICHIREN SECT

(1) The Nichiren Sect. (2) A mystic night in the temple of Ikegami. Mr Nichisho, bonze of the sect, relates to me the strenuous life of Nichiren, who was a great saint as well as a great Japanese patriot, and expounds the doctrine of the sect. The Lotus of the Good Law, unique Truth, and the Three Esoteric Principles. (3) Mr Z. Kazawa, bonze and professor at the Faculty of Letters of the Nichiren Sect at Osaki, gives me further details. Some canonical texts. (4) Mr Kyozui Oka, bonze and professor at the same Faculty, believes in the ultimate triumph of *The Lotus of the Good Law*. (5) A pilgrimage to the temple of Minobu.

1. *The Nichiren Sect*

Founded, as its name indicates, by Nichiren (1222-1282), who was a great saint as well as a great Japanese patriot, this sect claims only one text: *The Lotus of the Good Law* (Japanese: *Myôhorenge-Kyô*; Sanskrit: *Sadharmapundarika-sutra*). The Nichiren sect counts 3650 temples or monasteries, the most celebrated of which are those of Ikegami and Minobu, more than 9000 priests, 1,400,000 perpetual members and 38,000 occasional or Shinto members. It has also created 73 social works. After the death of its founder, differences of interpretation in matters of doctrine led to the creation of nine branches whose perpetual members number more than 500,000.

2. *The ardent life of Nichiren, Japanese prophet and patriot. The doctrine of the Sect—the Lotus of the Good Law*

On the night of the thirteenth of October, anniversary of the death of Nichiren, we repaired to the temple of Ikegami. As every year at this season, some twenty or thirty thousand pilgrims were wending their way towards the sanctuary, to celebrate the death of the saint. From the station of Omori to the Hommonji, numerous processions were being formed under the multi-coloured fires of paper lanterns. The pilgrims all chanted the sacred formula of the sect: *"Namu-Myoho-Renge-Kyō"* (Adoration of the Lotus of Perfect Truth), to the sound of wooden drums and to the rhythm of *getas* striking the ground. The mystic night was in progress. We had visited the *Daimoku-Ko* where the faithful were repeating this same formula, and the *Shaka-Do* where other worshippers were, according to custom, passing this holy night in prayer. In the *Shoshi-Do*, the "Hall of the Founder," the delicious concerts of painted angels represented on the walls seemed to accompany the chanting and invocations. Behind the altar an unknown artist had skilfully depicted the chief incidents in the life of Nichiren, whose story my master proceeded to relate to me.

"Nichiren," he said, "was born in 1222. His father was a fisherman who lived in a little village in the province of Awa, on that coast of Japan which is the first to be lit by the rays of the sun.

"When, as a child, he awoke at sunrise, at the hour when his father was preparing his nets and his oars, he and the other inhabitants of that privileged coast were the first to perceive the sun's golden light. Later, in his Memoirs, he noted how deeply he had been impressed by the rising of the sun in his native land.

"Mystery of cosmic influences! The sight of the Ocean incites one to mysticism, and dazzles the soul with prodigious vision. Nichiren was both a mystic and a visionary. The Sun is universal light. Nichiren created a religious doctrine which in his thought was to be universal light, that is to say, absolute truth, and destined to all men. He was born under the sign of the sun, in this land of Nippon which he never left, and for which he professed an ardent love. He was a patriot, passionately devoted to the independence and glory of his country, then threatened by the Mongols. Japan and Buddhism were as one in his heart."

"So he was really a Buddhist and nationalist prophet?" I asked.

"Yes. And his mysticism always preserved the savour of the soil. His strong personality founded and moulded it, as much as his erudition. His whole thought can be resumed thus: *Truth is contained in the Lotus of the Good Law*. It devolves upon Japan, for its own salvation and that of humanity, to make this Truth irradiate upon the whole world. As long as there remains in the world a single man unconverted to Buddhism, that is not believing in the efficient virtue of the Lotus, there will subsist a dark blemish on Buddha himself, the Light of the World.

"At the age of twelve Nichiren became a disciple of the Shingon sect, the mysticism of which nourished his exhaltation. A few years later, having made miraculous progress in the study of Buddhist texts and thought, he was admitted to priesthood. It was at this time that he adopted the Buddhist name of Nichiren, which signifies *Lotus of the Sun*, and under which he became celebrated. One can add one other reason to those already mentioned which determined the choice of this name. It is said that Nichiren's mother conceived her son after a dream in which she saw the sun and a marvellous lotus. She had thereupon concluded that the child was predestined to accomplish some high and pure mission—the lotus being the emblem of purity and light.

"For in the days of Nichiren all was dark in the history of Japan. From the middle to the end of the thirteenth century calamities succeeded each other. Mongol invasions polluted the Land of the Gods, until then inviolate, and which was suddenly threatened with a shameful subjection. Earthquakes, epidemics, famines followed each other, as did our own errors, of we Japanese who had established the capital of the time at Kamakura, where reigned a military dictatorship and was the scene of fratricide struggles. Some offered their services to the Emperor at Kyôto—others to the Shôgun. There was no unique commandment. What was to become of Japan? Death, like a great black bird, hovered over the country. Comets appeared in the sky. The terrified population saw in them the warning of a final catastrophe. Men lamented themselves. 'What have we done to deserve these evils?' they asked. 'What gods, what devils in their wrath are preparing to avenge themselves upon us?'

"Now all this time Nichiren was studying and meditating. The teaching of the Shingon sect no longer sufficed him. In 1252 he went to Mount Hiei to study the Tendai doctrine under the direction of the most authorised masters. But Nichiren had far too original a mind to content himself with copying. A personal conception was gradually ripening within him. In the course of his life he revealed to the world his Law of the Three Esoteric Principles. Each time he succeeded in formulating one of these Principles, he did so as if by a flash of genius, by a sudden enlightenment, after years of reflection.

"Here is a short summary of Nichiren's doctrine which is comprised in these few words: 'The Lotus and the Three Esoteric Principles.' At the basis we find the text which one must never lose sight of: the Myoho-Renge-Kyō, or Hokke-Kyō (Lotus of the Good Law), which is the only truth. You know that Buddhists recognise three decreasing periods from the point of view of men's capacity of comprehension concerning the pure thought of Buddha—for men make no progress on this point, but, on the contrary, regress. The first period, called the period of True Buddhism, is of one thousand years, counting from the death of Buddha. The second period extends for the following thousand years and is the period of 'Copied Buddhism.' Then begins the third period of degeneracy: this is our period, the period of the Later Law, or of the 'Men of the Latter Days.' We are now too corrupt to understand alone the whole light of Buddha. An act of faith in the sacred text which is suitable for the men of our time is necessary.

This text is *The Lotus of the Good Law*, the last and perfect word of Buddhism.

"The Three Esoteric Principles conceived by Nichiren are both the practical form under which all men, without exception, can utilise the wisdom and the efficacious virtue of the text, and the occasion for them to regain the knowledge that they can all be saved since all are formed of Buddhist spirituality. Naturally a superior mind, like Nichiren, possesses a clear vision of this consciousness such as we have not. But, by the effect of their sincere faith in the *Lotus* and in the Practice of the Three Esoteric Principles, the ignorant claim final salvation as well as the intelligent, and pretend also to absolute peace of heart, to *Nehan* (Nirvâna).

"These Three Esoteric Principles are :

"(i) The uttering of the holy title : *Namu-Myoho-Renge-Kyō* (Adoration of the Lotus of Perfect Truth).

"(ii) The Graphic and Symbolic Representation of the Supreme Being.

"(iii) The Forces of Universal Irradiation of Buddhism. These are called *Daimoku* (Title), *Honzo* (Object of Worship) and *Kaodan* (the Daïs from which the Buddhist Principles are proclaimed)."

"Must I understand," I asked, "that you are alluding to mere formulas, to mechanical repetitions of the title of a sutra, or, on the contrary, to some profound thought which escapes me ?"

"To both," answered the priest. "He who wishes to conquer souls must concentrate his thoughts into formulas—a wise proceeding. But these formulas should be like so many pieces of Truth, so that, joined together, *they are Truth*. The identical essence of Buddhist spiritual things results in Truth having two faces—the inexpressible and the expressed. The second aspect, which allows the most ignorant man in the world to share in the task of Buddhist salvation, does not change the foundation, which is the light of Buddha. That is why these Three Principles are Three Mysteries, and are not mere words. *They identify themselves with Truth.*"

"Are these Three Principles founded on a text?" I then asked.

"Yes. The genius of Nichiren extracted them from the chapter of the *Lotus* entitled 'Duration of the Life of Tathâgata,' in which the whole doctrine is hidden like a diamond buried in the earth. One reads therein of the permanency of the Three Bodies of Buddha—the Spiritual body (Sanskrit: *Dharma-Kaya*); the body of Beatitude (Sanskrit: *Sambhaya-Kaya*); and the body of Transformation (Sanskrit: *Nirmana-Kaya*)—from which the mystical virtue of the Three Esoteric Principles proceeds by effect of the 'supernatural power of the Tathâgata.' A moment ago, whilst we were standing before the basin of lustral water, I said to you: 'Water can be liquid, vapour, cloud, snow or ice, yet it always remains identical in its essence. In the same way the light of Buddha may be either wisdom, or the essence of the cosmos, or the thought contained in the text, or the formulas of this text, yet it always remains the light of Buddha.'"

"Can you give me a few precisions concerning each of these Three Esoteric Principles, or Mysteries of Nichiren?" I questioned.

"I have just spoken of the first of these which one can see in action this very evening. It is none other than the mystic formula: '*Namu-Myoho-Renge-Kyo.*'"

The innumerable pilgrims were chanting "*Namu-Myoho-Renge-Kyo!*" Their chant resembled the sound of the sea. I allowed myself to be gained by that mystical, sonorous wave, which rose higher, higher still, bearing within it a state of consciousness unknown to Westerners who are always sceptical: the state of absolute conviction. Shall we call it fanaticism? My reply to this question is that the exact term which would qualify absolute conviction does not exist in French. Not possessing the thing, how could we possess the word describing it? Meanwhile the immense procession of pilgrims bearing a thousand pink, green and yellow paper lanterns entered the holy precincts. Some of these lanterns were weirdly shaped, and represented ships, houses or flowers. A thousand others constellated the sky like as many stars. And the song of the pilgrims rose ever louder. It seemed to me as if the whole world, and even the stars of heaven, were chanting: "*Namu-Myoho-Renge-Kyō.*" Nothing is as foolish as the pride of not understanding. I did not wish to be so foolish this evening. Therefore, walking by the side of the kind priest who sets me an example, and gives me the tone, I also began chanting: "*Namu-Myoho-Renge-Kyō!*"

"The second principle, or mystery," continued the priest, "is the graphic symbol of the Supreme Being which synthesises the whole of which we are a part, and brings to light the fact, essential to our salvation, that all living creatures partake of the same nature as Buddha. Buddha is the Universe itself. That is why Nichiren imagined a diagram bearing in its centre the words *Myoho-Renge-Kyō,*" around which are grouped the names of all that exist.

"The third principle, or mystery, the *Kaodan* (daïs) is the place from where the doctrine will illuminate the world. This, for each of us, is our own body whose words and acts must propagate the Buddhist faith in our own radius. This favoured spot was to have been a monastery which Nichiren had planned to build on the side of Fuji, the sacred mountain."

We had drawn near to the *Katsu-Do*, the reliquary pagoda, whose rounded flanks rest upon an immense stone lotus. The clamour of the pilgrims re-echoed more strongly than ever. "*Namu-Myoho-Renge-Kyō! Namu-Myoho-Renge-Kyō!*"

The bonze continued:

"Let us resume the short biography of Nichiren I had interrupted in order to give you a brief explanation of his doctrine.

"At the age of thirty our saint and prophet, after long

meditations, reached the conviction that the cause of the many calamities Japan was then enduring—invasion, famine, etc.— was the misunderstanding of the true doctrine of Buddha, as it was expressed in the *Lotus*—a unique, complete truth—and in particular the adulteration of the pure Buddhist precepts, the result of the errors of the teachings of Hônen, of the sects of the Pure Land and of the Zen sect. Nichiren has often been blamed for his fanaticism. We should not forget, however, that he was, at a critical epoch of his country's history, an ardent patriot, who very justly reminded his compatriots that in order to face the peril threatening them, they must create anew their national and political unity, which could only subsist in institutions if it existed in the hearts of the people. The multiplicity of religious sects was dividing the nation. Now, the Truth is One—one sole government, one religious doctrine, etc. Political and moral unity alone could save the country. Nichiren expressed his views in a remonstrance which he addressed to the Government, and entitled: 'The Book of the Right Law and of National Salvation' (*Risoho-Ankoku-ron*). He declared that the sects practising the worship of Amida and of Hônen had, in particular, misrepresented and betrayed Buddhism. They had perniciously and arbitrarily accustomed the people to substitute another name for that of Buddha. The teachings of early Buddhism and of Dengyô-Daishi had been voluntarily repudiated and trodden underfoot. The Zen sect, on account of its individual eccentricities, was but 'an invention of the devil.' The Shingon sect was a 'traitor to the country.' Nichiren implored the Government to intervene, to forbid those false cults, to definitely establish the true doctrine, the *Lotus*, and to re-establish, together with political unity, the spiritual unity of Japan. At the same epoch he formulated the First Principle, or Mystery.

"In 1253 Nichiren decided to start his campaign for the triumph of his ideas. He went to the monastery where he had spent his youth in order to convert his former masters and colleagues.

"Seated before him, in the attitude of meditation, the priests awaited gravely his communication. With his customary vehemence and frankness, Nichiren proceeded to expound his faith and to tear the other sects to pieces. His audience was at first astonished, then alarmed, then revolted. Nichiren was taken for a lunatic, or at least an arrogant maniac. Banished and reviled by all, the Prophet descended the mountain he had scaled so joyfully a few hours earlier and went to Kamakura. There he summoned the Government to do its duty, and even appealed directly to the people, preaching in the street.

"At Kamakura the Government, indisposed by the virulence of his harangues, secretly excited the population against him. At that time the Prophet was proclaiming in the streets : 'Cursed be those who have deformed the true doctrine! They are the causes of the misfortunes of this country. Other catastrophes await you if you do not accept the light!' Or again : 'Awake! Awake! Men, awake!... Look! There is only one Truth and not several! Has one ever seen a man with two fathers or two mothers? Look at the sky above your heads! There is only one Sun!"

"But the crowd stoned him, and tried to murder him, and Nichiren only escaped death by favour of night.

"He wandered in the woods and in the country surrounding Kamakura. Once again he found his dear solitude. He loved solitude, finding therein a secret strength. His whole life was a rhythm of solitary meditation and energetic action. At night the sound of the wind amidst the leaves or of the stream flowing over its mossy bed, the delightful song of insects under the moon, brought him mysterious encouragements. A few months later he returned to Kamakura and resumed his preaching with the same fervour. Exasperated, the Regent, Hojô-Tokiyori, exiled him to the peninsula of Izu, where solitude again welcomed him. Whilst there, he lived in the direst poverty, deprived of even the bare necessities of life, but all the time his thought continued to pursue its dream, lulled by the great voice of the waves. Before immensity,

the spectacle of which exalted him strangely, he became fully
conscious of his mission in the world and wrote down his plan
of action. Was he not one of the 'Saints' announced for the
Latter Times—an emanation of Buddha?

"Returning from exile three years later, he pursued his
campaign with the same ruthlessness. Nichiren was a rock
which no tempest could overthrow. Like the Japanese soldiers
he never capitulated, was never discouraged, and never made
any compromise whatever. He believed that Truth is
One, and that one should either stake one's soul for Truth or
stand against it. Ardent disciples accompanied him. The
Prophet denounced the errors of the times, and stirred up the
passer-by. The people wished to forbid him to speak. The
Regent ordered his arrest, and he was thrown into a subterranean prison with six of his most faithful disciples.

"Soon the news came that Nichiren was condemned to
death. His execution was to take place the twelfth day of the
ninth month of the year 1271. At the very instant the execu-
tioner lifted his sword to strike—lo! a violent storm broke
out, and a flash of lightning darted across the lurid sky! The
weapon fell from the hand of the trembling headsman, now
convinced that he had been about to kill a saint. Panic reigned
amongst the executioners. The Regent Tokimune, who had
already been deeply impressed by a recent dream, ordered that
the life of the condemned man should be spared. The Prophet
was exiled in the North, in the island of Sato. Was it hoped
that the terrible climate and hardships of all kinds would
overcome this indomitable man? Nichiren crossed the waves
of a rough sea and was landed in the island. He was perfectly
calm. He was thinking of what he had already accomplished
and of what still remained to be done. Under the roof of a
miserable hut, lacking both food and fire, Nichiren meditated
all through a long, icy winter, during which snow fell heavily.
He never belonged to himself. He never saw himself live.
He was the man of a cause. Any other man would have died
under similar conditions. But the luminous spirit of Buddha

lived in him. He quietly gave a form to his conception of the second Mystery: the graphic symbol of the Supreme Being. And this also was miraculous.

"In 1274 the Prophet was pardoned. He returned to Kamakura, where the population gave him a triumphant welcome. Changing its tactics, the Government now tried to win him over, and offered him its official patronage. Nichiren refused it. He retired to Minobu, on the western side of Fuji, where, alone in a hut, he meditated upon his third Mystery: the foundation of a Universal Buddhist Church. Enthusiastic disciples flocked there to cull the watchword from his own lips. He entrusted one of them to choose at the foot of the sacred mountain the site of the future monastery, from whence Truth would irradiate upon the world. His heart expanded with joy at the thought that Japan was called to accomplish this sublime mission.

"In 1282, having reached his 61st year, Nichiren, who had come here, to Ikegami, fell seriously ill. He understood that the time had come for him to leave this world of illusions and shadows. At midnight on the thirteenth day of the tenth month (and that is why we are here tonight, together with these thousands of pilgrims) he begged his disciples draw nearer to him. Here is the very place where stood the house in which he died, marked by a reliquary, and the pillar against which he leaned during his last moments. Nichiren, his soul serene, recited the celebrated passage of the *Lotus* called the 'verses of Eternity,' and all his followers sang them in chorus with him. Then he closed his eyes for ever."

"*Namu-Myoho-Renge Kyō!*" sang thousands of voices in the night to the sound of wooden drums. All this chanting, all this noise had stirred up in me I know not what power of evocation. I imagined that I saw the Prophet slinging his imprecations like Ezekiel, then revealing to the whole world the wisdom of the *Lotus*. Before the thousands of lantern fires illuminating the delirious crowd, I thought of the legend a pilgrim had told me. . . . When Nichiren spoke during the night, the stars descended from the sky and hung to the branches of the trees to listen to him. Certain sceptical minds objected that they were not stars at all, but merely fireflies. But the wise deemed that these luminous points were neither fireflies nor stars, but thousands of Buddhas, come from the Ten Directions, to listen to the word of the Prophet.

3. *Mr Z. Kazawa, bonze and professor at the Faculty of Letters of the Nichiren Sect, at Osaki, gives me further explanations*

"I congratulate you for having undertaken the study of Japanese Buddhism and of Nichiren's philosophy," he said to me with a smile.

"I always advise students to read two contemporary works on the subject in which you are interested : they are written in Japanese by two of my compatriots, and are, *The Philosophy and Religion of Nichiren*, by Professor Umada, and *The History of the Nichiren Sect*, by Professor Kayeyama. Amongst the works by Nichiren himself I must mention the *Nichiren Jônin Goïbun*, which can be considered his philosophical testament, and his *Hyûgaki*, or Travelling Diary. Naturally one should, before all, study *The Lotus of the Good Law*,[1] the canonical work of the Nichiren sect, and of which certain chapters, and in particular one dealing with the *Duration of the Life of the Tathâgata* (Chapter XV) is especially recommended as a subject of meditations.

4. *Mr Kyozui Oka, bonze, and professor at the Faculty of the Nichiren Sect, believes in the future triumph of the Lotus of the Good Law*

"Let us give but one canonical basis to Buddhist thought, *The Lotus of the Good Law*; I have myself translated this admirable work into Japanese. The idea of building a Buddhist

---

[1] *The Lotus of the Good Law*, translated into French by Burnouf. Maisoneuve ed. See Appendix.

temple in Paris fills me with joy, but the Buddhist teaching which will be given there will necessarily have to be dominated by this luminous text. For my part, I have consecrated my life to it. I have written two other volumes, *The Essence of the Hokkekyô (Lotus of the Good Law)* and *The Philosophical Principles of Nichiren*, which are, as you know, exclusively inspired by the fundamental text. But you will object that this text is Indian, and that Japan did not reveal it to the world. True, but the Nichiren doctrine has crystallised the wisdom of the *Lotus of the Good Law* into practical formulas of vulgarisation. It was the Japanese method of simplification, the spiritual discipline of our sect, which allowed all people to assimilate and to use in daily life the truths contained in this holy text, and also to propagate them successfully, thus ensuring, I hope, their universal irradiation."

5. *At the temple of Minobu, sanctuary and reliquary of the Nichiren Sect*

The Kuonje, or temple of Minobu, was founded by Nichiren on the western slopes of Fuji, the sacred mountain. I reflect that the Prophet used perhaps to walk in this very place meditating upon his dream of a Universal Buddhist Church. The conceptions of Nichiren were ambitious, practical and mysterious, obstinate and grand. They bear the hallmark of genius, yet it is preferable that they should not have been completely realised. Their intolerance would have destroyed the other sects, those more subtly shaded philosophies of which I admire the variety, and which have made of Buddhism a scale of all spiritual aspects—a wonder unique in the world. The genial effort of Nichiren remains none the less admirable, however, and even useful, for it is a valuable counterweight opposing itself to the dangers of the philosophical and cultural particularism of the other sects.

I pass under the massive doorway and visit the sanctuary. From the Kaisan-Do, or temple of the Founder, I catch sight of the ways leading to the temple of Relics, or Shaka-Do, to the temple of Posthumous Tablets, to the Kakyu-den, the Pilgrims' Halt, and to the Taimen-jo, or Reception Hall.

Does that magnificent Hall of the Kaisan-Do chant the glory of Buddhism? One would almost believe it. As soon as he has crossed the porch, decorated with sculptured dragons, storks and tortoises, the visitor sees widening before his eyes a marvellous room, the woodwork and pillars of which are lacquered red and black. The impression is majestic. In the centre hangs a golden baldaquin. I notice the golden pillars, the red lacquer of the altar, on which shine golden peonies and lions. Then in a golden reliquary, the statue of Nichiren, a gift of the inhabitants of Tôkyô. Men have covered conquerors with glory. But had he not indeed the soul of a conqueror this Prophet who wished to transform the world into a garden for Buddha? To the amateurs of energy I recommend the page written by Nichiren whilst he was in exile, undergoing the worst hardships.

. . . even if the celestial beings deprived me of their protection, if all perils threatened me implacably—even then would I consecrate my life to the cause. In happiness as in torments, to deviate from the *Lotus of Truth* signifies that one shall fall into Hell. I will remain until the end faithful to my early vows.

If someone said to me, You can ascend the throne of Japan if you consent to reject the Book, and reach future joys by believing in Buddha Amida, or Your parents will be sentenced to death if you do not utter the name of Buddha Amida, yet would I face unshaken such threats and temptations. I would never be moved by any of them, unless my own principles were destroyed by the refutations of a sage.

Perils, whatever they may be, will be like grains of dust before a storm.

I will be the Pillar of Japan! I will be the Eyes of Japan! I will be the Great Vessel of Japan.[1]

Let us enter into the Shinkotsu-Do, the Reliquary Temple, where the bones of the saint are preserved. A gallery leads

[1] Translated by Mr Anezaki.

from the sanctuary to the very heart of the temple. I enter. It is a small octagonal edifice, delicately decorated—a fairy dream of gold and bright colours so disposed and combined that they attenuate each other and harmonise delightfully with the whole. On the walls, against a golden background, are painted white lotus flowers, emblems of Buddhist purity. I remember all I have heard about Nichiren. His name—Nichiren—which signifies the Lotus of the Sun. His mother's dream of a lotus, and *The Lotus*, the sect's sacred book. A mysticism of the lotus has been evolved in Japan. This flower could by itself become the object of a cult and inspire noble sentiments. These black and gold tones alternate to the ceiling. I meditate, though dazzled. The effect is weird. The Hôto, or Shrine, offered by the piety of the inhabitants of Owari, is a small two-storied pagoda in gold lacquer. It contains the reliquary resting upon a silver lotus, placed in its turn upon an overturned lotus of jade.

And that marvellous shrine contains a few bones—all that remains of that astounding man *who tried to regenerate the world by Thought*.

CHAPTER XII

IN THE MARGIN OF CANONICAL BOOKS

A Buddhist mountain hermitage. *The Notes of the Little Hut*, written by the hermit and bonze Kamo Chomei. *The Wild Grass of Idle Moments*, written by the bonze Kenkô-Kaneyoshi. I leave some of my heart behind me in Japan.

The Japanese like fantasy, which is, in their eyes, the expression of the variety of the world. In their opinion the methodical colloquies we have just been reading would lack something essential, such as an unexpected walk not foreseen in the programme, or a philosophical escapade in the margin of orthodox teaching, or a free and unlooked-for discovery. Buddhistic charm likes to liberate itself from the limits of the canon.

"You would like to understand the Buddhist *état d'âme*?" asked Mr Koyama, who is a bonze and a fine scholar. "Well, in that case you will follow my advice. You will abandon your texts and philosophical queries and we will retire amidst the mountains, just like two good hermits. I will read you the Note-books of two bonzes who, tired of the world, and being convinced of the impermanency and frailty of all things, lived and observed life like the wise men they were. They were called Chomei, the bonze-hermit (1154-1212), who wrote the *Hôjôki*, or *Notes of the Little Hut*, and the bonze Kenkô, who some time around 1335 composed a collection of short sketches, anecdotes and essays entitled *Tzure-Dzure-Gusa*, or *The Wild Grass of Idle Moments*. We Japanese consider that these two delightful Buddhist works are two literary masterpieces."

"But they surely are not canonical?"

"Certainly not. How would you like an impromptu walk and a reading in the margin of the canonical books?"

I welcomed this suggestion with joy, and a few days later we took the road which was to lead us to the slopes of Fuji, the sacred mountain. My quest was ended. The hour was fast drawing near when I would have to separate myself from my Buddhist friends and regain my own land. This perspective threw a veil of sadness over our last conversation. In Japan, when two friends are about to leave each other, it is not rare that one of them should invite the other to share some delicate pleasure with him for the last time. Thus the host may reserve for his guest the surprise of some rare object of art— or of a flower, or of a simple stone polished by rain and time. And, gazing at the rare object, they will both express their concentrated emotion by a few phrases, and then they will enjoy in silence the great happiness of passing this last moment together. The Buddhist sentiment of impermanency, which is the law of the world, forbids vulgar emphasis and imposes restraint.

Today, obeying this same delicate feeling, my master wishes to make me appreciate the souls of these wise and disillusioned Buddhist hermits, and the charm of their peaceful lives. I will listen to him as he reads and will say little.

A pale, blond light filtered through some thin clouds. We occasionally took cross-roads, walking through the dew. We halted an instant on the banks of a stream, and sat down amongst the reeds. My master seized this opportunity to read me the beginning of the *Hôjôki*.

The current of a running stream flows on unceasingly, but the water is never the same. The foam of the eddies now vanishes, now forms again, but never lasts. Such are in life men and their habitations.

In a magnificent capital, the dwellings of the exalted and the lowly joining their roof-trees side by side, and alternating the colours of their tiles, seem to have stood there for many generations, and to be there for ever. Look at them more closely: only a few of them are really ancient. Some were destroyed last year to be rebuilt this year, others, poor and miserable, have replaced palaces which have disappeared. Their inhabitants are as ephemeral as they are. If we have lived long in a place where we have a number of acquaintances, we find that only one or two are left of twenty or thirty we knew formerly. Some die in the morning, some die at night. Such is life. It may be compared to foam upon water.

Whether they are born, or whether they die, men know not whence they come nor whither they go. And in fact what do they know? Do they even realise during their short passage through this world of what use their efforts and agitations can be? Do they even know how to discern that which might make their happiness, and be the joy of their eyes? Uncertainty and instability are our lot. I do not know which is the most subject to change—a house or its master. Men and things pass away.

Men and things are like dew on the convolvuluses. The dew may fall, leaving the flower behind, but even so the flower fades with the morning sun. Again the flower may wither and the dew remains. But even so it cannot last until evening.

We started to walk again. On the way the bonze resumed for me the passages of the *Hójóki* in which Chomei gives a detailed account of the terrible events he witnessed, and which led him to understand the "heart of things," that is the essential truth that all is vain and fleeting. These events were the fire which destroyed the capital in 1177, the cyclone which swept away houses "like leaves in the winter wind," famine, earthquakes, etc.

After having walked all day, enjoying for the last time the pleasure of being together, smiling at the beauty of the landscape, we reached at nightfall a small abandoned hut on the mountain side. It was covered with thatch and half-buried under golden autumn leaves. Doubtless it had sheltered some pilgrim. We decided to stop here for two or three days. My master sat down in front of the door on a pile of dead leaves. I did the same, and listened in silence whilst he continued his reading.

The miseries I have just spoken of, the tribulations through which I had passed, and which are the common lot of human beings, demonstrate the vanity of life and the impermanency of all things. Under these circumstances what can we do with our brief life?

In order to safeguard my inner peace, my only possession, I have decided to retire from the world.

Having no wife, child, function or honour capable of retaining me, I left everything and went away. Man who lives in the world loses his liberty. He can neither go nor come at will, nor laugh if he wants to laugh, nor cry if he wants to cry. If he wishes to please others and craves their smiles, he will use his life at it. If he tries to resist them he will be considered mad. If one depends upon a powerful person, one becomes his slave, and trembles before him like a little sparrow who has built its nest next to that of a falcon. If one protects somebody, one will be obliged to love him always, and one will therefore also lose one's independence.

I left everything, and for five springs and five autumns I made my bed amongst the clouds which hover around the luminous summits of Mount Fuji.

Now I am old. I have reached the age when dew does not easily evaporate (*i.e.* the age when sadness is not easily dissipated). I am sixty. I have built myself a small hut, the last leaf on the naked branch. I have built myself this cabin, something like the shelter a traveller might erect for one night's lodging—or the cocoon spun by an aged silkworm. It is not the hundredth part so convenient as the habitation of my middle age. As my life declines with every year, so my dwelling becomes ever smaller.

I glanced around our little hut and thought: "How happy our life could be if we only knew how to be simple." One of the highest virtues of Buddhism is surely to have taught men the nobility of a simple life, and to have endowed renunciation with the colour of wisdom.

The bonze resumed his reading.

My dwelling is no ordinary house. It is hardly ten feet square and only seven feet high. As it was not meant for a fixed abode, but was designed to accompany me wherever I go, I did not dig any foundations; the ground around it was simply trodden hard. The walls are of mud, and it is thatched with rushes. The joints are fastened with rings and staples. Thus I can easily remove it according to my fancy, when this site will cease to please me.

It is here, in the fastnesses of Mount Hino, that I now live ignored by the world from which I have hidden my traces. On the south I have set up a sort of temporary shade, made of reeds and of ferns, and beneath which I have spread a bamboo mat. On the west I have placed a rustic domestic shrine, decorated with an image of Amida-Buddha. The rays of the setting sun illumine each evening his transparent forehead. To the right and to the left I have hung pictures of Fugen and Fudo.[1] Then on a hanging shelf of bamboo I have placed a few black leather cases containing the *Ojôyôshu*, poems and music, and two or three books. On the eastern side I have made myself a bed of ferns and straw. Before the window I have placed my low table on which I write these notes. Near to my fern pillow I have dug a little hole in which I occasionally burn up brushwood. To the north of my little dwelling I have enclosed with a hedge a small garden in which I grow herbs and flowers. Such is my temporary home.

In the springtime I admire the rippling blossoms of the fragrant wistaria. In summer the *Hototogisu* [2] invites me to follow him to Mount Shide (the other world). In autumn the songs of the cicadae fill the air, sounding like lamentations over this life as void as the shell they have just shed. In winter I like to see the snow accumulating like human errors, soon to disappear.

When at dawn I see the white foam of the waves on the lake, my thought rejoins that of the novice Mansei gazing at the boats of Okanoya.

Here the bonze interrupted his reading to observe:
"Chomei is alluding to the following verses:

> *To what can I compare life?*
> *To the ship's wake?*
> *To the foam left by the wake?*
> *To dawn?*"

He then resumed his reading:

At night, when inclined to do so, I play on my lute the 'air of the autumn breeze.' The wind in the pine trees accompanies me.

[1] Fugen, a Buddhist divinity, patron of those practising the Hokke-zammai, or contemplative ecstasy. Fudo, Buddhist divinity to whom is attributed the power of chasing away evil spirits.
[2] A kind of cuckoo.

Or again, I softly accompany the murmur of the stream by playing the air of the flowing fountain. I play for myself only, not for auditors. I also sing to myself. I have no talent. I merely strive to put a little joy into my heart.

As for clothing, I am content with a blanket woven from wistaria fibres, and with a hemp cloak. As I do not go into society, what need have I of fashionable clothes? For nourishment, the fruit and berries of the forest and of the flowering fields suffice me. And if the harvest is not always plentiful, I only appreciate all the more their delicate, natural taste. I compare my past and my present and am obliged to admit this: I am a thousand times happier now than I was of yore. I live without desire, without fear, and without the slightest worry. I have no preoccupation whatever. I trust heaven to direct my destiny. I am as thoughtless and light as a happy little cloud floating in the azure sky. I do not make too much of myself. I take my joys one by one as they come, each hour, each instant. At night I dream smiling dreams on my pillow of ferns. During the day one of my very great joys is to marvel at the passing colours and lights which change delightfully with the seasons.

How can I render the charm of this reading by a simple-hearted bonze in this lost mountain nook? Whilst listening to him, my throat contracted more than once. My past life? Lost time. The essential for man would be to find a peaceful heart. The trees, flowers, herbs, live in the truth; that is *naturally and without ambition*.

The bonze said to me:

"There really exists for man only one boon."

"And what is it?" I inquired.

"Interior peace."

Then he resumed once more his reading:

I have built my little hut for myself alone. The hermit crab loves its shell because, being alone in it, it knows that it is sufficient for it. The osprey lives in the recesses of distant rocks because it fears men. I am like them.

Why, and for whom should I have built a larger hut? I desire neither friends nor servants. Friends seek rich companions who can be of some use to them. Servants see only their wages and profits, they fear punishments, yet do not aspire after a peaceful life near a good master. In the actual state of the world one can have faith in no one. And if I must have friends, I have my harp and lute, the moon and the flowers.

Our heart forms our destiny and command the Three Worlds. Without inner peace, of what use will thy treasures, thy horses and thy cattle be to thee? The more palaces thou wilt have, the more thou wilt desire. But here, in this solitary spot, under my roof of reeds and leaves, I possess interior peace and a heart which is always gay. If I lived in the capital, I would be ashamed to have become a tramp. Living here, I pity the fools who give themselves such trouble to catch the dust of fortune. I love my poverty, my solitude and my hut. The fish is happy in water, but in order to understand its heart, one should be a fish oneself. The bird loves its forest, but to understand its heart one should be a bird oneself. Even so, my poverty, my solitude are a joy to me, but to understand this, it is necessary to be what I am.

Light was failing. A rosy glow aureoled the holy mountain. My master, who had stopped a moment, continued his reading so as to end it before night fell:

At the foot of my mountain there is another hut made of brush-wood, where a forester lives. He has a young son who sometimes comes to see me. When *ennui* threatens me I take him for a walk, and although there is a great difference in our ages—he is sixteen and I shall soon be sixty—we both enjoy the same pleasures. We pick the great rush flowers or berries, we gather wild potatoes and parsley. Sometimes we go down to see the rice-fields at the foot of the mountain, and glean the fallen ears, with which we make posies and garlands.

When the sky is serene we climb to the summit of some lofty peak, from whence I can see my native place in the distance. We can also see Kobata-yama, the village of Tushimi, Tola and Hitsukishi. Fine scenery is not private property and no one can prevent me from enjoying it.

On our way back we break off cherry blossoms, or if it is autumn we gather branches of red maple, or young shoots of the bracken, or else we gather berries, pine cones and nuts, according to the season. After having given Buddha his part, we share our harvest.

Although it was still light, the sky grew darker from one instant to another. I helped my companion to prepare a wood fire. Our shadows danced in the clearing surrounding our hut. In the sky I noticed the moon, which was still very pale. Under the foliage shadows, lights and shades, a thousand indistinct objects awakened weird visions. The snapping of branches betrayed the presence of some animal. I heard the screech of an osprey, so despairing that my own heart contracted with pain.

The bonze resumed his reading :

When, on calm nights, I gaze at the moon, whose rays penetrate my hut, I think with emotion of people of yore, of my dead parents. And when I hear the cries of the monkeys, I wet my sleeve with my tears. In the distant meadows fireflies resemble the fishermen's cressets on the island of Maki. At dawn the rain sounds like leaves fluttered by a gust of wind. And when the golden pheasant utters its cry, *horo-horo!* I ask myself with a strange emotion if it is my father or my mother who have returned to earth as vagrant phantoms?

The mountain stags visit me fearlessly. The familiarity of these animals is for me the proof that I am definitely separated from the world. At night, whilst stirring the ashes of the fire, I sometimes see the vision of a vanished friend who has come back to me. The hooting of the mountain owl fills me with a sweet sadness.

Night was falling. My master had great difficulty in distinguishing the Chinese and Japanese characters of the little book open upon his knees.

Once again I enjoyed Buddhist peace. The sky, the earth, the trees themselves were bathed in peace and serenity. The world was fading away. I had often spoken of death with my Buddhist friends. One of them had said to me :

"Death is a gentle thing . . . an evening."

These words now came back to my memory, as the bonze finished his reading in a low voice :

The moon of my life is approaching its decline and will soon disappear behind the mountain full of shadows. Is it seemly that I should still occupy myself with all these earthly things, simple and modest as they may be? The hour draws nigh when I must depart for the obscurity of the Three Ways.

One calm morning I reflected long upon all these things and I questioned myself sincerely: I said to myself:

The goal for which thou didst abandon the world and for which thou hast made the forest, the mountain, the flowers and the moonlight nights thy familiar companions, was to acquire interior peace, and to follow the ways of Buddha. But although thy outward appearance is that of a holy man, thy heart remains impure. Thy hut is but an unworthy imitation of that of Saint Jômyo,[1] and thy spiritual conduct does not even equal that of the simple-minded Han So Ku.[2] Is it the effect of human nature to be mentally imperfect, or that of those obscure passions still stirring in thy heart?

To that my heart made no answer. Then spontaneously my lips uttered the invocation to Buddha. That is all.

We spent several delightful days in our hermitage. Then our dream ended. We were obliged to redescend the mountain in order to board at the nearest station the train for Tôkyô. From the capital I would gain a port where I would embark for France. As soon as we were on our return journey, my master and friend, obeying to a truly Japanese delicacy of heart, only spoke to me to express in a poetic and veiled form the regret our coming separation would cause him. And in the *Tzure-Dzure-Gusa*, by Kenkô Bôshi (1282-1350), he had marked the following passages, which harmonised well with his own state of mind:

The ephemera does not reach night. The summer cicadae knows neither spring nor autumn.

Or again:

Life is inconstant. Time passes. Men and things pass. Joys and sorrows come and go. What was formerly a place full of charm is now simply a deserted heath. And if the dwelling remains what it was of yore, those who lived in it are no more. Neither the peach nor the pear tree can speak. Therefore with whom will I be able to speak of days gone by?'

[1] A saint who miraculously assembled thousands of people within his *hôjô*, or ten-feet-square hut.

[2] A simple-minded man who followed the teachings of Buddha.

And lastly the bonze read me the following extract :

Although the breeze does not touch it, the flower of the human heart changes also of colour. If one should one day consider the past, or throw a glance backwards on the time when one had a friend now far away, living in another land, let me remember the words which were exchanged, the emotions experienced in common. How sad is all this—sadder perhaps than the separation which comes from death! How melancholy it is to remember ceaselessly that all ways must necessarily separate at the cross-roads.

This was a delicate allusion to our coming separation.
Thus ended our last interview.

THE COMING BUDDHISM

The general sense of the evolution of Buddhism, and its actual moral value, appear sufficiently clearly, we believe, from our inquest. Yet if an express conclusion were necessary, the following incident would provide us with the pretext for drawing one. Professor Inuye Tetsujiro, of the Imperial University of Tôkyô, formulated a few years ago certain propositions tending to rejuvenate and modernise Buddhism, propositions which, be it said, caused quite a sensation.

"The pessimism of India," he said, "which constitutes the essence of Japanese Buddhism, is not appropriate to our national needs. Pessimism is that state of soul of a decadent nation which, in the hour of adversity, when all becomes dark, no longer finds within itself the possibility of reacting. This may be a natural attitude for old India, but pessimism cannot suit a nation which practises a high ideal. Japan, with its modern pretensions, demands a religion of hope, full of lofty ideals and aspirations. Buddhism must rid itself of its pessimism, or renounce addressing itself to our people."

I have consulted numerous bonzes on this last point, and their declarations inspire me to write the following lines as conclusion.

I was told in substance that the summons of Professor Inuye Tetsujiro were not indispensable. Buddhism has evolved naturally from pessimism, and from its methods of negative meditations, towards the optimistic conceptions of universal salvation. It has passed from darkness to radiance. It seems superfluous to trace a programme for it in this direction, as its normal development has already done so. Rich in diverse doctrines, Buddhism, as far as the inhabitants of the Far East understand it, possesses the privilege of reserving, and of causing to blossom at its chosen hour, those philosophical and religious systematisations best appropriate to spiritual needs throughout time and space. Accommodating itself easily to the social and moral exigencies of a determined *milieu*, it will also adapt itself easily to modern civilisation.

We have seen how it succeeded in satisfying the human craving to believe in some superior force of sympathy and love, in tempering itself with indulgence for human frailties, and in becoming, under more or less accentuated or *nuancé* doctrinal forms, a source of spiritual encouragement, consolation and hope.

The future of Buddhism, such as present facts allow us to foresee it, is to *crystallise* itself (to use the expression of Mr Ono, bonze and professor at the Faculty of Letters of Taishô) around that optimistic conception of a kindly, humane force, acting for the salvation of all creatures. And its different sects will no doubt one day be only concentric spiritual circles in which philosophies, interpretations and *nuances* of thought will graduate around this central idea.

Under this aspect, which will become still more accentuated, Buddhism may perhaps lose some of its interest, of its spiritual depth and of its philosophical particularities, but, on the other hand, it will gain ground as a religion and as a faith, and also by its charitable works. It is in this direction that it has engaged itself and that its future development should be considered. Those curious minds who, in the words of Lafcadio Hearn, seek in Buddhism "the strangeness of the intellectual landscape," or the "land of the fairies," and who delight in the thought that it comprises, as it is said, 84,000 doctrines, are apt to be disappointed. Buddhism will indeed tend more and more to free itself from different or too subtle philosophies, for the sole use of wise men and thinkers of exceptional aptitudes. Whilst remaining an essentially human philosophy, it will become a religion comparable in many aspects to the

religions of the West—that is to say, a system of practical
morality and of spiritual salvation, addressing itself especially
to the masses.

This said, we must not forget, nevertheless, that one cannot
speak of Buddhism as of a unitary doctrine evoluating as a
whole. The multiplicity of sects in which its thought is
subdivided and expressed will always allow to the minds of
men the possibility of special points of view to which each
sect attributes a particular value, and which each is astonished
to see neglected by others. Thus the Zen Buddhists hold to
the originality of their conceptions and consider Amidism a
rather vulgar doctrine. A philosophical particularism will
therefore subsist, which should not, nevertheless, be confounded with the "chapel spirit." In a general way, all the
living sects have admitted the necessity of making hope
accessible to all, and of adapting their conceptions to the
human scale.

However, whatever may be the extreme simplifications in
which Buddhist thought becomes "crystallised," even if the
bonze of tomorrow were to appear to us under the aspect of a
sort of pietist or salvationist clergyman, Buddhist conceptions
would none the less remain endowed with a particular seduc-
tion, impregnated with a special charm, and bathed in a special
light. It is not without reason that we ended this book with
the confession of a solitary bonze, who lived with a peaceful
heart and was content with little. This Buddhist wisdom,
true treasure of the humble, which Art and Literature have
both illustrated, this wisdom which is not indigency but
elegance of thought, denoting the sensitive soul of a poet
and artist, of a philosopher happy to live obscurely and with a
"pure heart," has coloured and perfumed all Buddhist états
d'âme, and will subsist through all doctrinal evolutions.

It sometimes happens that one discovers an object in an old
wooden Japanese box. From the box arises, blended with the
perfume of precious wood, that smell of incense which one
of my Japanese friends so aptly calls The odour of my country,

and the object contained in the box is also perfumed by it. Just so, Buddhism charm and wisdom, made of simplicity of heart and serenity of soul, perfumes the doctrines, thoughts, gestures of all Buddhists—even modern ones. All the doctrines which we have reviewed in this book contain what one reads in them and also something else which overflows from them : the charm, perfume, light and prestige of Buddhism. These are the adorable qualities which Buddhism brings in its wake, and which it gradually incorporates into our pacified soul, whatever may be the doctrinal form under which it presents itself. The view of a little temple lost in the depth of a wood, inhabited by a venerable bonze, often awakens in us, even better than a text, the desire to live a simple, sincere life. Those kakemonos, so charming by their composition, colours, and by the expressions of the personages depicted, in which one sees Buddha in the centre of a legion of Bodhisattvas, or, again, Kwannon flying through the world to the aid of sinners, evoke, far better than a text, the idea of Love irradiating throughout the Universe and acting on our behalf. And because the name of *Butsu* (Buddha) has become charged with sublimity with the passing of centuries, the sole fact of uttering these two syllables brings a balm to the faithful in the hour of sorrow. Is it necessary to remind you of the impressive beauty of Buddhist religious ceremonies ? I should say that Buddhist teaching, whatever form it may assume, liberates imponderabilities which oblige us to smile even in the face of Death.

As long as Buddhism will bring with it this affluence of sentiments, ideas and emotions predisposing the soul to peace, it will fulfil its rôle, and hold its place in the world. The danger for it is that a too hasty or clumsy modernism would deprive it of its light, colour and perfume. But nothing authorises me, however, to believe that such a danger will realise itself.

The evolution of Japan, which has become a modern nation, and that of Buddhism, both provoke the same question. Will

Japan adapt herself to modern civilisation without losing her racial qualities, or will she become absorbed by this civilisation? To this Japanese laymen and priests both reply: "We will assimilate it. But we will always preserve our deep, fundamental originality."

Need it be said that all true friends of Japan and of Buddhism share this hope?

TEXTS

(1) A List of Canonical Texts. (2) Extracts from some canonical or fundamental texts. (a) *The Lotus of the Good Law.* (b) The Kegonkyō, text of the Kegon Sect. (c) The Sukhâvativyûha, text of the Jôdo and Shinshu Sects.

I

A LIST OF CANONICAL TEXTS OF THE DIFFERENT SECTS

HOSSO SECT

Kegonkyō.	(Avatamsakasutra).
Gejimmikyō.	(Sandhinirmocanasutra).
Abidatsumakyō.	(Abhidarmasutra).
Ryogakyō.	(Lankâvatârasutra).
Kôgonkyō.	(Ghanavyuha).
Yugashijiron.	(Yogâcârabhûmi).
Daijôshogonron.	(Mahôyânasûtralankâra).
Shûryôron.	(Pramânasamuccaya).
Shôdaijôron.	(Mahâyânasamparigraha).
Jûjiron.	(Dasabhûmi).
Nijûquishikiron.	(Visamtika).
Benchûbenron.	(Madhyantavibhaga).
Abidatsumazôshûron.	(Abhidarmasangiti).

KEGON SECT

Kegonkyō.	(Avatamsakasutra).

TENDAI SECT

Hokke-kyō.	(Sadharmapundarika).
Konkômyô-kyō.	(Suvarnaprabâsasutra).
Nehan-gyō.	(Nirvânasutra).
Dainichikyō.	(Mahavairocanabhisambodhisutra).
Kongôchôkyō.	(Vajrasekharatantrarâja-sutra).
Soshijikyō.	(Susiddhikâramahâtantrarâja).
Bodaishiron.	(Bodhihrdayasâstra).

SHINGON SECT

Dainichikyō.
Kongôchôkyō.
Soshijikyō.
Yugikyō.
Daibirushanabussetsuyâryakunenjukyō.
And the works of Kōbō-Daishi.

JÔDO AND SHINSHU SECTS.

Muryôjukyō.
Kammuryôjukyō.
Amidakyō.   (*Sanskrit*: Sukhâvativyûha).

NICHIREN SECT

Myôhôrengekyō.   (*Sanskrit*: Sadharmapundarikasutra).
And the works of Nichiren.

2

EXTRACTS FROM SOME CANONICAL OR FUNDAMENTAL TEXTS

(a) *The Lotus of the Good Law.*

  (*Sanskrit*: Sadharmapundarikasutra. *Japanese*: Hokke-kyō, or Myôhôrengekyō.)

Chapter X.   The Interpreter of the Law.

. . . Now, ô Bhâichadjyarâdja, if any person, man or woman, came to say : 'which are the beings who in some time to come will become venerable Tathâgatas?' thou must, ô Bhâichadjyarâdja, show that person the one amongst the sons and daughters of quality who is able of understanding, teaching and reciting, be it only one stanza of four verses of all this interpretation of the law, and who welcomes it with respect. It is this son or daughter of quality who will in some time to come surely become a venerable Tathâgata. That is how thou must envisage the question. Why so ? Because, ô Bhâichadjyarâdja, he who understands, be it only one stanza of this interpretation of the Law, must be recognised as a Tathâgata by the world formed by the union of the Devas and the Mâras. With so much the more reason what shall be said then if he would grasp, understand, repeat, possess, explain, write or cause to be written, or remember after having written, the whole of this interpretation of the Law, and who would honour, respect, venerate, adore this Book, who would worship it, render it due respect and homage, by offering it flowers, incense, perfumes, garlands, unctuous substances, scented powders, clothes, parasols, flags, standards, instrumental music, demonstrations of respect, such as the act of holding the hands joined, of expressing adoration, and of prostrating oneself? That son or daughter of quality, ô Bhâichad-jyarâdja, must be considered as having reached the summit of the supreme state of Buddhahood, perfectly accomplished. One must consider him as having seen the Tathâgatas, as being full of kindness and compassion for the world, and as having been born through the influence of his prayer, in the Djambudvîpa amongst men in order to explain properly this interpretation of the Law. One must admit that, when I shall have entered into complete Nirvâna, such a man must be born here out of compassion for mankind and for its good in order to explain completely this interpretation of the Law, with the exception of the sublime conception of the Law and the sublime birth in a land of Buddha. And that son or daughter of quality who, when the Tathâgata shall have entered complete Nirvâna, will explain this interpretation of the Law, will explain and communicate it, be it even in secret and privately to a single being, must be considered as the messenger of the Tathâgata, as his servant, as his envoy.

Again, ô Bhâichadjyarâdja, should a man whoever he may be, be he wicked, a sinner or cruel of heart, who during a whole Kalpa should revile the Tathâgata to his face, and, on the other hand, should a man address a single disagreeable word, be it justified or not, to one of those interpreters of the Law, and possessors of this sutra, be they householders or partakers of religious life, I declare that of these two men 'tis the latter who commits the gravest fault. Why is that? Because, ô Bhâichadjyarâdja, that son or daughter of quality should be considered as decked with the ornaments of the Tathâgata. He, ô Bhâichadjyarâdja, who after having written the interpretation of the Law and having bound it into a volume, carries it on his shoulder, is indeed carrying the Tathâgata himself on his shoulder. In whatsoever place he goes to, all beings should accost him with joined hands; they should honour, respect, venerate and adore him. This interpreter of the Law must be honoured, respected, venerated and adored with offerings of divine flowers, with incense, with perfumes, with garlands of flowers, with unctuous substances, with powdered scents, etc., with food, rice, beverages, chariots, with masses of precious stones heaped up. Heaps of precious stones should be presented with respect to such an interpreter of the Law. Why is that? Because this son of quality need explain, be it only once, this interpretation of the Law, for all creatures having heard it too rapidly reach in great multitudes the supreme state of Buddhahood, perfectly accomplished.

The Bhagavat then pronounced on this occasion the following stanzas:

1. He who wishes to maintain himself in the state of Buddhahood, he who longs for the science of self-existent being, must honour the beings who observe this rule of conduct.

2. And how shall he who desires omniscience succeed in obtaining it promptly? By understanding this sutra and by honouring he who has understood it.

3. He who out of compassion for the creatures expounds this sutra, has been sent by the Guide of the World to convert all beings.

4. It is after having left a good existence that the sage who out of compassion for all beings possesses this sutra came here below.

5. It is thanks to the influence of his former existence that he was able to appear here below expounding the supreme sutra at the time of his latter birth.

6. One should honour this interpreter of the Law by offering him divine and mortal flowers, together with all kinds of perfumes. One must cover him with divine clothes and scatter gems over him.

7. Men hold constantly their hands joined together in sign of respect as they do before the self-existent Indra of the Djinas, when they are in the presence of he who, during this dreaded epoch of the end of time, possesses this sutra of the Buddha who has reached complete Nirvâna.

8. One must donate Kôtis of food, rice, beverages, vihâras, beds, seats and clothes to honour this son of Djina, even if he has only expounded the sutra once.

9. He who, during this last epoch of the Kalpa, writes, possesses and hears this sutra, accomplishes the mission which the Tathâgatas entrusted to him, and for which he was sent by me in human form.

271

10. The man who would dare revile the Djina during a whole Kalpa, by frowning whilst harbouring bad thoughts, would doubtless be committing a sin the consequences of which would be very serious.

11. Well, I declare that he who would address insulting or angry words to a personage who, understanding this sutra, would expose it to the world, would commit a still graver sin.

12. The man who, holding his hands joined in sign of respect during a whole Kalpa, celebrated me to my face in several myriad Kôtis of Kalpas, in order to obtain that supreme state of Bodhi—

13. That man, I declare, would receive many merits for having celebrated me thus with joy. But he who would celebrate the praises of those virtuous personages would receive still far greater merit.

14. He who during eighteen thousand Kôtis of Kalpas would worship these images of Buddha, by rendering them the homage of sounds, forms, savours, perfumes and divine touch—

15. Would surely have obtained a great marvel if after having thus honoured these images during eighteen thousand Kôtis of Kalpas, he heard this sutra, be it only once.

I will speak to thee, ô Bhâichadjyarâdja, I will teach thee. Yes, I have made of yore many interpretations of the Law, I still do so, and I will continue to do so in the future. Of all these interpretations of the Law, the one I am making today must not receive the assent of the world. It must not be welcomed with faith by the world. That is, ô Bhâichadjyarâdja, the great secret of the supernatural knowledge which the Tathâgata possesses, secret guarded by the force of the Tathâgata and which has not been divulged as yet. No, this thesis has not been expounded until this day. That expounding of the Law, ô Bhâichadjyarâdja, is the object of contempt of many people, even while the Tathâgata exists in this world. What will it be therefore when he has entered into complete Nirvâna ?

Besides, ô Bhâichadjyarâdja, they must be considered as clothed with the mantle of the Tathâgata.

Chapter XV. Duration of the Life of the Tathâgata.

Then Bhagavat uttered the following stanzas :

1. Inconceivable are the thousands of Kôtis of Kalpas which have elapsed since I reached the supreme state of Bodhi, and since I have not ceased to teach the Law.

2. I convert numerous Bodhisattvas and I establish them in the science of Buddha. Since numerous Kôtis of Kalpas, I am bringing to perfection infinite myriads of creatures.

3. I select the land of Nirvâna and I expound my means with the purpose of disciplining creatures. And yet I do not enter Nirvâna at the very moment I speak of it. In this very place I explain the Laws.

4. Then I bless myself, and I also bless all creatures. But ignorant men whose intelligence is warped and perverted do not see me, even whilst I am in this world.

5. Believing that my body has entered complete Nirvâna, they render diverse homages to my relics, and not seeing me, they long to see me. By this means their intelligence becomes straight.

6. When men are straight, gentle, and kindly, and despise their bodies, then, calling an assembly of Grâvakas, I reveal myself on the summit of Mount Gridhrakûta.

7. And I speak to them after this fashion : 'I did not enter here, nor in such a time, into complete Nirvâna. I have simply made use, ô Monks, of my skill in the use of means, and I reappear on several occasions in the land of the living.

8. Honoured by other creatures, I teach them the supreme state of Bodhi which is mine. Yet you do not listen unto my voice unless you hear that the Leader of the World has entered into complete Nirvâna.

9. I see the utter destruction of men, and yet I do not show them my own form. But if perchance they yearn to see me, I expound the Good Law to those beings who thirst for it.

10. My blessing has always been such as I have just described it, since an inconceivable number of Kôtis of Kalpas, and I do not leave the summit of Gridhrakûta to go and seat myself on myriads of other seats and beds.

11. Even when beings see and imagine that this universe is afire, even then the land of Buddha which belongs to me is peopled with men and Maruts—

12. Who partake therein of varied games and pleasures. They possess there Kôtis of gardens and divine chariots. That land is enhanced with mountains made of diamond, and is full of trees covered with flowers and fruit.

13. And the Devas strike drums over this land, and they shower down upon it Mandara flowers with which they cover me, as well as

my Grâvakas, and those other sages who have reached Buddhahood.

14. It is thus that my land subsists continually, whilst other beings imagine that it is the prey of flames. They see this dread universe destined to misfortune and abounding in a hundred kinds of miseries.

15. And they remain during numberless Kôtis of Kalpas without even hearing the name of the Tathâgata, or of the Law, without knowing an assembly such as mine. Such is the result of their guilty actions.

16. But when gentle and kindly beings are born in the world of men, hardly are they here than, thanks to their virtuous conduct, they see me busy explaining the Law.

17. And I never speak to them of this unending task which I am ceaselessly pursuing. That is why a long time has passed since I have shown myself, and why I say to them: 'The Djinas are difficult to meet.'

18. Such is the strength of my science, that radiant strength to which there is no end. And I have reached this long existence, which is equal to an infinite number of Kalpas, because I accomplished of yore the duties of a religious life.

19. O sages, do not conceive any doubt on this subject. Renounce absolutely all kind of incertitude. The word I utter is true. No, my word is never untrue.

20. Just as a doctor who, versed in the use of proper means, would, though still alive, declare himself dead in the interest of his children whose minds would be turned towards contradiction, and just as this would result from this doctor's prudence, and not be an untrue statement—

21. Just so, I, who am the father of the world, self-existent being, I, the leader and doctor of all creatures, when I see them disposed towards contradiction, I show them my Nirvâna, although I have not as yet entered therein.

22. Why should I show myself continually to men? They are unbelieving, ignorant, deprived of light, indolent, carried away by their desires, whilst their drunkenness leads them into an evil way.

23. Having realised what has ever been their conduct, through all time, I sometimes say to the creatures: *I am the Tathâgata*, in order to convert them by this means to the state of Buddhahood, and to put them in possession of the Laws of the Buddhas.

Chapter XVI. Proportion of the Merits.

Bhagavat then addressed himself as follows to the Bodhisattva Mâhasattva Mâitrêya:

All those who, whilst this indication of the duration of the existence of the Tathâgata was being given (which is an interpretation of the Law), have given a proof of confidence, be it only by one thought, or who give credit to it, what immense merit will they derive from it, those sons and daughters of quality? Listen to this, and engrave well in thy mind what an immense merit they derive from it. Let us suppose on the one hand, ô invincible one, a son or daughter of quality who, longing to reach the supreme state of Buddha perfectly accomplished, would fulfil during eight hundred thousand of Kôtis of Kalpas, the duties of the Five Perfections, *i.e.* the perfection of charity, the perfection of morality, the perfection of patience, of energy, of contemplation, and of wisdom. And let us suppose on the other hand, ô invincible one, a son or daughter of quality who, after having heard this indication of the duration of the existence of the Tathâgata (which is an interpretation of the Law), would give a proof of confidence, be it only by a single thought, or who would have given credit to it. Well, compared to this latter mass of merits, the first mass of merits and virtues acquired by the accomplishment of the Five Perfections, practised during eight hundred thousand of myriads of Kôtis of Kalpas, does not equal the hundredth, or the thousandth, or the ten-millionth, or the trillionth part of the second mass of merits which surpasses all number, all calculation, all comparison, all similitude. A son or daughter of quality, ô thou invincible one, who is possessed of such a mass of merits, can never turn himself away from the supreme state of Buddha, perfectly accomplished. No, that is not possible.

Then the Bhagavat pronounced the following stanzas on this occasion:

17. A man seeking to obtain the science of Buddha, which is unequalled, should take in this world the vow to practise the Five Perfections.

18. He should use eight thousand Kôtis of Kalpas to give, on several occasions, charity to the Buddhas and Grâvakas.

19. (He should) entertain myriads of Pratye Buddhas and Bodhisattvas, by giving them food, rice, beverages, clothing, beds and seats.

20. He should have erected here for these persons sandal-wood dwellings and Vihâras, agreeable hermitages with places to walk in.

21. He should pour out upon this world varied and diverse sorts of gifts, and having made such offerings during thousands of Kôtis of Kalpas, he may think of the state of Buddhahood.

22. In view of the science of Buddha, he should observe the pure rule of morality, which has been described by all the Buddhas, which forms a continuous whole and is praised by the wise.

23. Full of patience, he should be established on the ground of moderation, he should be full of constancy and memory, and should stand many insults.

24. In view of the science of Buddha, he should endure the disdain of those arrogant beings who rest in pride.

25. Ever attentive to display his strength, ever endowed with a firm memory, he should remain, during thousands of Kôtis of Kalpas, occupied with the same thought.

26. In the forest he inhabits, be he walking or standing, or else when he arises, he should, during Kôtis of Kalpas, live a stranger to both sleep and sloth.

27. Abandoned to contemplation, to the great contemplation, in which he finds his pleasure, and being always self-concentrated, he should pass eight thousand of Kôtis of Kalpas meditating thus.

28. In his heroism he should demand by this meditation the excellent state of Bodhi, and by saying: 'May I obtain omniscience!' he may reach the perfection of contemplation.

29. Well, the merit such a man could acquire by accomplishing during thousands of Kôtis of Kalpas the duties I have just described—

30. Is much inferior to the infinite merit which might acquire that man or woman who, having heard, if even only an instant, this relation of the duration of my existence, and having given credit to it—

31. He who renouncing to doubt, anxiety or pride, would grant this relation, be it only a moment of confidence, must glean the fruit I have indicated.

32. The Bodhisattvas who, during thousands of Kalpas, have fulfilled the duties which are imposed upon them, will not be awed on hearing this inconceivable relation of the duration of my existence.

33. They will say, bowing their heads: 'May I also, in some time to come, be like this Buddha; May I save Kôtis of creatures.'

34. May I be like the leader Sakyamuni, like Sakyasimha, the Great Solitaire. May I roar like a lion, being seated in the very bosom of Buddhahood.

35. And may I also, in the future, being honoured by all men, and seated in the very bosom of Buddhahood, likewise teach that my existence has a similar duration.

36. The men endowed with extreme application, who, after having heard and possessed this explanation, understand the sense of my enigmatical language, doubt no more.

Yet another thing, ô invincible one. He who, after having heard this information as to the duration of the life of the Tathâgata, which is an interpretation of the Law, would understand it, fathom it, and be versed in it, that man would reap a mass of merit far surpassing the one I have just mentioned—of merits able to lead him to the science of Buddha. And with still more reason, he who having heard an interpretation of the Law like unto this one, would transmit it to others, and would repeat it, write it down and, after having enclosed it in a volume, would honour it, offering it perfumes, flowers, incense, garlands, unctuous substances, scented powders, clothing, parasols, flags, standards, lamps burning oil, clarified butter or odoriferous oils, that man, I declare, would reap a still far greater mass of merits able to lead him to the science of Buddha.

And when, ô invincible one, a young man or woman of quality shall have heard this information as to the duration of the life of the Tathâgata, which is an interpretation of the Law, and shall give it his or her confidence with an extreme application, this is the sign by which this application shall be recognised. He or she will see me established on Mount Gridhrakûta, teaching the Law, surrounded by a crowd of Bodhisattvas in the midst of an assembly of Crâvakas. He will see this land of Buddha I inhabit—that is the Saha Universe—made of lapis-lazuli and presenting a level surface covered with enclosures traced checker-wise with golden cords—strewn with trees of diamond. He will see there Bodhisattvas living in high-storied houses. Such is, ô invincible one, the sign by which one can recognise that a young man or woman of quality gives his or her confidence with an extreme application.

Better still, ô invincible one, I declare that they give their attention with an extreme application those who, when the Tathâgata shall have entered into complete Nirvâna, having heard this of the Law, shall not despise it, but, on the contrary, shall be satisfied by it. And with still more reason do I say as much of he who will remember it, and recite it. He carries the Tathâgata in his arms who, after having enclosed this interpretation in a volume, shall carry the volume itself in his arms.

O invincible one, such a one need build me neither Stûpas nor Vihâras.[1] He need not present to the assembly of monks the remedies destined to the sick, nor furniture. And why? Because, ô invincible one, this son or daughter of quality has rendered my relics the worship due to the relics of Buddha. He has built Stûpas formed of seven precious substances, rising to the firmament of Brahma, and covered with a parasol proportioned to their circumference, decorated with banners resounding with the sound of bells. He has rendered to these Stûpas containing my relics different kinds of honours—offering them flowers, incense, perfumes, garlands, etc., and making resound near these monuments the agreeable and gentle music of all kinds of instruments—large and small drums, timbrels and tabrets, and causing dances, choruses and all sorts of chantings to be performed.

In a word, these homages have lasted during an immense number of hundreds of thousands of myriads of Kôtis of Kalpas. He who since my entrance into complete Nirvâna has possessed this interpretation of the Law, and who has recited it, written it, or explained it, that man, ô invincible one, has built for me spacious and extended Vihâras, of red sandal-wood, containing thirty-two palaces, eight stories high, and having in their vicinity a wood in which to walk, all furnished with beds and seats, and able to serve as habitation to a thousand monks, embellished with flowers, gardens, and containing remedies destined for the sick, as well as beverages and food, and furnished with all kinds of convenient furniture.

These beings, be they very numerous, be they incommensurably numerous, should they number a hundred, a thousand, a hundred thousand, ten millions, a hundred Kôtis, or a thousand myriads of Kôtis, must be considered as having been presented before me to form the assembly of my Crâvakas.

He who after the entrance of the Tathâgata into complete Nirvâna will possess this interpretation of the Law, and will recite it, teach it, write it or cause it to be written, shall, I declare, ô invincible one, have no need to erect me any Stûpas, when I shall have entered complete Nirvâna, nor shall he need to honour the assembly. With still more reason, ô invincible one, he who possessing this interpretation of the Law, shall perfect himself

[1] Stûpa = a Buddhist monument. Vihâra = Buddhist temple or monastic establishment.

in charity, morality, patience, energy, contemplation or wisdom, shall certainly reap a still greater mass of merits able to lead him to the science of Buddha—of immense, incommensurable infinite merits. But, ô young man of quality, just as the element ether is unlimited, in whatever direction one may turn oneself, be it to the east, the west, the south or the north, above and beneath us, so the mass of merits able to lead to the science of Buddha, which that son or daughter of quality will reap, is no less immense and no less innumerable. He who possesses this interpretation of the Law, will recite it, teach it, write it or cause it to be written, will have a care to worship the monuments erected in honour of the Tathâgata. He will celebrate the Crâvakas of the Tathâgata, and, celebrating the hundred thousand myriads of qualities of the Mahasattvas Bodhisattvas, he will explain them to others. He will be accomplished in patience. He will be moral. He will possess all the conditions of virtue. He will have happy friendships. He will be patient, master of himself, exempt from all envy, and from all wrathful thoughts. He will never think of harming others; he will be endowed with memory, strength and energy. He will be constantly striving to seek the qualities of the Buddhas. He will be absorbed in contemplation. He will attach great price to profound meditation, and will indulge in it frequently. He will know how to solve easily all questions which may be asked him. He will free himself from a hundred thousand Kôtis or questions.

O invincible one, the Mahasattva Bodhisattva who, after the Tathâgata shall have entered Nirvâna, will possess this interpretation of the Law, will have the qualities I have just enumerated. Be he a young man or woman of quality, he must be considered in the following way: 'Entered into the pure essence of the state of Bodhi, that young man or woman of quality draws near to the trunk of Bodhi tree in order to reach the state of perfect Buddhahood.' And, ô invincible one, in whatever place this son or daughter of quality may stand, sit or walk, there must be erected a monument to the Tathâgata. This monument must be erected by the world united to the Devas in this thought: 'This is the Stûpa of the Tathâgata.'

Then Bhagavat pronounced the following stanzas on this occasion:

37. He who is versed in this sutra will possess a mass of merits which I have celebrated more than once, when the Guide of Mankind will have entered Nirvâna.

38. Such a one has worshipped me, he has erected Stûpas to contain my relics, Stûpas made of various precious substances, beautiful to look at and resplendent.

39. Equalling in height the world of Brahma, covered with lines of parasols of appropriate circumference, beautiful and decorated with standards.

40. Resounding with the tintinnabulation of bells shaken by the wind, enhanced with silken garlands. These Stûpas indeed derive their magnificence from the relics of Djina.

41. He has paid them extensive homage with flowers, perfumes and unctuous substances, with musical instruments, with tissues and with the sound of tymbals.

42. He has caused sweet-sounding musical instruments to be played near these edifices. He has surrounded them on all sides with lamps fed with odoriferous oils.

43. He who is versed in this sutra, and who will teach it during the period of imperfection, will have rendered me the varied homage I have just spoken of.

44. He has erected many Kôtis of excellent Vihâras, built in sandal - wood, formed of thirty - two palaces of eight stories each.

45. Furnished with beds and seats, filled with food and courses, provided with excellent hangings, and containing thousands of rooms.

46. He has donated hermitages and fine walks, decorated with gardens and filled with flowers, as well as numerous cushions of various forms and covered with diverse designs.

47. He has rendered in my presence a varied cult to the assembly, he who shall be versed in this sutra when the Guide of Mankind shall have entered Nirvâna.

48. A man may be full of excellent dispositions, yet he who will recite this sutra, or who will write it, will reap from this action far greater merit than him.

49. If a man should have this sutra written and enclosed in a volume, and if he should later render homage to this volume, whilst offering it perfumes, garlands and unctuous substances—

50. If he should offer it ceaselessly in sign of respect a lamp fed with odoriferous oils, with oblations of beautiful blue lotuses, with pearls and Tchampaka flowers—

51. If a man, in a word, should render a cult of this kind to the sacred volumes, he will reap such a mass of merits as cannot be measured.

52. Just as there exists no measure for the ether, whatever side of the ten points of space one may direct oneself, just so there exists none for this mass of merits.

53. What shall one say, therefore, if a patient man was in question, a man master of himself, meditative, faithful to morality, and whose whole activity is devoted to meditation—

54. If a man free from wrath and wickedness, honouring respectfully the monument (of Buddha), prostrating himself ceaselessly before the monks, knowing neither pride nor sloth—

55. Endowed with wisdom and firmness, who does not become angry when questioned; and who, having his heart full of compassion for the creatures, gives them a teaching proportioned to their strength—

56. Yea, if such a man, versed in this sutra, exists, he possesses merit without number.

57. If anyone meet such an interpreter of the Law, versed in this sutra, let him treat him with respect.

58. Let him deck him with divine flowers and clothe him in divine vestments, and after having saluted his feet by touching them with his forehead, let him hold this thought: 'This is a Tathâgata.'

59. At the sight of such a personage he will immediately make the following reflection: yea, he will go towards the tree and he will acquire there the supreme and fortunate state of Buddhahood, for the good of this world, united with the Devas.

60. In whatever spot this sage may walk, be he standing or sitting, or should he, full of constancy, stop to lie down, reciting only one stanza of this sutra—

61. Upon these different places varied and beautiful Stûpas should be erected for the Best of Men, to the intention of the holy Buddha, the Guide (of the World), and homage of all kinds should be rendered to these different edifices.

62. I have certainly possessed the region of the earth where this son of Buddha was to be found. I myself have walked in that spot. I myself have sat down there.

Chapter XX. Effect of the Supernatural Power of the Tathâgata.

. . . Then Bhagavat addressed himself as follows to the Maha-sattvas Bodhisattvas, whose leader was Vicichtatchârin : ô young man of quality, those venerable Tathâgatas, who are perfectly and completely Buddhas, possess a power which surpasses the imagination. If even, in the intent of communicating this interpretation of the Law, I should pass several hundreds of thousands of myriads of Kôtis of Kalpas exposing the numerous enumerations of the advantages it possesses, making use of diverse introductions to the Law, I could not reach the limit of the merits of this interpretation of the Law.

All the Laws of Buddha, their superiority, their mysteries, their great depth, all these are taught by me briefly in that interpretation of the Law (*The Lotus of the Good Law*). That is why, ô young man of quality, when the Tathâgata will have entered complete Nirvâna, you must, after having worshipped (this Law), possess it, teach it, recite it, explain it and honour it. And in whatever part of the earth this interpretation of the Law may be recited, explained, taught, written, meditated, preached, read, reduced in a volume, be it in an hermitage or in a Vihâra, in a house, in a wood, or near a tree, in a town, a palace, an edifice or a cavern—in that place a monument must be erected to the Tathâgata. Why should this be ? Because that place must be considered the place where all the Tathâgatas acquired the very essence of the state of Buddhahood. For it must be recognised that in that place all the venerable Tathâgatas have reached the supreme state of perfectly accomplished Buddhahood, and that in that place all Tathâgatas have entered complete Nirvâna.

The Bhagavat pronounced on this occasion the following stanzas :

1. The condition of those beings established in the science of supernatural knowledge, who, endowed with infinite sight, manifest here below their magical power to rejoice all creatures, is a condition which escapes intelligence and is useful to the world.

2. The organ of speech (of these Buddhas) which reached even to the world of Brahma, by throwing forth a thousand rays, revealed a prodigy, by the effect of a supernatural power, which was apparent for those who had attained the supreme state of Bodhi.

3. The Buddhas expelled their voice forcibly out of their throats, emitting once the noise made by the snapping of fingers. They attracted the attention of the whole world of those universes situated in the ten points of space.

4. Full of compassion and kindness, they manifest their qualities as well as those miracles and other similar ones, so that these beings, filled with joy, may possess this sutra when the Sugata will have entered complete Nirvâna.

5. Even if I were to spend several thousands of Kôtis of Kalpas singing the praise of those sons of Sugata who will possess this eminent sutra, when the Guide of the World shall have entered complete Nirvâna—

6. I could not reach the limit of their qualities which are as infinite as those of the ether, in the ten points of space. For the qualities of those who are always versed in this beautiful sutra are beyond the comprehension of intelligence.

7. They see me, as well as all the Guides of Mankind, and as that Guide of the World who has entered into complete Nirvâna. They see all these Bodhisattvas who are as numerous as the four assemblies.

8. Such a son of Sugata fills me with satisfaction. He enchants all those Guides of the World, and also that Indra of the Djinas who has entered Nirvâna, as well as those other Buddhas established in the ten points of space.

9. The Buddhas of the ten points of space, both past and future, have been, and will be seen and adored by he who is versed in this sutra.

10. He knows the Mysteries of the Best of Men, he soon succeeds in meditating as they do on that which is the object of their meditations in the intimate essence of the state of Bodhi, he who is versed in this sutra which is the true Law.

11. His power is limitless. Like that of the wind it meets no obstacles. He who is versed in this eminent sutra knows the Law, its sense and its explanations.

12. He always knows the relation between the sutras which the Guides of the World have expounded after having reflected upon them. When the Guide of Mankind entered complete Nirvâna, this sage understood the true sense of the sutras.

13. He shines like the Moon and the Sun, he is resplendent with the light and brilliancy he sheds around him. Travelling over the world in all directions, he forms a great number of Bodhisattvas.

14. Thus the wise Bodhisattvas who, after having heard an enumeration of the advantages of this sutra, similar to the one I have just made, will be versed in it at the time I will enter into Nirvâna, will without any doubt reach the state of Buddhahood.

(b) *The Kegonkyō* (*Avatamsakasutra*).

Chapter VIII.

At this moment rays of light emanated from the feet of the Most Honoured One, illuminating Universally the Three Great Parts of the World, and revealing all things as contained in them and in their light. Thanks to the miraculous power of Buddha, all the Bodhisattvas were present at the holy assembly, and the Bodhisattva Manjusru uttered the following gâthas or prayers:

Even when one reaches light and deliverance,
And one is detached from the wrongs which flood one,
And one knows that one should not attach oneself to worldly things,
One may not as yet have acquired a gaze of pure wisdom,
But if one understands the Tathâgata as free from all idea of possession,
And if one knows how things vanish and are finally destroyed,
Then one may soon attain the state of Buddhahood.

If the soul follows the path of similitude
And understands the truth of non-duality
It will be beyond comprehension.

The sage knows that things innumerable are only one thing,
And that this one thing is in innumerable other things,
And that things are not real because they undergo a perpetual transformation.
In consequence he knows not fear.

Seeing how sentient beings are oppressed by suffering
And blinded by their follies,
How they are goaded by their covetousness and by their passions,
The Bodhisattva seeks the incomparable Truth,
And this is the teaching of all the Buddhas.

He is neither a nihilist nor a realist,
And seeks all things as they have been and as they will be,
He preaches the incomparable Cycle of the Law which has never been preached before.
Through innumerable existences (kalpas)
The Bodhisattva preserves himself by wearing the armour of the great vows.
For he wishes to carry all beings across the Ocean of Birth and Death,
And that is the Way of the Great Sages.

To struggle courageously to vanquish all ills,
To put all beings at their ease with charming words,
Such is the incomparable Way of Mercy.

To preserve interiorily the deepest wisdom,
In order to destroy all wicked passions
And to see all things in a single thought,
Such is the ornament of a power which is free and unfettered.

Beating the Drum of the Perfect Law,
The sound of which re-echoes through the Ten Quarters,
The Bodhisattva does everything to reach incomparable Truth,
For such is the Way of he who is interiorily initiated.

He does not disturb innumerable states of things,
He passes through all countries, equally innumerable,
And he attaches himself to no particular reality,
He is, indeed, as free as a Buddha.

When you think of the Tathâgata,
As pure and immaculate as space itself,
Your heart expands into an unequalled joy,
And all its needs are abundantly met.

Penetrating into the lowest of Hells,
For the salvation of suffering beings,
The Bodhisattva may suffer an eternal torture;

But his heart remains as pure as He who cannot be surpassed.
He whose life and acts are always devoted
To the cause of all the Buddhas,
And whose patient heart practises all praiseworthy acts,
Will reach the virtues of the age of the Tathâgata.

Abandoning all earthly and heavenly pleasures,
The Bodhisattva contains a great and pitiful heart
In the aim of saving all creatures.

Believe in Buddha with the simplicity of thy heart,
Be unshakable in thy faith,
And never cease thinking of all the Buddhas,
To leave the ocean of Birth and Death,
Enter in the torrent of Buddhism,
To reach the beauty and the calm of Wisdom.

Consider the real nature of thine existence,
And know that all await in the serenity of Faith.
Thy heart will thus free itself of all doubts as to the self and the non-self.

In gazing at the bottom of the heart of all creatures,
Detach thyself from perfidies and lies,
So as to reach a world of realities.

Measure all the worlds,
Fathom all the oceans,
And thus become the possessor of a great and miraculous power.

How exquisite is our physical eye,
It has not the power to see our condition,
The affirmation of its power betrays an illusion,
And it is inapt to understand the incomparable Law.

No one in this world
Is able to see the form of the Tathâgata.
One can think of him during centuries,
And yet, how can he realise his divine presence ?

The Tathâgata has no countenance.
He is serene and faceless ;
And yet, thanks to his transcendent nature,
In which one finds all things,
He manifests himself in answer to our needs.

The Perfect Law of all the Buddhas is incomprehensible.
For it surpasses the power of our comprehension.
It never unites nor divides,
It is eternally serene.

The Tathâgata is not a physical body,
And if you think truth without attaching yourself to a figure,
You will reach unfettered clairvoyance,
Which will allow you to be in his presence.
The Tathâgata is to be found where words are at a loss
And thoughts struggle in vain.

Surpassing the dualism of soul and body,
The Tathâgata is liberated from all obstacles,
Both interior and exterior,
And his thoughts are of an eternal unity,
Of an unfathomable depth, and perfectly unconstrained.

The Tathâgata in his light
Illumines all the worlds,
His pure gaze knows all,
Penetrates everywhere, both far and near.

He is the one who reveals himself in immensity,
And immensity is he.
Knowing the nature of all things,
The Tathâgata reveals himself everywhere.

286

The Body has no space,
It knows no limit,
It is unreal,
And yet manifests itself under many forms.

All the worlds are born in Illusion,
There is no material existence,
And Buddha alone knows
The true essence of all this.
He who understands thus
Sees the Master.

Buddha's wisdom is impenetrable.
And his deep doctrines are unparalleled.
He has reached the other shore,
Beyond the ocean of Birth and Death,
His life is unlimited.
His light is incomparable.
Eternally free from the devouring fire of the passions,
He has acquired great merits.

Even when he fathoms the depths of Buddhism,
As if they were his own nature,
Considering the past, the present and the future,
He experiences no fatigue.

He embraces the sentient world,
But his mind is free from all illusion.
He sees all things, without nevertheless thinking of them,
He reveals himself in person without however constraining himself to do so.

Interiorily he is tranquil in his meditation,
Although he is unfettered in his thoughts
He considers things such as they are.
He understands them truly.
His mind is concentrated in a loyal thought,
And he always puts into practice the Truth of Nirvâna.

Holding fast to the Dharma which is difficult to practise,
The Bodhisattva exerts himself night and day,
And is never tired or discouraged.
Whilst crossing the ocean it is difficult to cross
He roars like a lion:
'I now wish to help all beings to cross it.'

They float aimlessly and helplessly about in the sea of Birth and Death,
They sink beneath the waves of covetousness and passions,
They are entangled in the nets of madness and error,
They tremble with fear in obscurity and ignorance.

They are left alone and without a guide,
They have wandered long in the ways of evil,
The fires of avarice, of wrath, and of pride,
Have always devoured them.
And they know no way of deliverance.

Walking thus, straying from the right path,
They fall into the ways of evil.
Because they cling to the thought of self,
It is an endless chain of Birth and Death.

The sage who has destroyed the causes of ignorance
Holds high above him the torch of intelligence.
Or builds the Arch of the divine Law,
Or edifies the Bridge of the Law,
Over which he carries all that must be carried
Across the Ocean of Birth and Death.

In the prison of Birth and Death
Secret sufferings are endured,
Old age, illnesses and death
Follow each other,
Perpetually, day and night.

By understanding the profound verity of all things,
By practising the wisdom of the 'able stratagem,'
The Bodhisattva has vowed to save all beings from these sufferings,
Such is, indeed, the life of a Bodhisattva.

He listens to the incomparably profound teaching of Buddha,
And, believing in him, he admits not the shadow of a doubt in his mind,
Whilst understanding the calm and serene truth,
His heart is emptied of all fears.
Revealing himself everywhere, he identifies himself with all forms.
He is the greatest teacher of men and Gods.

Eternity is seen in a single thought.
Where there is neither arrival, departure, nor even any suffering.
The Bodhisattva understands the whole truth,
Of all the things which are, and which are not.

His unequalled name resounds through the lands in the Ten Quarters
And saves us from the perils of Life and Death.
He reaches the furthermost confines of the world,
Preaching the doctrine charged with deep significations.

Even since he made his first offering to Buddha,
The Bodhisattva rejoices in acts of deep patience and meditation.
He analyses the truth full of significations,
And leads all creatures, rejoicing, towards the Tathâgata.

Wherever the Bodhisattva practises his teaching,
He will soon realise the unsurpassed truth.
A heart full of pure and incommensurable delights
Will expand everywhere in the Ten Quarters,
Preaching the truth to the inhabitants of all countries,
Who will thus be purified of all defilement,
And will come to sojourn in the truth of resemblance.

When the Bodhisattva behaves himself thus,
He will become a companion of the Tathâgata.
The Tathâgata surpasses all form and is eternally serene,
But allows no one to behold him in an apparition.
If he shows himself, he is like a blind man.
One can stand in front of the Tathâgata, and yet know nothing of it.

Those who attach themselves to Illusions
Cannot see the Tathâgata.
But he who is free of all idea of possession
Will see the true Buddha.

Sometimes incommensurable numbers of beings
Start off in crowds,
The faces which are within and without the Ten Quarters
Surpass all measure.
Thus also the person of Buddha fills all points of space.
He who knows this is indeed the great leader of men.

He is like unto those lands filling all space,
Whose situation and centre it is impossible to know,
Whose dates of creation and destruction no one knows.
Thus the person of Buddha fills all space.

(c) *The Sukhâvativyûha.* (Text of the Jôdo and Shinshu Sects.)

. . . Then Dharmakara spoke thus:

1. O Bhagavat, if in my land of Buddha there should be Hell,
or Birth as it exists in the animal kingdom, in the kingdom of
departed spirits, or the body of Asura, then may I never obtain

perfect omniscience. (Literal translation: the highest perfect knowledge.)

2. O Bhagavat, if in my land of Buddha the beings which are born there should have to fade (die), and fall into hell, or into the body of Asura, into animal birth or the kingdom of departed spirits, then may I never obtain perfect omniscience.

3. O Bhagavat, if the beings born in my land of Buddha should not be of one same golden colour, then may I never obtain perfect omniscience.

4. O Bhagavat, if there should exist in my land of Buddha a difference between gods and men other than that spoken of by the people when they say, 'These are gods and men, but only of imperfect and ordinary language,' then may I never obtain perfect omniscience.

5. O Bhagavat, if the beings born in my land of Buddha were not endowed with the highest Paramitas, with a miraculous power and a self control which would allow them to jump into the shortest period of a thought beyond hundreds of thousands of Kôtis of lands of Buddhas, then may I never reach perfect omniscience.

6. O Bhagavat, if the beings born in my land of Buddha did not all remember their preceding births so that they could remember at least one hundred thousand nyutas of Kôtis of Kalpas, may I then never obtain perfect omniscience.

7. O Bhagavat, if the beings born in my land of Buddha did not all possess the divine eye allowing them to see at least one hundred thousand nyutas of Kôtis of worlds, then may I never obtain perfect omniscience.

8. O Bhagavat, if the beings born in my land of Buddha were not all to acquire the divine ear allowing them to hear the Good Law at the same time in at least one hundred thousand of nyutas of Kôtis of Kalpas of lands of Buddhas, then may I never obtain perfect omniscience.

9. O Bhagavat, if in my land of Buddha all the beings that are born there were unable to read the thoughts of others, so as to know at least the thoughts of one hundred thousand nyutas of Kôtis of lands of Buddhas, then may I never obtain perfect omniscience.

10. O Bhagavat, if in my land of Buddha the beings which are born there were to conceive the slightest idea of property, be it only in what concerns their own bodies, then may I never obtain perfect omniscience.

11. O Bhagavat, if in my land of Buddha the beings which are born there were not all firmly established in absolute truth, until they reach the Mahaparinirvâna, then may I not obtain perfect omniscience.

12. O Bhagavat, if when I have obtained perfect omniscience some one was able to number the disciples which will belong to me in my land of Buddha, even if all the beings contained in the three millions of spheres of worlds, after having become Pratyeha-buddhas, were to count during one hundred thousand nyutas of Kôtis of Kalpas, then may I never obtain perfect omniscience.

13. O Bhagavat, if when I shall have obtained perfect omniscience my light should be measurable in my land of Buddha, even with the measure of one hundred thousand nyutas of Kôtis of lands of Buddhas, may I never obtain perfect omniscience.

14. O Bhagavat, if when I have obtained perfect omniscience the life of the beings born in my land of Buddha was capable of being measured otherwise than by the power of their own prayers, then may I never obtain perfect omniscience.

15. O Bhagavat, if when I have reached Bodhi the measure of my life could be limited even by one hundred thousand nyutas of Kôtis of Kalpas, then may I never obtain perfect omniscience.

16. O Bhagavat, if (when I shall have reached Bodhi) the name of sin could even exist for the beings of my land of Buddha, then may I never obtain perfect omniscience.

17. O Bhagavat, if innumerable and incommensurable Buddhas in incommensurable lands of Buddhas do not glorify my name when I shall have reached Bodhi (Buddhahood), if they do not proclaim my fame, and do not shout my praise all together, then may I never obtain perfect omniscience.

18. O Bhagavat, if those beings who have directed their thoughts towards perfect omniscience in other worlds have meditated upon me with serene thoughts after I have reached Bodhi ; and if at the moment of their death, having drawn near them, surrounded with an assembly of Bhikshus, I were not to hold myself upright before them, adored by them so that their thoughts be not troubled, then may I never obtain perfect omniscience.

19. O Bhagavat, if the beings of the innumerable and incom-mensurable lands of Buddha who have heard my name after I reached Bodhi, should direct their thought towards being born in my land of Buddha, and with this object in view, bring their merit

to maturity—if those were not born in my land of Buddha, even those who had only repeated ten times that thought (of the land of Buddha), always excepting those beings who have committed the (five) Anantarya sins, and who have opposed or abused the Good Law, then may I never obtain perfect omniscience.

20. O Bhagavat, if when I have reached Bodhi the beings born in my land of Buddha were not bound to one birth only before obtaining perfect omniscience, always excepting those special prayers of the noble-souled Bodhisattvas who have donned the whole armour (of the Law), who understand the welfare of all creatures, are devoted to all creatures, and strive to make all creatures reach Nirvâna, and wish to accomplish the task of a Bodhisattva in all the worlds, desiring to serve all the Buddhas, and to lead beings as innumerable as the grains of sand of the Ganges to perfect omniscience, and who, besides, turn themselves towards higher practices and excel in the practice of the *samantabhadra* discipline, then may I never obtain perfect omniscience.

21. O Bhagavat, if the Bodhisattvas born in my land of Buddha, when I shall have reached Bodhi, should not all be capable, after having been in other lands of Buddhas and taken their single morning meal, of adoring hundreds of Buddhas, thousands of Buddhas, hundreds of thousands of Buddhas, numerous Kôtis of Buddhas, etc., and even several hundreds of thousands of nyutas of Kôtis of Buddhas, with the objects which give all sorts of pleasures, and that thanks to the favour of Buddha, then may I never obtain perfect omniscience.

22. O Bhagavat, if when I have reached Bodhi the Bodhisattvas of my land of Buddha should wish that their merits should grow under the following forms : gold, silver, gems, beryls, shells, corals, crystal, amber, red pearls and diamonds, etc., or in that of any other jewel, perfumes, flowers, garlands, ointment, powdered incenses, mantles, parasols, flags, banners or lamps. Or with all sorts of dances, songs and music. And if such gifts do not come to them as soon as they have thought them, then may I never obtain perfect omniscience.

23. O Bhagavat, if when I have reached Bodhi the beings born in my land of Buddha did not all recite the history of the Law which is accompanied by omniscience, then may I never obtain perfect omniscience.

24. O Bhagavat, if the Bodhisattvas of my land of Buddha, when I shall have reached Bodhi, were to think as follows: May we,

living in this world, honour, venerate, esteem and adore the blessed Buddhas of innumerable and incommensurable Buddhistic regions, with clothing, begging bowls, beds, chairs, refreshments, drugs, implements, flowers, incense, lamps, perfumes, ointments, powder, mantles, parasols, flags, banners, different sorts of dances, songs and music, showers of jewels, and if the blessed Buddhas did not accept them when they were produced as soon as thought, then may I never obtain perfect omniscience.

25. O Bhagavat, if the Bodhisattvas born in my land of Buddha were not, when I have reached Bodhi, all in possession of a physical strength equal to that of the diamond of Narayana, then may I never obtain perfect omniscience.

26. O Bhagavat, if one being of my land of Buddha, when I will have reached Bodhi, were to learn the limit of the beauty of its ornament, even if he possessed the divine eye, and should know its varied beauty and say: 'This Buddha land possesses such a quantity of beauty and magnificence,' then may I never obtain perfect omniscience.

27. O Bhagavat, if when I have reached Bodhi, one Bodhisattva of my land of Buddha, having even very little merit, were not to perceive the Bodhi tree, so nobly beautiful, of at least one hundred yaganas in height, then may I never obtain perfect omniscience.

28. O Bhagavat, if when I have obtained Bodhi the beings in my land of Buddha were to teach, or to learn, and not all be in possession of perfect science, then may I never obtain perfect omniscience.

29. O Bhagavat, if when I have reached Bodhi my land of Buddha was not brilliant enough for one to see from it on all sides, the incommensurable, innumerable, inconceivable, incomparable, immense lands of Buddha just as one sees a round shape in a round and very burnished mirror, then may I never obtain perfect omniscience.

30. O Bhagavat, if in my land of Buddha, when I shall have reached Bodhi, there was not one hundred thousand vases full of different subtle perfumes, made of all kinds of jewels, and from which the smoke of incense was continually ascending, suitable for the adoration of the Bodhisattvas and the Tathâgatas, and rising towards the sky far beyond the gods, men and all things—then may I never obtain perfect omniscience.

31. O Bhagavat, if in my land of Buddha, when I shall have reached Bodhi, there were no more showers of jewel flowers, and

if there were no sweet-sounding clouds, then may I never obtain perfect omniscience.

32. O Bhagavat, if the beings which will belong to me when I will have reached Bodhi, and whose splendour is visible in the incommensurable, innumerable, inconceivable and incomparable worlds, were not all to enjoy a pleasure far greater than that of gods or of men, then may I never obtain perfect omniscience.

33. O Bhagavat, if when I have reached Bodhi, the noble-souled Bodhisattvas of the immense, incomparable, inconceivable and innumerable lands of Buddha, after having heard my name, were not delivered from birth by the merit deriving from the fact that they have heard my name, were not strong enough in the science of the Bhasanis to obtain the very throne of Bodhi, then may I never obtain perfect omniscience.

34. O Bhagavat, if when I have reached Bodhi, the women of the immense, incommensurable, inconceivable, innumerable and incomparable lands of Buddha, having heard my name, should allow negligence to be born in them, and should not concentrate their thoughts on Bodhi, and delivered from birth, were not to despise their womanhood, and if, having been born again, they were to assume a second time a woman's nature, then may I never obtain perfect omniscience.

35. O Bhagavat, if when I have reached Bodhi, the Bodhisattvas of the innumerable, incommensurable, inconceivable, incomparable and immense neighbouring Buddha lands, of the Ten Quarters of the worlds, heard my name and prostrated themselves, adoring me, and if whilst they fulfilled their duty as Bodhisattvas they were not honoured by gods or men, then may I never obtain perfect omniscience.

36. O Bhagavat, if when I have reached Bodhi, the Bodhisattvas were obliged to do all dyeing, sewing, cleaning and drying of their clothes, and did not see themselves covered, swift as a thought, with superb, newly made clothes, given them by the Tathâgata, then may I never obtain perfect omniscience.

37. O Bhagavat, if the beings born at the same time in my land of Buddha, when I shall have reached Bodhi, were not to obtain a happiness equal to that of the Bhikshu saint, who was delivered from suffering, and who obtained the third meditation, then may I never obtain perfect omniscience.

38. O Bhagavat, if the Bodhisattvas in my land of Buddha did not create trees of different jewels, and the quantity of magnificent ornaments desired by them in this land of Buddha, may I never obtain perfect omniscience.

39. O Bhagavat, if the Bodhisattvas born in other lands of Buddha, after having heard my name after my acquisition of Bodhi, were to suffer the least diminution of the strength of their senses, then may I never obtain perfect omniscience.

40. O Bhagavat, if, when I have reached Bodhi, the Bodhisattvas were not to acquire at the sound of my name the Samadhi (ecstasy) called Suvibhaktavati, thanks to which the Bodhisattvas will see, second by second, incommensurable, innumerable, inconceivable, incomparable and immense blessed Buddhas, and if between time their Samadhi should cease, then may I never obtain perfect omniscience.

41. O Bhagavat, if, when I have reached Bodhi, beings after having heard my name in other Buddha lands than this one, were not, thanks to the merit which the knowledge of my name assures them, born again into a noble family until they had reached Bodhi, then may I never obtain perfect omniscience.

42. O Bhagavat, if when I have reached Bodhi, the Bodhisattvas living in other lands of Buddha, after having heard my name, and by that very fact having increased their merits so as to obtain Bodhi, were not all to obtain the alliance of their merits with the joy and happiness of their life as Bodhisattvas, may I never obtain perfect omniscience.

43. O Bhagavat, if when I have reached Bodhi, the Bodhisattvas, as soon as they shall have heard my name in other worlds, failed to obtain the Samadhi called Samantanugata, by which the Bodhisattvas honour one after the other the innumerable, incommensurable, inconceivable, incomparable and immense blessed Buddhas, and if their Samadhi was to end before they had reached the throne of Bodhi, then may I never obtain perfect omniscience.

44. O Bhagavat, if when I shall have reached Bodhi, the beings born in my land of Buddha were not to hear, swift as a thought, the teachings of the Law as they wish it, then may I never obtain perfect omniscience.

45. O Bhagavat, if when I shall have reached Bodhi, the Bodhisattvas of this land of Buddha, or of any other, were to turn away

from perfect omniscience as soon as they have heard my name, then may I never obtain perfect omniscience.

46. O Bhagavat, if, when I have reached Bodhi, and shall have become a teaching Buddha, the Bodhisattvas who will hear my name in the lands of Buddha, and who will reach the first, second and third degree of endurance, as soon as they have heard my name, should turn away from Buddha, the Law and the Church, then may I never obtain perfect omniscience.

AN ELEMENTARY AND ANNOTATED
BIBLIOGRAPHY OF JAPANESE BUDDHISM

HISTORY

TETSU SAKAINO, *Indo Bukkyô Shikô.* (Historical Sketch of Indian Buddhism.)

KOYA SAKAINO, *Shina Bukkyô Shikô.* (Historical Sketch of Chinese Buddhism.)

DR S. MURAKAMI, *Nihon Bukkyô Shikô.* (Historical Sketch of Japanese Buddhism.)

DR E. MAEDA, *Daijo Bukkyô Shiron.* (Historical Sketch of Mahayana Buddhism.)

KAKEYAMA, *Nichirenshu Zenshi.* (History of the Nichiren Sect.)

DR S. MURAKAMI, *Shinshu Zenshi.* (History of the Shinshu Sect.)

BIOGRAPHY

PROFESSORS T. INUYE AND K. HORI, *Shakamuni-den.* (Life of Sakyamuni.)

DAIJO TOKIWA, *Shakamuni-den.* (Life of Sakyamuni.)

JUNKEI WASHIO, *Nihon Bukka Jimmei Jisho.* (Bibliographical Dictionary of Japanese Buddhist Priests.)

DR ANEZAKI, *Hokke Gyoja to shite no Nichiren.* (A very remarkable work on Nichiren which has been translated into English under the title : Nichiren, the Buddhist Prophet.)

ISHIZUKA, *Hônen, the Pietist Saint* (in English). (A remarkable work on Hônen, his life, his work.)

TEXTS AND COMMENTARIES

Dai Nippon Bukkyô Zenshô. (A collection of 200 volumes containing the Chinese *Tripatika*, original Japanese works, and Commentaries.)

Kokuyaku Daizokyo. (The Canonical Texts translated into Japanese.)

Shingonshu Seiten. (Principal Texts of the Shingon Sect with Commentaries.)

Zenshu Seiten. (Principal Texts of the Zen Sect with Commentaries.)

Jôdoshu Seiten. (Principal Texts of the Jôdo Sect with Commentaries.)

Shinshu Seiten. (Principal Texts of the Shinshu Sect with Commentaries.)

Zenso-Mondo. (Dialogues of Zenist Bonzes.)

DRS MURAKAMI AND MAEDA, *Bukkyô Seiten.* (Extracts from the principal Buddhist Texts.)

SOEN SHAKU, *Hekiganroku Kowa.* (Commentaries.)

TOKUNO OTA, *Hokkekyô Kogi.* (Lectures.)

TEI TADA, *Shoshinge Kowa.* (Commentaries.)

YAMABE, *The Buddhist Psalms of Shinran.* (Translation.)

Some texts of a capital importance have been translated into French from the Sanskrit by well-known scholars. Thus *The Lotus of the Good Law* has been translated into French by Burnouf (Maisoneuve ed.), whilst the *Abhidharma Kosa Sastra,* and the *Siddhi of Hiouen Tsan* have been translated by De La Vallée Poussin (Geuthner ed.).

ESSAYS AND STUDIES

DR B. MATSUMOTO, *Butten no Kenkyu.* (Studies on the Japanese Canon.)

DR S. MURAKAMI, *Bukkyô Gairon.* (Essay on Buddhist Doctrines.)

DR S. MURAKAMI, *Bukkyô Toitsuron.* (Fundamental Principles, various Essays.)

DR ANEZAKI, *Kompon Bukkyô.* (Fundamental Principles.)

DR S. MURAKAMI, *Daijo Busseturon Hiban.* (Critical Essay on the Mahayana.)

DR ANEZAKI, *Genshin Butsu to Hoshin Butsu.* (The Buddha and His Law.)

SHINKYO MOCHIZUKI, *Jôdokyo no Kenkyu.* (A Study on Jôdo.)

KYUKEI YABUKI, *Amida Butsu no Kenkyu.* (Study on Amida Butsu.)

RAIFA GONDA, *Mukkyo Koyô.* (Essay on the Teachings of the Mystery.)

DR E. MAEDA, *Tendaishu Koyô.* (Essay on the Tendai Doctrine.)

T. SUZUKI, *Outline of Mahayana Buddhism*. (Containing the translations of the Chinese texts. The passages quoted in this book from Nagarjuna have been taken from this work. The *Thû-ron-kwan*, or *Book on the Meditation of the Middle Way*, by Nagarjuna, has been translated into Chinese by Kumarajiva.)

GESSHO SASAKI, *A Study of Shin Buddhism*. (Excellent work on the Shinshu Sect.)

RYANON FUJISHIMA, *Le Bouddhisme Japonais*. (In French.) (The author, who knows France, is one of the most distinguished Bonzes of Japan.)

TCHICADZUMI, *Buddhism in Japan*.

S. MOTOYOSHI, *Buddha and Buddhism*.

TAKA KUSU, *Buddhism as I find it in Japan*.

TOKI, *Buddhism in Japan*.

MASAHARU ANEZAKI, *Quelques pages de l'histoire religieuse de Japon*. (A collection of excellent lectures, especially on the Prince Shotoku, Dengyo and Kōbō, Hônen and Nichiren.)

OKAKURA, *The Book of Tea*. (See, in particular, the chapter on Zen.)

TEITARO SUZUKI, *Essays in Zen Buddhism*. (A very remarkable work which should be read by all who are interested in Zen, and, in particular, in its history, its practical methods of instruction, the *satori* and the Hall of Meditations.)

KAITEN NUKARIYA, *The Religion of the Samurai*. (An excellent work on Zen.)

UMADA, *The Philosophy and Story of the Nichiren Sect*.

SEISHIN KATO, *Dainithi-Nyorai Kenkyu*. (Essays on Dainithi-Nyorai. The author declares that Dainithi-Nyorai and Shaka (Sakyamuni) are one same Body.)

—— *Kyorishi yori mitaru Kokudai enguiron*. (Six great theories of causation, from an historical, doctrinal and religious point of view. This work contains also a criticism on other opinions.)

—— *Hizoki no Sakusha ni Tsuki*. (Essay on the author of the Secret Notes, which, according to Mr Kato, are not by Kōbō Daishi, but by Engyo.)

—— *Kyogyô Daishi no Jôdokan*. (The doctrine of the Pure Land explained by Kyogyô Daishi. The author explains his personal ideas on death, and believes that the body is Buddha, here below.)

SEISHIN KATO, *Kōbōdaishi kaso setsu.* (On the cremation of Kōbō-Daishi. It is generally believed that Kōbō-Daishi was buried on Koyasan. The author declares, however, that the saint's body was burnt.)

—— *Shaka to kyôjutsu.* (Shaka and deceitfulness. A thesis in competency in the means used.)

—— *Mikkyo yori mitaru uchu.* (The universe according to the secret doctrine. The author expounds what he believes to be Buddha's secret concerning the world, and combats the belief that even *things* can become Buddhas.)

—— *Guendai shiso to mikkyo.* (Modern ideas in relation to the secret doctrine.)

E. TOMOMATSU, *Shinjidai no Bukkyô.* (Present-day Buddhism.)

—— *Bukkyô to Shakai.* (Buddhism and Society.)

SPECIAL BIBLIOGRAPHY OF THE SHINSHU SECT

OTANICHI HONGWANJI. (Principal Teachings of the Sect of the True Land.)

SHINRAN, *Kyo-Gyô-Shine-Sho.* (The teaching, practice, belief and goal.)

—— *Gutoku-Sho.* (Note-book of the simple-hearted bald man.)

—— *Jôdo-moneruī jushô.* (Extracts from sutras relating to the Pure Land.)

—— *Nyu-Shutsu* and *Nimone-ge.* (Buddhist Psalms and Stanzas.)

—— *Jôdo-wassane.* (Hymns of the Pure Land.)

—— *Kossô-wassane.* (Hymns to the Seven Great Patriarchs of Shinshu.)

—— *Shozô-matsu-wassane.* (Hymns.)

—— *Matto-shô.* (Enlightenment and the final period.)

—— *Go-Shozoku-shu.* (Letters to the venerable Shinran.)

—— *Nyoshine-Tâne-i-shô.* (Works open to discussion. Shin.)

KAKUNYO, *Godene-Shô.* (Honourable Biography. The Life of the holy sage of Hongwanji.)

—— *Shuyi-kotoku-dene.* (The Life of the old sage.)

—— *Kudene-Shô.* (Teachings of Shinran transmitted verbally by Nioshine to Kakunyo.)

—— *Shu-dzi-shô.* (On reciting the name of Amida.)

—— *Sai-yô-shô.* (On the eighteenth vow of Amida.)

KAKUNYO, *Shu-se-gwane.* (On the signification of Sakyamuni's apparition on earth.)

ZONEKAKU, *Roku-yô-shô.* (Commentaries. Ten volumes.)

—— *Sene-Jyaku-shu-tchu-ge-shô.* (Commentaries on the work of Hônen.)

—— *Jôdo-shin-yo-shô.* (Treatises on the essential doctrines of the Pure Land.)

—— *Hokke-monedo.* (Controversies with the Nichiren Sect.)

—— *Busene-shô.* (Work in which the teaching of the Pure Land is compared to an easy sea voyage, and that of the Way of the Wise to a painful journey on foot.)

—— *Jimyô-shô.* (On the salvation of women.)

—— *Jôdo-kemmone-shu.* (On the conception of this world, and the joys of the Pure Land.)

DICTIONARIES ON BUDDHISM

DR U. HAGIWARA, *Bonkan Taiyaku Bukkyô Jiten.* (Sanskrit–Chinese Buddhist Dictionary.)

HOMPA HONGWANJI, *Bukkyô Daijirin.* (Great Dictionary of Buddhism.)

TOKUNO OTA, *Bukkyô Daijiten.* (Great Buddhist Dictionary.)

FUJIE AND SHIMAJI, *Bukkyô Jirin.* (Buddhist Dictionary.)

—— *Tetsugaku Daijisho.* (Great Philosophical Dictionary.)

—— *Zenshu Jiten.* (Dictionary of the Zen Sect.)

HOBOGIRIN. (Encyclopædic Dictionary on Buddhism, published under the patronage of the Imperial Academy of Japan and under the direction of Messrs Sylvain Lévy and G. Takakusu.)

CHIEF BUDDHIST PERIODICALS

1. *Dealing with Buddhism in General*—

"Kanso." Published in Tôkyô, its chief contributors being the professors of the Tôyô-daigaku.

"Gendai-Bukkyô." Editor: Takakusu, Tôkyô.

"Chuô-Bukkyô." Published in Tôkyô.

"Young East" (in English). Published by the Association of Buddhist Students of the Imperial University, Tôkyô.

"Tobo Bukkyô." Editor: Washio, Tôkyô.

"Bukkyô Bijutsu, on Buddhist Art." Published at Nara.

"Seichô." Published by the Association of the Sensôji Temple, Tôkyô.

2. *Periodical devoted to the Tendai Sect—*

"Myôjô." Published by the Tendai-Shûgaku-in, Sakamoto, Shigaken.

3. *Periodical devoted to the Shingon Sect—*

"Mikkyô-Kenkyû." Published by the Professors of the Koyasandaigaku.

4. *Periodicals devoted to the Zen Sect—*

"Zengaku-Kenkyû." Published by S. Hisamatsu, Kyôto-fu.

"Zen-No-Seikatsu." Editor: Yamada, Tôkyô.

"Daijo-Zen." Editors: S. Harada and T. Tida, Tôkyô.

"Daiichigi." Published in Tôkyô.

5. *Periodical devoted to the Jôdo Sect—*

"Bukkyôgaku." Published by the Taisho-Daigaku of Tôkyô-fu.

6. *Periodicals devoted to the Shinshu Sect—*

"Eastern Buddhist" (in English). This review is particularly recommended to Westerners who wish to understand Buddhism, and is conceived in a very large-minded way, and publishes articles on all the sects. It has published Mr Suzuki's articles on Zen, as well as his translations of the Kegonkyō and of the Hekigan-roku.

"Kanshô." Written by the professors and pupils of the Otanidaigaku.

"Gedatsu." Editor: Noyori, Tôkyô.

"Shinran-Shonin-Kenkyu." Editor: Umehara, Tôkyô.

"Butsuzu." Edited by the Butsuzu-sha Association, Kyôto.

"Honi." Edited by the Honi-sha Association, Kyôto. Editor: Y. Fujiawa.

"Ryukoku-Daigakurono." Kyôto.

LEADING SOCIETIES FOR THE STUDY OF BUDDHISM

RYÛKOKU-DAIGAKU. Kyôto.

BUKKÔ-GAKKAI. Messrs Yutsugi and Akamatsu.

SHIGAKKI. Messrs Miura, Yamauchi and Tsumagi.

BUTSUZA-SHA. Messrs Kaneko and Soga.

BIBLIOGRAPHY

OTANI-DAIGAKU. Kyôto.

BUKKYO-KENKYÛKAI. Messrs Teramoto, Akanuma and Yamabe.

INDO-GAKKAI. Mr Izumi.

BUKKYÔ-SHIGAKKAI. Mr Hashikawa.

EASTERN BUDDHIST KYÔKAI. Mr Suzuki.

KOYASAN-DAIGAKU.

HACHIYÔ-GAKKAI. Mr Mizuhara.

KOMAZAWA-DAIGAKU.

WAYÛSHA. Messrs Nukariya and Yamakami.

TOBO-BUKKYÔ-KYÔKAI. Tôkyô.